Contents

Notes on contributors

Sheila Aikman is a lecturer at the University of London, Institute of Education. She has worked for many years on issues of intercultural and bilingual education in Latin America and has carried out long-term ethnographic fieldwork with the indigenous Harakmbut peoples of south-east Peru.

David Coulby is Professor of Education and Dean of Education and Human Sciences Faculty at Bath Spa University College, United Kingdom. He has published widely on intercultural education and special education in Europe. His current book *Old Knowledge, New Societies* is shortly to be published by Falmer.

Robert Cowen is a Reader in Comparative Education in the Academic Group, Culture, Communication and Societies at the London Institute of Education. He normally writes on comparative education theory, on changing higher education systems and from time to time on changing patterns of educational studies and teacher education. His main current interest is a new theory about 'educational rosettas' which he thinks of as a fresh way to 'read' educational systems comparatively. He has been privileged to work in a number of countries in East Asia, in Europe and in North and South America. He is also delighted to be member of the Editorial Board of the journal *Comparative Education* and a member of the Comparative Education Society in Europe.

Roger Dale has researched, published and taught in the area of political sociology and policy studies over almost three decades. Following a prolific and extended period of time at the Open University in the United Kingdom, he moved to New Zealand to take up a Chair at the University of Auckland. He continues to publish in leading journals and book collections on matters of governance, markets, state formations and globalization.

Jan Derry is a lecturer in the School of Education at the University of Birmingham. She has a special interest in contemporary Iran. Her current research interests are technology mediated teaching and learning with particular reference to the field of Vygotskian studies.

Candido Alberto Gomes is Professor of Education at the Catholic University of Brasília, Brazil, and was a Legislative Adviser for educational affairs at the Federal Senate. Consultant to several international organizations, he is the author of more than 100 articles published in his country and abroad. His most recent books are *A nova LDB: uma lei de esperança* (The new Law of Directives and Basis: a law of hope, Brasília: UNESCO/Universa, 1998) and *Financiamento da educação especial* (Financing special education, Brasília: UNESCO/Ministry of Education and Sport, 1996). He was president of the Brazilian Comparative Education Society, as well as member and chair of the Research Committee of the World Council of Comparative Education Societies.

Nigel Grant was formerly Professor of Education at the University of Glasgow. He is an expert on education in the former Soviet Union and in Europe. He has a strong interest in Scottish history, language and identity. His research interests concern comparative and intercultural education.

Mirjam M Hladnik is an Assistant Professor at the University of Ljubljana where she teaches sociology of education at the Faculty of Education. Her main theoretical interest is the politics of education combined with the history of empowerment. Her first book *The School Reform is a Paper Tiger* (1986) is a documented history of the civil opposition against the notorious educational reform in the 1980s. Her second book, *Schools and Teachers in Slovenia* (1995) is a historical analysis of the establishment of the national educational systems and reasons for the feminization of the teaching profession. Her third project, *The Collected Works of Angela Vode* (1998–99) consists of three volumes on a leading feminist, anti-fascist and woman union leader in the 1930s, who was ostracized and had her work erased after the Second World War. She is a co-author of textbooks on ethics (1998, 1999) for the elementary school and author of many articles published at home and abroad.

Crispin Jones is Senior Lecturer in Education at the Institute of Education, London University, United Kingdom, where he works in the International Centre for Intercultural Studies and the Culture, Communication and Societies academic group. His especial interests are in urban and intercultural education. Much of his recent work has been in the areas of education and conflict resolution and the educational needs of refugees. Currently he is working on a book with David Coulby on the interrelationship between the educational systems of Europe and war and violence. He has been associated with the *World Yearbook of Education* since 1992 and became one of the series editors in 1995.

Andreas M Kazamias is Professor of Educational Policy Studies at the University of Wisconsin-Madison (United States). He is also Professor Emeritus at the University of Athens (Greece) and a Member of the Academy of Athens. His research and teaching interests are in the areas of Comparative Education,

Comparative Social History, and History of Educational Thought. He is the author, co-author or editor of several books and articles in English and Greek, including *Tradition and Change in Education: A comparative study; Politics, Society and Secondary Education in England 1895–1926; Education and the Quest for Modernity in Turkey; Herbert Spencer on Education* and *Education in Greece: Perspectives on reconstruction and modernisation* (in Greek). He served as Editor of the *Comparative Education Review* and he is President of the Greek Comparative Education Society.

Terri Kim graduated from Yonsei University in Seoul, South Korea. She then came to England to study Comparative Education at the Institute of Education, University of London for both MA and PhD degrees. After her MA, she worked as a researcher for the Korean Educational Development Institute in Seoul in 1993. On the completion of her PhD, she was invited to write a consultancy paper on the globalization of higher education for the OECD in 1999. She has a strong comparative research interest in, and has been writing on, the academic profession at university level, the social construction of merit in different cultural and knowledge traditions, and globalization and its impact on the uses of the university and knowledge. Currently, she is translating her doctoral thesis into Korean for publication.

Katalin Kovacs is an educational researcher at the Research Centre of the National Institute of Public Education (OKI) in Budapest and a part-time lecturer at the Teacher Education Institute of the Janus Pannonius University, Pecs, Hungary. She is a founding member of the association that introduced the *Facing History and Ourselves Holocaust* education programme in Hungary.

Ben Levin is Professor and Dean of Continuing Education at the University of Manitoba. He also holds a position in the Department of Educational Administration, Foundations, and Psychology. His research interests include international school reform, education and poverty and educational finances. He is the author (with J A Riffel) of *Schools and their Changing World: Struggling towards the future* (Falmer, 1997).

Charles Posner was formerly a lecturer in the Department of Sociology at the London Institute of Education. He currently runs a major doctoral programme jointly between the London Institute and universities in Mexico. His research interests include innovative and alternative forms of education.

Susan Robertson has researched, published and taught political sociology and political studies in education in Australia, Canada and New Zealand. She has recently taken up an appointment at the Graduate School of Education, University of Bristol in England. Susan has published in a range of journals on matters of education and the state – her interest is in policy formation, critical policy analysis and teachers' work. Her book, *A Class Act: Teacher, globalisation and the state* will be published shortly by Falmer.

Nick Taylor has a PhD in mathematics education. He taught mathematics and science at the high school level for 10 years. He then served as Subject Adviser (mathematics) in Soweto, where he was responsible for the in-service development of teachers. In 1988 he joined the Education Policy Unit at the University of the Witwatersrand, from which he co-ordinated the National Education Policy Investigation (NEPI). The NEPI research project spanned 12 areas of education, involved over 300 researchers and was published in 13 volumes in 1993. Since 1994 he has been director of the Joint Education Trust, a development agency based in Johannesburg.

Janusz J Tomiak was a Senior Lecturer in Comparative and Eastern European Education in the University of London Institute of Education and the School of Slavonic and East European Studies between 1966 and 1988. He is the author of *The Soviet Union* in World Education Series; the editor of *Soviet Education in the 1980s* (Croom Helm, 1983); *Western Perspectives on Soviet Education in the 1980s* (Macmillan, 1986); *Schooling, Educational Policy and Ethnic Identity* (with K Eriksen, A Kazamias and R Okey, European Science Foundation, 1991) and numerous journal articles and book chapters.

Penny Vinjevold taught at secondary schools designated for African pupils from 1981 to 1987 in Mmabatho and Soweto and then at the Soweto Teachers Training College from 1988 to 1993. At the end of 1993 she joined the Joint Education Trust, a funding and development organization based in Johannesburg. There, as General Manager, Research and Evaluation, she conducted and supervised evaluations of teacher development initiatives in the period 1994–99. She has also been involved in an audit of NGO teacher development projects for the National Department of Education and research projects on teacher development for the National Commission on Higher Education.

Jon Young is Professor and Head of Department of Educational Administration, Foundations, and Psychology at the Faculty of Education, University of Manitoba. His research interests are in the area of educational administration and anti-racist education. Recent publications include *Understanding Canadian Education: An introduction to educational administration* (2nd edition) 1998.

Evie Zambeta is a Lecturer in Comparative Education in the Department of Early Childhood Education at the University of Athens. Her first degrees are in Education and in Philosophy and her PhD is on Educational Politics. Her main research interests include policy analysis in education and identities in the new Europe. She has published books and articles on educational politics in the Greek and European education systems.

Acknowledgements

Thanks to Christine Flenley of Bath Spa University College for her assistance in the administration of this publication.

1. Fine-tuning educational earthquakes?

Robert Cowen

The theme of this volume of the *World Yearbook of Education* is education in times of transition. The phrase is deliberately ambiguous and was chosen precisely because of the immediate questions stimulated by the vagueness of the phrasing. Clearly, the 'times' are not merely in transition; on the calendar which many people in the world use, the times are also millennial. What that may mean for us all, we do not yet know. However, most educationists – teachers, policy-makers, administrators, new educational entrepreneurs and a lot of concerned parents – know that education is 'in transition'. The evidence is lived through daily – new examination systems, new curricula, new kinds of teacher training, expanding university systems, new financial responsibilities, new forms of accountability. More generally, it is becoming more obvious that the educational forms of the 19th century – state-provided schools, educational *systems* – which we have lived with for most of the 20th century, are collapsing. Education systems, and what it is to be educated, are in transition.

So the theme of this volume is a big one and one which cannot be easily controlled, either in real life by educational planners, or in written scripts by the editors. Societies and economies are changing dramatically; education is in transition. There are a number of ways in which it is possible to develop such themes, but it is probably important to clarify what we are not trying to do in this volume, before we sketch what we did ask our contributors to worry about.

Transitions in education are not educational problems that are there to be solved. They are not routine puzzles in educational systems, puzzles for which a well-organized international or domestic conference can probably find solutions. One of our larger professional myths – embedded in research and policy literature and marked by the availability of money for meetings – is that of pragmatism. Indeed, some conferences in some countries are culturally expected to conclude with a summary statement of the proposals, made during the week, for solving problems. These proposals are then sent to the Minister of Education if (s)he does not happen to be present. The custom has its charm; it is a marvellous ritual of good manners, and of 'paying the piper'. The custom may even help academics to address the 'real' educational world, though that tends to assume the Minister knows what and where that is and

how it can be understood. But the custom is reassuring. It affirms the pragmatic.

Our professional myth implies that the major international and regional
policy agencies in education, together with those doing educational research
in think-tanks or universities, can take a good shot at defining useful
up-to-date thinking and pulling together useful evidence. In consequence, at
almost any given moment, well-organized international or regional agencies,
Ministries of Education, and individual scholars can identify a range of useful
solutions to practical educational problems in several countries. Quite so; the
constant theme of being 'useful' is important. Our professional assumption is
that we can, with enough money and enough socially organized intelligence,
fix things.

We act or write as if literacy problems, or the decentralization of educational systems, or creating good management systems in higher education are
technical problems, capable of solution in a decade or less. This is our professional ideology, through which we conduct our day-to-day educational practices, in policy-making, in research and in what we say to students and in what
we encourage them to read. Of course, the ideology of pragmatism glides over
a few difficulties. We have been struggling with literacy problems for rather
longer than a decade. We cannot guarantee that the benefits we predict for the
decentralization of educational systems will follow in practice. The important
question to be asked about good management in higher education – good for
what? – demands a theoretical answer before techniques for the delivery of
good management can be constructed.

Nevertheless, we carry on in our assumptions that the world of education is
a technical universe – predictable, difficult, but only routinely so, and manageable. Indeed, *under certain circumstances* it is all those things – fairly predictable, only routinely difficult and, with the skills and professional training of
dedicated educational leaders, more or less manageable.

We have, however, tended to assume that this condition of stability, the
routines of historical change, the mundaneness of things educational, are normal conditions. Such relatively stable historical and social circumstances and
periods of routine educational reform can be noted. There was a nice normal-
ity to the debates and policies on the expansion of educational opportunity in
France, West Germany, Denmark, Norway, Sweden, Australia, Canada, New
Zealand and most of the United Kingdom in the period between about 1950
and 1980. There were steady patterns and routines in the reforms to education
in the Soviet Union, and, for that matter, in Poland, Hungary and Czechoslovakia and other countries in Central and Eastern Europe, in approximately
the same period. Even in the United States, despite the drama of specific historical moments – such as the 1954 decision of the Supreme Court on the inherently unequal effects of racially segregated education – there was a
steadiness in the trajectories of educational policy and in the idea of a publicly
organized school system. The domestic and international politics of the

United States framed a range of educational developments which could be understood by reference to US legal and constitutional traditions, the histories of immigration, race and settlement in the United States, and the cold war. Even in Latin America, though there were strong variations between countries such as Argentina, Brazil and Chile in the styles of their democratic projects in the 1950s and early 1960s, there was a pattern. There were dramatic regional and urban inequalities, class, race and gender discrimination, and the heavy administrative centralization of many educational systems. There was also a nicely stable rhetoric from Latin American governments, drawn partly from Christianity and partly from the international agencies, about the need for and the directions of educational reform. In Africa, there was a steady pattern in the commitment to elite training and some vocational training, coupled with under-investment in basic education, in most of the French and British colonies, north and south of the Sahara, after 1945 and before political independence.

These gradual, incremental patterns of educational change – the slow movements in the invention of a complex social technology called an educational system – have setbacks, interruptions, heroes and villains. But they make a coherent narrative which is only occasionally interrupted and made dramatic. There is a strike, a protest, an organized movement for reforms, and victory: educational legislation which slowly produces consequences that were unexpected or are disliked. The social and political processes to rearrange the social technology – the educational system – start again.

Within such gradual incremental patterns of educational change in such social contexts, an ideology of pragmatism is attractive and perhaps a bit of social engineering, though not a lot, would be useful. We can fix education systems sector by sector: educate a good elite, train some teachers, add some vocational technical education and elementary education, and then the system can be slowly expanded. In the end, sooner or later, equality of educational opportunity will probably be achieved. It is remarkable how much of the contemporary history of education in so many countries in the last 50 or even 100 years can be written up in those terms.

The metaphor is one of fine-tuning; or needlepoint; or the steady progress and occasional dropped loop in the hypnotically attractive rhythms of the skilled knitter. Fine-tuning and needlepoint and knitting take for granted a stable social world. Similarly, the ideology of pragmatism and piecemeal educational reform takes for granted a relatively stable domestic and international politics and economics.

Indeed, it is within this vision and from this pragmatic ideology that many (though not all) of the *World Yearbooks of Education* from 1950 to about 1990 were constructed. There were 'problems', for example, in the curriculum for schools, in teacher training, in the expansion of secondary education, in changing university systems, or in the relation of church and state. By using comparative examples, or, far more difficult, by thinking comparatively, new educational policies might be devised in one country wishing to take advantage of the experience of others.

Every now and then, though, things go wrong. The knitting has to stop. The ideology of pragmatically oriented explanation and expectations about gradual change and permanent fine-tuning in a stable universe suffers a severe test. Instead of an expected spring shower or the monsoon rains, a tidal wave clears an inhabited shoreline, a twister flattens parts of a major modern city, a typhoon sweeps across the South China Sea. The system – the weather system, the social system, the educational system – goes crazy.

Of course the system – the weather system or the social system – has not 'gone crazy'. There is enough academic understanding of weather systems to be able to offer abstract explanations of tidal waves, of twisters and of typhoons. We know how they work internally, how they are powered and re-powered, the rules of their apparent chaos. We are even combining old and newer ways of predicting, in practice, their occurrence, their patterns of movement and their eventual ending. We also know enough about social systems to have some labels; we speak or write of political revolutions, *coups d'état*, rebellions, resistance movements, cultural revolutions, and so on. We also tend to make confident predictions which are wrong, or right so late that it is too late, or banally correct: Communism will triumph, Yugoslavia will collapse.

Our relative failure to explain violent disturbances to social systems, our difficulties in labelling and in identifying the relations and consequences of such disturbances, are even more pronounced in our failure to notice, label and explain collapses and rapid reconstructions of educational systems. What should we call such rapid collapses and re-shapings? Educational revolutions? Transformations? Transitions? Rolling transformations? Interrupted transitions? Educational hiccoughs? And how may any one of those labels be defined and justified? These are reasonable enough questions, probably. But it is equally important to note, in the process of trying to avoid a lengthy and abstract excursion into labelling and defining, that what we have seen in the last few decades, for example since the 1960s, is an increasingly widespread pattern of the rapid collapse, or destruction, and the reconstruction of educational systems.

There were in the 1960s, for example, major educational redefinitions in Cuba and Brazil following sudden changes in the control of the central state. There was the Chinese Cultural Revolution, at whose centre were educational 'reforms'. In Africa, there were not merely the redefinitions of educational systems which followed from the escape from colonialism into new political systems, there were also the dramatic and contemporary educational events of South Africa as it has thrown off an apartheid of colour. Since the 1970s there has been major reconstruction (and a great deal of destruction) of the educational systems of England [*sic*], New Zealand, Canada, and the United States. Since the late 1980s, almost all the countries of Central and Eastern Europe, including 'East' Germany, have been redefined educationally.

So this *World Yearbook of Education* is about a major set of events which we have trouble even labelling. In fact, we cannot yet be sure there is 'a set'. What is clear is that the metaphor for these modes of educational change should break away from ideas about pragmatic fine-tuning, or the slow knitting together of new social and educational fabrics. A new metaphor needs to be drawn from ideas about styles of chaos – a typhoon, a tidal wave, a twister, an earthquake – and an urgent sense that how we have thought about educational systems needs a new vocabulary. Of course, we could merely continue to write about educational reform.... .

For this *Yearbook*, the editors rather hoped that the contributors would not do that. We hoped that our contributors would get rid of old ideas and that they would try to avoid adding yet another essay on educational reform to an already large literature. We advised them that the theme of the volume would be 'education in times of transition' and we noted that the word *transition* was becoming widely used. We suggested first that it would probably help the contributor and the readers of the volume (and us) if a particular moment in the last decade, or so, were identified as a point of 'transition'. We ourselves suggested that particular dates, such as the moment of Thatcher, or the moment of Deng, could be taken as marking a transition; or that dates could be identified for particular countries – Latvia 1991, Romania 1989, and so on. We thought that in many other places, such as Bolivia, or South Korea or Brazil, it might be more difficult to be precise about a date for the 'transition', but setting a date was the first problem that faced our contributors.

We hoped that they – and the readers of the volume – could and can see a particular date as a symbol of a concentration of particular events. These events and processes, the markers of transition, would probably include 1) a new clarity and determination in the role of central (or several regional) governments to reconstruct society; 2) a moment of new alertness (by a variety of agencies and publics) to the need to reorder the economic and social stratification systems; 3) a new political vision of the future; and 4) a fresh definition of the political–cultural thrust of the educational system. We invited the contributors in the analysis of 'their' transition to comment on the rhetoric of the participants, to identify some of the immediate consequences of the transition for political parties, or land and property distribution, or the emergence of new elites, or other obvious markers of shifts in power in their own country.

It was against these moments and processes of political, economic and social 'transition' that we invited contributors to ask about the new political visions of the future expressed in the redefined educational system. What was the educational system, as a major carrier of cultural messages, now 'saying'? How did it redefine the social past – how is it rewriting history, as it were? How is the educational system, as a message carrier, defining the old or the new nation, or the old and the new minorities? Who, in other words, are the old and the new secular devils, or, for that matter, the religious ones?

Within the educational system itself we asked contributors to pay particular attention to two themes: what are the new techniques of surveillance and
what are the new epistemological principles? In other words, in the 'transition' picked by the author, we hoped that it might be possible to say how the
state (in particular) had – or had not – made the new education system open to
public scrutiny. One of the major characteristics of really serious educational
change is an increase in the intensity of surveillance. This can be seen in most
'transitions', for example, in the 'purification' of the teaching force after defeat
in war or in a political and social revolution. Currently, even in countries that
have not experienced war or violent revolution, a new cultural and professional emphasis has been given to the 'management' of educational systems.
The educational manager, as cultural hero or heroine, is armed with new techniques. New agencies of surveillance – the rhetoric is typically that of quality
control and the word 'surveillance' is not used – have dramatically increased
in many places. The new agencies of surveillance can tell you, as an educator,
and the state as the guarantor of quality whether professional errors are (or are
not) being committed. In a well-managed world, institutional punishments or
rewards follow.

More broadly, we wondered if new definitions of social and educational error and truth were on offer. We asked our contributors to consider whether
some knowledge considered to be bad before the transition, is now considered to be good. We invited them to indulge in some 'de-coding', for example,
of words such as 'effective and efficient', 'Islam', 'the market', 'internationalization' or 'national culture'. Clearly, the words and their meanings vary according to national context. Overall, we hoped that this kind of analysis
would give the author(s), us and the readers of the volume a sense of 'transi-
tions-in-education' in different places. This left the problem of time, or 'times
of transition'.

Asking for a rather recent date for the analysis is very much within the tradition of the *World Yearbooks of Education* that have sought out relatively 'hot',
contemporary topics. However, as the theme of the volume, while very immediate, is one about which we know very little, we suggested to the contributors
that they might wish to set their own analysis in a longer perspective in the
Conclusion to their own chapters. We also encouraged some to pick a moment
of transition that was not of the 1990s if they felt that this was crucial to their
analysis and the context of their own country.

Thus, this volume is about education in times of transition and about 'educational transitions'. Educational transitions can be defined, for the purposes
of getting a first grip on the theme, as the more or less simultaneous collapse or
destruction and then reconstruction of state apparatuses, political visions of
the future, economic and social stratification systems and the deliberate incorporation of the education system, as an active agency and as a message system, into this social transition. In the context of such social drama, the
educational system itself is redefined, fully or partially. The educational sys-

tem is both changed by the broader transition and (after rapid redefinition) contributes to the social transition.

A rather firm decision was taken about time, and the idea of times of transition. In the same way as we wished to avoid receiving general essays on educational reform, so we wished to avoid receiving general essays on educational history and the slow genesis of contemporary crises. Thus we advised our contributors that educational transitions should be taken to mean social processes that happened and were made to happen in about a decade. Such a time distinction is arbitrary but it has two advantages. It distinguishes educational transitions – for us here – from a more general and an even more difficult book on education and revolutions; and it directs attention away from a fixation on the question of the causes of things.

Thus, the editors wished to stay within the tradition of the *World Yearbooks*. That is, they wanted contributors to write about major contemporary educational events of interest to educationists and policy-makers in many countries within a broad international framing of the topic of the volume. The consequence is worrying. While almost all of the *Yearbooks* are frightening – the number of unresolved educational problems is very large – this *Yearbook* is especially so.

The *Yearbook* covers what is probably a major set of educational happenings, many of which have occurred in the last couple of decades. It is difficult to know how to label them. Educational transitions? Maybe; or at least maybe for now. It is difficult to work out a way to analyse any one of them. And in the present state of our knowledge it is just about impossible to make sense of them as a category of happenings. Educational earthquakes? Yes, or at least intuitively and metaphorically, yes. The educational world has indeed changed dramatically. But do we understand it? I think the worrying answer is, only little bits of it and probably not the most important bits.

2. Education in times of transition: Eastern Europe with particular reference to the Baltic states

David Coulby

Introduction: transitions in Eastern Europe

Some political transitions are highly visible. The destruction of the Berlin Wall gave visible expression to the collapse of the iron curtain, the end of Soviet domination of Eastern Europe and the eventual reunification of Germany. Sometimes the visible moments are themselves misleading. Romania had to wait several years after the demise of Ceausescu before the *securitates* relaxed their grip on power and the modernization of the economy and the state could proceed.

Some transitions, equally fundamental, are less readily identified. Reagan came to power in 1978, Thatcher in 1979. In the period since then, the United States, the countries of the expanding EU and the states of Eastern Europe and the former Soviet Union have all undergone major transitions. With the introduction of the common currency for eleven EU members in 1999 and with the planned movement of the Union to the east, along with the expansion of NATO, a further period of social and political turbulence is likely. At the same time international capital has never been more rootless and information communication technology (ICT) developments are transforming all modes of production, distribution and consumption (Castells, 1996; 1997; 1998). The European countries are in the midst of profound and by no means completed transitions.

This chapter focuses on the transitions in Eastern Europe, making a particular case of the Baltic states. It attempts briefly to identify and differentiate important features of these transitions. It then goes on to examine some of the concomitant changes within education systems. Eastern Europe is unfortunately a political rather than a geographical term. Greece and Finland are actually further east than Poland or the Czech Republic. The continued use of the discourse of east and west may reflect the anachronistic, divisive thinking of the cold war period. What is intended here is a shorthand to cover the states of the former Soviet Union (where the transition began in 1991 with the break-up of that state, as Russia followed the lead of the Baltic states in opting for independence) and those over which it had influence (where the transition began in 1989 following Soviet non-involvement in the liberalization of East Germany, Hungary, Czechoslovakia and Poland and the death of Ceausescu in Romania).

In Eastern Europe features that characterize this transition so far include:

- political freedom;
- economic liberalization;
- nationalism;
- the breakdown of social order;
- a renewed interest in the West.

These matters are clearly linked and not all states display all these features. They constitute the generalizations within which individual examples can be identified.

The extent, or for that matter the benefits, of political freedom must not be overstated. While speech, publication, worship and media are certainly substantially freer in a great many states, from the Czech Republic to Estonia, there are many groups who would question the nature of their new-found freedom: Crimean Tartars, Russian-speakers in Latvia, Chechens everywhere. Nevertheless, in many parts of Eastern Europe there is an exceedingly widespread awareness of a greatly enhanced perspective of personal freedom and renewed political participation. The former Communist parties themselves have in many cases performed a miraculous transformation into electable democratic organizations.

This political liberalization has been the accompaniment, if not the precondition, for economic liberalization. With varying degrees of pain, the Eastern European economies are being transformed to participate in the global market. The pain has been extreme in many cases: between 20 and 40 per cent reductions in industrial output; mass unemployment at the same time as the social security net has been removed; the irresponsible introduction of Thatcherite economic policies, which had already been abandoned in the West. Nevertheless, while massive inflows of international capital are still, in most states, eagerly awaited, some economies are on clear convergence with their Western neighbours as is recognized by the planned admission of Estonia, Poland, the Czech Republic, Hungary and Slovenia (along with Cyprus) to the EU. (The status of Latvia's application is discussed in the final section.) A further tranche of east European countries are almost certain to follow. The admission of Poland and Estonia will give the EU further land boundaries with Russia. The recent economic crisis in Russia, combined with the persistently worsening economic performance in countries such as Romania, indicates that not all states will be able to make as smooth a change of economic system as that effected in, say, Hungary. Indeed, commentators in Romania have begun to question the notion of 'transition'. Without substantial internal reform and equally solid investment from the West, Bosnia, Serbia, Bulgaria, Albania and Romania may not emerge to a future of economic liberalism and prosperity but rather remain trapped in post-Communist conflict, bureaucracy and poverty. The lexicon of transition is inherently optimistic, that of a difficult period which can be passed through to happier times. It is then more obviously applicable to Estonia and Latvia, say, than to the Former Yugoslavian Republic of Macedonia (FYROM) and Georgia.

Apart from applications to membership of the EU, the renewed interest in the West is also manifested in the expanded membership of the Council of Europe and NATO. Tourism and commercial and educational visits have increased from east to west as well as from west to east. Western products and styles are much in demand. Western broadcasts can now be received across Eastern Europe and their popularity is all too often in inverse proportion to the quality of their content and the impartiality of their reporting.

This transition has not been without its downside. The breakdown of social order and the re-emergence of nationalism being among the two most notable aspects. Crime rates have exploded in Sofia as well as in Moscow and St Petersburg. Drug abuse and vandalism have accompanied Microsoft and Coca-Cola into Eastern Europe. The processes of privatization have allowed for collaboration between *aparatchiks* of the previous regime with local and Western criminal organizations to make huge, illegal and semi-legal fortunes at the public expense. Particularly in Russia, organized crime, linked to the police and political structures, has become exceedingly prevalent.

Especially for the older generation, there is a widespread perception of a breakdown of social order that, along with the perceived tardiness of Western financial commitment, provides much of the groundswell towards the refashioned Communist parties. Those countries identified above as being more entrenched in poverty than emerging from any economic transition are also the ones that the Western institutions, notably NATO and the EU, are most reluctant to accept. Progressive politicians in Romania, for example, have demanded economic change and sacrifice on the basis that it would lead to a successful application to join the EU (and associated economic paradise). When the application was turned down in 1998, there was a risk that extremist political parties, nationalist as well as Communist, might benefit to the further detriment of economic progress.

The manifestations of re-emergent nationalism have varied from the citizenship laws of the Baltic states, discussed below, and the break-up of Czechoslovakia, to civil wars in Yugoslavia, Georgia and Chechnia. This nationalism has highly particularistic loyalties and is capable of generating the most intense passions. It is exacerbated by apparent economic disparities, between Slovenia and Serbia or between the Czech Republic and Slovakia. It constitutes a major threat to the stability of many parts of the region: currently including Kosovo, Macedonia (FYROM), Vojvodina and Bosnia. Furthermore Russian nationalism and its uneasy relationship with that of many of its new

neighbours – the Baltic states, Georgia and Moldova – may also come to constitute a continental threat. If the period of transition in Eastern Europe is not to
be even more bloody, then some control over nationalist sentiments and activities as well as greater economic and political stability in Russia would appear
to be essential.

Education in times of transition

The transitions in Eastern Europe, then, were associated with the democratization of the central state and the attempt to involve it in the reintroduction of
capitalist modes of production, distribution and consumption. In many states
this engaged a rhetoric of restored freedom and national identity. In most
states it involved a rejection of Communism and of Russia. Property was re-
distributed from the state often to those who could claim to be the former
owners. In this process much of the land and industrial capital actually came
into the hands of the former *aparatchiks*. This group maintained economic and
often political power in some countries such as Romania. Elsewhere, as described for the Baltic states below, nationalist forces were sufficiently strong to
break the *aparatchiks'* grip on wealth and power.

Just as states differ in the extent to which they are involved in the transitions described above, so they differ in the extent to which they seek to adapt
their education systems to address these changing circumstances or to which
the transition itself is driven by educational processes. While there certainly
are structural aspects to this adaptation – the emergence of private, selective
and streamed institutions – it is on curricular aspects that this chapter particularly concentrates. To what extent have the curricular systems of Eastern European schools and universities been adapted to recognize and facilitate the
wider transitions? This section of the chapter focuses on curricula and nation-building and nationalism in Eastern Europe generally, and the final sections take up the case of the Baltic states.

Education had not been the only instrument of Russification. Other, less
subtle techniques had been used: mass murder, mass deportation, the influx
of Russian speakers, party and citizenship restrictions on national language
speakers. But language and educational language policy were key elements of
Russification across the former Soviet Union. The Soviet approach to asymmetric bilingualism had been at best assimilationist, at worst attempted destruction of nations such as the Inguchetians, the Chechens and the Crimean
Tartars. National language speakers in the three Baltic states felt that their languages too had been taken to the edge of elimination. Language, then, was a
critical area of nation-building in many of the newly independent states. The
transition was widely characterized by changes in national and educational
language policy. In Estonia, Latvia and Lithuania, Russian ceased to be the

language of many schools and is rapidly being replaced in the universities. The first foreign language in a great many states ceased to be Russian and became English.

Other important changes involved the abandonment of Marxist–Leninism as the paradigm discourse for a variety of subjects from sociology to biology in schools and universities across the former Soviet Union and Eastern Europe. The transitional states rapidly used educational policy to redefine the nature of truth and error. History had to be fundamentally rewritten and Soviet internationalism revealed as a further aspect of the centuries-long expansion of the muscovy state. 'In the former Soviet Union', the joke goes, 'the past is always unpredictable'. Across Eastern Europe paragraphs on Soviet friendship and brotherhood were deleted from history and social sciences textbooks and replaced by ones on the suppression and ultimate triumph of the national destiny.

National culture, no longer in the shadow of the Moscow-financed state culture machine, found itself with a central dimension in the curricula of schools. In Latvia, folk song and folk dance, manifestations of the rich national tradition, could take up the school time previously given over to dreary, polytechnical wishful thinking. Schools and universities were set free to celebrate the nation, to reinforce the strength of its language, to re-make its history and to re-shape its civil society. In Tajikistan the universities are introducing new courses in management, world culture, the history of religious ethics and ancient Tajik languages (Holdsworth, 1998). In this emancipatory, epistemological transformation, many states are still engaged.

As the example of the Soviet Union itself indicates, nation-building and nationalism-building are all too often closely connected. In many states of the former Soviet Union, nation-building took the form of the denigration of the Russian language and of Russia which too often had as its political accompaniment, harsh restrictions on citizenship. In Eastern Europe too the re-writing of history and the celebration of culture focused on a narrow definition of what was the nation, who were the true citizens and who had been the historical enemies. The rediscovery of the nation and national identity was accompanied by a rediscovery or recreation of the Other. The Serbs reasserted their difference from Bosnians and Croatians; more peacefully the Slovaks established their distinctiveness. Russians and Chechens threw off the fiction of peaceful, Soviet internationalism. In Latvia Russian speakers were stripped of their citizenship and many associated human rights. Latvia is only an extreme example here. The disenfranchisement of minorities is common across the region: the Czech Republic excludes gypsies and Slovaks from citizenship (Mazower, 1998). Of course, nationalism figures as a continuity as well as a transition. The treatment of Magyars and Gypsies in Romania has improved little in the new democracy from their conditions under the xenophobic Ceausescu regime.

In this reassertion of nationalism the schools and universities played their part. A surprising number of the most outspoken Serbian nationalists were academics, as manifest in the infamous memorandum of the Serbian Academy of Arts and Sciences (Mazower, 1998). In the invention of tradition, the school and university curricula stressed a particular view and period of history, the Battle of Kosovo, say or the 1939–45 period, which identified peoples of other languages, scripts or religions as Others; in extreme cases as enemies. In Bosnia, Croatian children are actually taught in schools that Tudjman is their president and Croatia is their country (Done, 1998). The sense of solidarity invoked by a literary masterpiece, folk song or common enjoyment of sacred landscape has too readily become a sense of solidarity against the Other.

The shift to English as the second language is leading to the neglect of the other languages of the state and of near neighbours. The attempt to internationalize, in some cases spectacularly successful, as in the case of Estonia, has been at the expense of a rejection of regional continuity. Neighbouring St Petersburg has the same population as Estonia and Latvia combined, and these five million people speak Russian. The unfortunate and, in some instances disastrous, concomitants of reawakened national identity have been revived xenophobia, language-based politics and regional isolationism: a process in which school and university curricula have played a significant part. In some instances, such as Serbia (Rosandic and Pesic, 1994), this has led to a curriculum that is potentially and actually destructive of democratic politics.

Linguistic nationalism in the Baltic states: a brief background

Distinctions between groups of peoples in the Baltic states are made on the basis of either religion or language. It is the latter distinction – in particular between Russian, on the one hand, and Latvian or Estonian, on the other – that forms the main focus of current politics. Language in this region is rather readily conflated with ethnicity. The transitional independent states have attempted to portray themselves as linguistic or ethnic nations (in this they reflect a more general trend described in Hobsbawm, 1987). It is possible that nowhere is the fallacy of the nation–state more potentially dangerous than in Latvia, Lithuania and Estonia.

To understand this danger and the way in which it concerns education and citizenship in a period of transition it is necessary to have some knowledge of the history of the Baltic states during this century. The difficulty is that the interpretation and even the facts of this history remain deeply contested (Mazower, 1998; Overy, 1998). Following the peace treaties that ended the First World War, Lithuania, Latvia and Estonia became independent states. At this point their demographic profile was substantially different from what it was in 1991. In all three countries there was a significant Jewish population, with some cities being historically and demographically important

components of the diaspora, such as Vilnius in Lithuania and Daugavpils in
Latvia. In all three countries, but especially in Latvia and Estonia, there were
also significant Russian(-speaking) minorities.

The independence betrayed by the Molotov–Ribbentrop Pact, during the
Second World War the Baltic states were successively invaded by the Red
Army, the *Wehrmacht* and the Soviets again. Baltic forces fought for both sides
as well as independence movements. This was a period of atrocities. Responsibilities for these remain contested. By the end of the war the Jewish population had been almost eliminated in local as well as distant death camps. The
German population had largely fled westwards. In 1945 Lithuania, Latvia and
Estonia became Soviet Republics. This was not the choice of their populations
but, following the defeat of Germany, reflected the military power of the Soviet Union across Eastern and Central Europe at that date.

The period of Russification of the Baltic states between 1945 and 1991 involved demographic, economic, political and educational processes. Through
waves of systematic purges, Lithuanian, Latvian and Estonian people were
transported *en masse* to Central Asia and Siberia. Many who resisted Soviet incorporation were murdered. Others fled as refugees to the West. A parallel
and opposite demographic movement of Russians into the Baltic states was
implemented. This rested on the Soviet development of industrial facilities in
the area and more particularly on the military installations rapidly established
in the warm water Baltic ports. The demographic profile, especially of Latvia
and Estonia, was radically transformed. In 1934 Estonians represented 88.2
per cent of the population, in 1989 they were 61.5 per cent (Estonia Institute,
1995). By 1993 Latvians represented only 54.2 per cent of the population of the
state (United Nations Development Programme, 1995), having been 75.5 per
cent at the high point of 1939 (Lieven, 1993). This demographic profile was
most visible in the cities. In Daugavpils, to take an extreme example, out of a
total population of over 120,000 in 1994, 56 per cent are Russian, while Polish
and Latvian speakers both represent about 15 per cent (Multinacional Culture's Centre, 1995): this probably underestimates the Russian population;
Lieven (1993) gives 87 per cent Russian speakers. Riga has 60 per cent Russian
speakers as against 37 per cent Latvian. Tallinn has just over 50 per cent Russian speakers (Lieven, 1993).

The economic processes were such that the Russians in the Baltic states during the Soviet period were often seen to have the best paid jobs, frequently in
the military or security services. Political processes supported this: the new-
comers were provided with new housing, while Latvians, for instance, sub-
sisted in poor conditions. The politics of Soviet internationalism were actually,
in the south and west as well as the north of the enlarged Soviet Union, those
of the continuation of 18th- and 19th-century Russian expansionism. The Baltic states were Russified.

Education played a major part in this process. Schools and universities
were adapted to the production of the ideal Soviet citizen. The history of the

20th century was accordingly rewritten – not for the first or the last time: its unpredictability has already been noted. The status of the Russian language became ever more important in schools and universities. Russian became the first language of many schools and of higher education. It became the second 'international' language of all other schools. Lithuanian, Latvian and Estonian, or for that matter Livonian, Polish and Ukrainian, did not have this status in the Russian-speaking schools where English or German were more likely to be the foreign languages. Thus, speakers of the Baltic languages spoke Russian but speakers of Russian did not speak the Baltic languages. Russian rapidly became the language of the military, of commerce and of education. Russian was the language of daily transaction in the cities, as indeed it still is in many. Educational institutions were used to implement policies of linguistic segregation and asymmetric bilingualism.

Dispersed and degraded, their language, their culture and their very 'people' seemed, especially to the Latvians and Estonians, to be being systematically wiped out. They were conscious of their history, as languages, cultures, independent states and major European trading cities, which goes back many centuries. It was as if it were all about to disappear under the onslaught of Russification, disguised as Soviet internationalism. 'The Latvian nation was moving inexorably towards that point where national dissolution and extinction could become irreversible' (Driefelds, 1996, p 50: though this source cannot be regarded as invariably impartial).

Given the current status of Russians, especially in Estonia and Latvia, given the actual history of the Jews in the Baltic states during the Second World War, the vociferousness and extremism of some Baltic nationalists may appear incongruous. Yet when the three states achieved independence, heralding the total dissolution of the Soviet Union, they had succeeded, from the point of view of many of the participants, in wresting political independence from the seeming brink of cultural ('ethnic') extinction. The education and citizenship laws that were rapidly put in place reflect this. It is to these that this chapter now turns.

Baltic education in transition

Laws were put in place so that in Latvia, Latvian is the one official language and in Estonia, Estonian was the official language. In both states only people who are literate in the official language were regarded as citizens by the law. People not regarded as citizens have no vote and cannot engage in political activity. (In Estonia non-citizens can vote in local elections only.) They carry a different passport from citizens and there are thus restrictions on their ability to travel. A large percentage of the populations of these countries thus suffer discrimination in terms of civic rights on the basis of their language. Further-

more, 'there have been changes in the Latvian labour law code permitting employers to lay off employees who cannot fulfil their professional duties due to
lack of Latvian language knowledge' (United Nations Development
Programme, 1995). The mass of 'non-citizens probably shun the naturalisation
system because they regard the language and history tests as too demanding
and at times even humiliating. This is contributing to a mistrust of institutions
and reflects the psychological estrangement of non-citizens from the state'
(United Nations *Latvia Human Development Report* 1997, cited in Vipotnik,
1998, p 7).

The ability of people to learn a foreign language can thus determine their
civil status. In this sense, in Latvia and Estonia education and citizenship are
vitally interconnected. To put it at its starkest: a pensioner, whose family have
been living in Riga for many generations, who might have actively participated in the independence movement, now has to take a language examination before being eligible to vote. Not official policy in either state, though part
of the political discourse in both, is the notion that Russians should go 'back' to
Russia. Although Russia has said that it will accept any who proclaim themselves to be Russian, the current political and economic climate in that state is
not one to encourage significant inward migration.

Educational policy in the region is now that characteristic of newly emer-
gent or re-emergent states. The change in language policy is the most obvious.
One asymmetric bilingualism has replaced another. Lithuanian, Latvian or
Estonian have become the predominant language of schooling in Lithuania,
Latvia and Estonia, respectively (for a full description of language policy in
Latvia see Kamenska, 1995). Attempts are also being made rapidly to shift the
language of higher education away from Russian. 'The Baltic universities increasingly operate only in the Baltic languages, and quietly discriminate
against Russian applicants' (Lieven, 1993, p 314). Russian-speaking schools
continue, though their numbers are being reduced, and in these either Latvian or Estonian is the first and compulsory foreign language. The foreign language of Estonian- or Latvian-speaking schools is no longer Russian but
German or predominantly English. Thus all young Latvians and Estonians
will soon speak the official language but only some of them will speak Russian, the language of many cities and of their neighbour, trading partner and
major regional power. English is replacing Russian as the *lingua franca* between the three states.

All three Baltic states rapidly shifted their curricula away from the objective
of creating ideal Soviet citizens. Their urgent concern was the invention or
re-invention of a national culture. Great poets and artists, important scientific
and technological developments, sacred landscapes and cityscapes are being
discovered, re-discovered or, if necessary, invented. The history of each state,
of its relations to the rest of Europe and the wider world and of the various
groups within the state are being rewritten. In this way a version of the state's
importance, its culture, its identity and its history are being encapsulated

within the school and university curriculum and thereby legitimated and re-produced to succeeding generations.

Religious education has been reintroduced as an optional subject in Estonia and Lithuania. The importance of Latvian and Estonian culture – in terms of folk music and dance – as well as in the discovery of a literary canon, is being stressed. Dance and music had been important components of the protected identities of groups, especially in Latvia during the Soviet period. This self-conscious identity indeed formed a part of the 'singing revolution' (Driefelds, 1996). Current and historic links with the West are emphasized in many activities: scientific, commercial, artistic, political. An official statement on education in Lithuania, for instance, stresses that, 'The educational system is based on European cultural values;... Educational reform is based on the ed-ucational experience of democratic Lithuania and Europe' (Lithuanian Minis-try of Education, undated; see also Zujiene, 1995).

The danger of these radical changes to school and university curricula is that these institutions are being involved in the encouragement of xenopho-bia as a mode of state building. This possibility is obviously attractive in newly re-emergent states. A sense of statehood may be encouraged by emphasizing difference from other states, perhaps even distrust of the inhabitants of other states or a stress on their historical role in subordinating the 'true' citizens. The curricula of schools and universities implicitly or explicitly shift towards the encouragement of warfare (Coulby and Jones, 1996). Such a temptation may be particularly attractive with regard to the state and inhabitants identified with previously colonizing powers.

It seems almost as if there were an element of revenge in the policies pur-sued by politicians, otherwise enlightened, with regard to the Russian speak-ers in Latvia and Estonia. Combined with other policies on housing and on the payment of pensions to previous Soviet military and security personnel still resident in the two states, this may well be the perception of the Russian-speaking people. And it may also be the perception of the much larger Russian population across the land borders within Russia itself. On the other hand, from the point of view of Latvian or Estonian speakers, these are essential steps to preserve the languages and cultures which Russification almost suc-ceeded in eliminating and to redress the economic and civil wrongs of the So-viet era.

The politics of this region are important in European and indeed global terms. All three Baltic states are actively pursuing political and economic links with the West. As capitalist democracies with a long history of Western links, and in close proximity to 'Western' Finland, these connections are readily fur-thered. The Estonian currency has been successfully tied to the deutschmark since shortly after independence. All three states wish to become members of the European Union (see below). They would furthermore welcome member-ship of NATO. In the medium term such developments would seem to be wel-come to these Western organizations. The Scandinavian countries in particular are keen to further their historical, geographical and commercial links with the Baltic states. They are also anxious to support all political developments that can assist in the establishment of stability in the region.

At this point it is worth mentioning the dimensions of each of the three states in demographic terms. The population of Estonia in 1990 was little over one and a half million (Estonian Institute, 1995); that of Latvia in 1993 was 2.6 million (United Nations Development Programme, 1995); that of Lithuania in 1989, 3.7 million (Lieven, 1993). Not one of them has as many people as, say, the adjacent city of St Petersburg. No matter what their success in transforming their economies, these states can never become world powers. They could not sustain the armed forces necessary to defend themselves against their militarily powerful neighbour. Russia has now almost completed its military withdrawal from the Baltic states though it maintains as its sovereign territory the naval base at Kaliningrad (Koenigsberg) on the Baltic coast between Poland and Lithuania. Russia is not the only post-Soviet nuclear power but it is unquestionably the main one. Events internally in Inguchetia and Chechnia, as well as externally in Georgia and Moldova, not to mention the confrontation at Pristina airport, make it clear that Russia is still prepared to use conventional military power. These military interventions have been made by a moderate, ostensibly pro-Western government. It is by no means clear that such an administration will continue in Moscow. The language and citizenship laws of the Baltic states, even without the actual or threatened expulsion of Russian speakers, are probably provocative to the people of Russia. They could certainly be made to seem so by any government with an expansionist eye on the Baltic ports and natural resources. Thus, these language and citizenship laws may become a source of regional and European instability.

It is notable that Lithuania has established a more positive foreign policy with regard to Moscow than the other two states. Legislators in Latvia and Estonia are faced with two sets of policy options. The first option is to abuse the civil rights of Russian speakers and to erode the importance and status of Russian as a language. This option depends on the continuation of Russian weakness in the area or on the calculation that the existing and ever strengthening links with the West would be sufficient to deter any Russian military intervention or the threat of such. An even less realistic calculation would be that, were there to be any such intervention, the Western powers in the shape of the EU or NATO would actively intervene. The second option is to recognize that the economic collapse of Russia will not continue indefinitely; that Russia will remain a major trading power; that Russian speakers in the three states are an economic and cultural asset and should have equal civil rights; that educational policies and particularly language policies should recognize these issues of social justice and economic and political fact. As the Baltic states come to recognize the importance of Russia to their own trading position, opening up the Latvian port of Ventspils in preparation for Russian oil, for example, there are hopes that this latter policy may prevail.

While, in the early years of regained independence, it was the first of these options that Latvia and Estonia followed, it is clear now that there has been an important policy shift in the case of both states. When all three applications were considered by the European Union, it was Estonia with its stable currency, its flourishing economy and its development of more progressive citizenship laws, which received approval to proceed to accession discussions. In the case of Latvia it was made clear that it was the citizenship laws which had prevented the state being considered for accession. This led to dramatic developments in 1998. A plebiscite of largely Latvian-speaking citizens resulted in a vote to widen the franchise and to include Russian speakers as citizens. This move, supported by the government, has resulted in the near certainty that Latvia will now proceed to accession discussions. It seems that a progressive attitude to diversity within the state and the move towards Europeanization are inextricably linked. What remains to be seen is the extent to which the school and university curricula, having oscillated between two extremes, can now establish content which genuinely reflects the multilingual population and the geographical position and economic potential of the three states.

This chapter and indeed this volume are an attempt to analyse processes which are far from complete. Certainly, the expansion of NATO in 1999 to involve Poland, Hungary and the Czech Republic might symbolize that at least a stage in the process had been achieved. Elsewhere further warfare in the former Yugoslavia and continued economic depression in Bulgaria and Romania question the very principle of transition: transition to what? What is clear is that the more simplistic assumptions embedded in the term transition – that Eastern Europe is in a period of being transformed into the likeness of Western Europe – must be rejected. The historical context is such that the political and educational actors do not see themselves as gaining independence, freedom, prosperity so much as regaining them. Their aspirations are no more towards Western cosmopolitanism than towards Soviet internationalism: on the contrary, they are towards national self-consciousness embedded in language, culture and historical narrative as much as in political and economic institutions.

Indeed, it is clear in these cases that education is not a consequence of political change; it is not a camp follower of the armies of transition. Rather, it is an indispensable part of the process of transition and one of the institutions which is invariably involved in the process from the very outset. The transitions in Eastern Europe are ideological and epistemological just as much as they are political and economic. This was evident before 1989 in the attraction to Western cultural forms and products from modern art to pornography and in the apparent resurgence of Catholicism in Poland and of Protestantism in East Germany. In the singing revolution of the Baltic states culture and language were both the mode and the goal of political contestation. The epistemological protocols that inform the school and university curricula in any state are important foundations of social control and reproduction. The educational transitions in Eastern Europe reveal the extent to which these protocols are profoundly contested and may not be taken for granted. They reveal further that this contestation is often dangerously predicated on nationalism. The hard lesson from Eastern Europe is that nationalism is far from a spent force. Its manifestations and self-perceptions are various – language, religion, 'ethnic identity', culture, historical narrative – but they are all latent within educational just as much as political processes. Nationalism is the bridge which links educational structures and knowledge on the one side to civil strife and warfare on the other.

References

Castells, M (1996) *The Information Age: Economy, society and culture,* vol. 1 *The Rise of the Network Society,* Blackwell, Oxford

Castells, M (1997) *The Information Age: Economy, society and culture,* vol. 2 *The Power of Identity,* Blackwell, Oxford

Castells, M (1998) *The Information Age: Economy, society and culture,* vol. 3 *End of Millennium,* Blackwell, Oxford

Done, K (1998) Unification: a slow process, *Financial Times,* Survey II

Driefelds, J (1996) *Latvia in Transition,* Cambridge University Press, Cambridge

Estonia Institute (1995) *Facts About Estonia,* Estonia Institute, Tallinn

Hobsbawm, E (1987) *The Age of Empire 1875–1914,* Weidenfeld and Nicolson, London

Holdsworth, N (1998) Tajiks opt for revival of the fittest, *Times Educational Supplement,* 15

Kamenska, A (1995) *The State Language in Latvia: Achievements, problems and prospects,* Latvian Centre for Human Rights and Ethnic Studies, Riga

Lieven, A (1993) *The Baltic Revolution: Estonia, Latvia, Lithuania and the path to independence,* Yale University Press, New Haven, CT

Lithuanian Ministry of Education (undated) *General Concept of Education in Lithuania,* Ministry of Education, Vilnius

Mazower, M (1998) *Dark Continent: Europe's twentieth century,* Allen Lane, Harmondsworth

Multinacional Culture Centre (1995) *Multinacionala Multinacional Daugavpils,* Multinacional Culture Centre, Daugavpils

Overy, R (1998) *Russia's War,* Allen Lane, Harmondsworth

Rosandic, R and Pesic, V (1994) *Warfare, Patriotism, Patriarchy: The analysis of elementary school textbooks,* Centre for Anti-War Action MOST, Belgrade

UNDP (United Nations Development Programme) (1995) *Latvia Human Development Report,* UNDP, Riga

Vipotnik, M (1998) Constant source of friction, *Financial Times*, Survey 7
Zujiene, I (1995) Education in Lithuania: an object of reform, in *Education in Europe: An intercultural task*, ed C Wulf, Waxmann, Munster

3.   Bolivia

Sheila Aikman

Introduction

Democratic government was returned to Bolivia in 1982 after almost two decades of military rule. The newly elected government faced economic crisis as
Bolivia and Latin America staggered under the debt crisis and the collapse of
an import-substitution-led economic model. In 1985 Victor Paz Estenssoro
was elected President and negotiated with the IMF a structural adjustment
programme, the 'New Economic Policy', ending the state capitalism which
had been predominant since the same president, Estenssoro, had led the
country through a period of transition of a very different nature, the 'national
revolution' of 1952.

Then, in 1952 the national revolutionary government included the new national union, the Bolivian Workers' Confederation (COB) which promoted the
participation of the wider Bolivian society by improving social conditions in rural areas and expanding the country's economic base beyond tin mining
(Rivera, 1992). Though COB's joint government only lasted until 1958, the unions held strong power and control over state–civil relations until the 1980s, except for a period of exile during the Banzer military dictatorship in the 1970s.
The national revolutionary government gave a prominent place to education,
encapsulated in the 1955 Education Code, as a means of incorporating the rural
population into national society through free and compulsory education. This
Code remained unchallenged until the Estenssoro government produced a
draft reform law in 1986. This was the beginning of a long process of deliberation and contestation between different sectors and powerholders within society that reached a climax with the passing of the Education Reform in 1994.

This chapter examines the Education Reform Law of 1994 and the nature of
the transition in Bolivian society implicit and explicit in this reform. It identifies the different currents of change throughout the 1980s and early 1990s, culminating in constitutional reform which finally paved the way for a break
with the country's 40 years of political and economic centralization and strong
control by union organizations. The Constitution included two historical
changes: the recognition of Bolivia as a country characterized by ethnic and
cultural diversity and the establishment of mechanisms for a participatory democracy through the decentralization of state power. The package of reforms

which followed soon after included the Education Reform, which was conceived of as an important and integral part of the wider change process, designed to alter radically the political and economic profile of the country and allow it to play its part in the new global economic order.

The Education Reform is based on the axiom that education should be intercultural, bilingual and participatory. This chapter investigates how in the educational transition this is articulated in the new education system and examines what it means from the perspective of the Lowland Amazon region or 'Oriente', a region which has traditionally been politically, socially and culturally marginalized.

Bolivia: the context

The 1992 census puts the population of Bolivia at approximately 6.5 million inhabitants (Erdinger, 1997). Bolivia has the largest indigenous population in South America. There are some 33 ethno-linguistic groups, the largest being the Quechua and Aymara peoples, who represent some 54 per cent of the total population of the country and live mostly in the Andean region. The monolingual Spanish-speaking population is 40 per cent. The other indigenous groups represent 16 per cent of the population, though the majority live in the eastern lowland areas where they can comprise the majority population in their territory: Guaranís – 60,000, Moxeños – 40,000, Chiquitanos – 30,000 and Guarayos – 10,000 (in Muñoz, 1997). The remaining groups are much smaller in number with many less than 500. Some of these peoples, such as the Quechua, Ayamara and Guaraní, live across international borders as do the Ese-Eja who live on both sides of the north-eastern border with Peru (ETARE, 1993, cited in Muñoz, 1997).

In terms of GDP, Bolivia is the third poorest country in Latin America after Nicaragua and Haiti with a rate of US $800 per capita (Erdinger, 1997). Education statistics indicate that 20 per cent of the population are absolute illiterates, never having attended school, while 35 per cent more are functionally illiterate, that is after 1–2 years of schooling they cannot read or write a simple letter. Only 11 per cent of children who begin school continue after Grade 5 and only 1 per cent of children in rural areas go on to secondary school. Statistics from the non-formal sector for literacy rates among marginalized out-of-school children and adults show a steady increase with an estimated 800,000 illiterates between the ages of 5 and 19 and more than 2 million adults (CENDES, 1994). The same source notes that because of the government focus almost exclusively on formal education, adult illiteracy will not have changed by the year 2000 because of high levels of educational marginalization and dropout from the formal system (ibid, p 12).

Information about literacy in a multicultural country such as Bolivia requires that we look closer at the changing relationships between languages. In what languages are people becoming literate and what languages do they speak? The panorama of bilingualism is complex and the relationship between Spanish and the indigenous languages differs between regions and between urban and rural contexts. Using data from 1980, Amadio and Zuñiga (1990) note the expansion of bilingualism in the Andean departments and the expansion of monolingualism in the Eastern Lowlands. The former, they explain, is due to growing opportunities for contact between Spanish, Quechua and Aymaran speakers leading to increased Spanish-Quechua and Spanish-Aymaran bilingualism. The latter illustrates a different dynamic whereby the sparse and low density indigenous population of the Lowlands continues on the whole with limited contact but there is a strong influx of monolingual Spanish-speaking colonists into the region in general (ibid).

Changing ideologies, changing society

We can look back to the radical moves taken by Estenssoro's government in 1985 to 'solve' the economic crisis by a definitive break with past political, economic and social ideologies and establishing monetarist and a free market, neo-liberal political economy as paving the way for a package of reforms including the Education Reform which saw the light of day a decade later. The nation was no longer looking to solve its crisis by distancing itself from the outside and 'going it alone' but, on the contrary the 'viability of Bolivia depends on... integration with the rest of the world through a policy of productive transformation' (Plan General de Desarrollo Económico y Social, cited in Erdinger, 1997). The orthodox structural adjustment which the country underwent was implemented quickly by a small team of well-trained technocrats and supported by an alliance with the political opposition in Congress (Brysk et al, 1995).

This New Economic Programme implied a decreasing role for state institutions and posed a serious challenge to union power, in particular the COB. Estenssoro achieved what his immediate predecessors had not – the undermining of organized labour through a series of measures including imprisoning 143 strike leaders and removing labour legislation and safeguards established in 1952, such as a minimum wage. The withdrawal of state subsidies led to the closure of many factories, redundancy for thousands of factory workers and the final demise of tin mining (Green, 1995).

Economic collapse and soaring inflation followed by strict adjustment policies affected not only labour opportunities for the small percentage of the population with a waged income but affected the predominantly subsistence rural population as food subsidies were lifted and budgets for state health and education services were slashed. The number of children leaving school early to support their family increased and by 1991 80 per cent of households were living below the poverty line (food, clothing, housing, health and education services) and 50 per cent were classed as being unable to feed their family (Green, 1995). Illiteracy rates began to rise, drop-out from schooling accelerated, infant mortality rates reached 200 per thousand and life expectancy was only 50 years (Brysk *et al*, 1995, pp 6ff.).

Estenssoro established an Emergency Social Fund designed to cushion the poorest sectors of society, most of whom are indigenous, against the effects of adjustment. The Fund was independent of state bureaucracy and supported NGO and local government small-scale projects. While Brysk *et al* (1995) question the extent to which the poorest really benefited from this Fund, Barríos (1995) is in no doubt that the structural adjustment process widened the gulf between social sectors and affected most seriously those in peri-urban and rural areas.

The 1955 Education Code was designed to provide schooling for the masses, to provide the human resources demanded by an economy based on an import-substitution model of industrialization. As such, it represented a victory over the former liberal elitist tradition while converting education into a powerful ideological instrument at the service of the national revolution. It viewed education as anti-imperialist, anti-feudal and an instrument of liberation, democracy, establishing the dignity of the *campesino* (peasant) and protecting the traditional and historical values of the nation. The Education Code recognized the organized participation of teachers in the guidance, implementation and supervision of education together with the state. In practice, this meant that COB took key political decisions while the teachers' unions controlled the appointment of all educational authorities in collaboration with the government, including having a say in the appointment of the vice-ministers (Rivera, 1992). In reality no one could be appointed to a position of influence without the approval of teachers' unions (Erdinger, 1997).

The implementation of the 1955 Education Code highlighted its inherent contradictions, which have undermined its important premises such as education for a democratic society and free and obligatory education for all. Barríos (1995) points out that a universal and unified education was implemented through a two-tier model with a different administration, teacher training and curriculum for urban and rural schools. This dual urban–rural education system encompassed teacher education, the curriculum and separate teachers' unions. While this guaranteed that rural teachers received extra remuneration for hardship postings, it also meant that rural education was seen by government as second class and low status.

Moreover, the notion of a unified system to incorporate the majority of people into Bolivian society revealed an ignorance of the multicultural and multilingual reality of Bolivia (ibid). The Code established a monolingual Spanish language education system with no reference to the different languages or cultural traditions of the majority of society. The term 'Indian' was outlawed and replaced by *campesino* which was a 'new rhetoric of nationalism that paid homage to the non-acquisitive, stoic virtues of selflessness of the peasant and pictured him as the worthiest of all Bolivians' (Pike, 1973, p 68). While the 1952 national revolution and 1955 Education Code had formally attempted to incorporate the indigenous population into Bolivian society through schooling, the question of ethnic identity had remained untouched and ethnic discrimination and political manipulation had continued unabated (Ticona, 1996).

By the mid-1980s the increasing hardship experienced by a large percentage of the population, together with the undermining of COB union control, had contributed to a change in the nature of political participation and popular movements within civil society. The indigenous/*campesino* sectors of the population began to organize around issues of ethnicity and/or on a national basis rather than the class-based alliances of previous decades (CEDOIN, 1996). Out of the new spaces being created the indigenous and *campesino* movements began to exert much more influence across the whole political sphere (Ticona 1996), though this was not created out of a vacuum. The Tupac Katari Revolutionary Movement, originally an Aymaran movement, had been growing through the 1970s with a view to 'recuperating and re-elaborating the history of the Indian' (ibid, p 13). The movement had three dimensions: cultural, syndical and political. The syndical dimension was established in 1979 with the CSUTSB (the National Confederation of Peasant Workers) and later a political party was formed. By the 1980s the 'Kataristas' had found their first ideologue in Victor Hugo Cardenas who emphasized that the movement was not concerned simply with either class or ethnicity but with the colonial character of both class and ethnicity and the structure of the state (Ticona, 1996).

In 1982 the different indigenous peoples of the Oriente – the Lowlands – established an interethnic organization to represent their demands and to press for recognition of their rights on a regional basis. CIDOB, the Indigenous Confederation of Eastern Bolivia, was formed with a mandate to work in defence of indigenous territories, for the recognition of their communal authorities and ancestral culture and the right to self-determination (Riester, 1989). Throughout the 1980s CIDOB struggled against abuses of indigenous territory and the sacking of natural resources by private entities protected by state laws. It questioned the political administrative structure which ran contra to traditional indigenous practices and demanded participation in the planning of development policies and programmes which affected the indigenous peoples (Zolezzi, 1989). In 1989 CIDOB worked together with the local organization CPIB (Indigenous Confederation of the Beni) to spearhead the campaign of the Chimane people for the demarcation of their territories which were being illegally invaded by colonists and plundered for timber by logging companies. In the following year some 750 indigenous people marched from the rainforest to La Paz in the Andes, a March for Dignity and Territory, where after three days of negotiations the government agreed to remove the logging companies and recognize indigenous rights to the area (IWGIA, 1990).

CIDOB was also active in promoting bilingual education and demanding the legal recognition of the indigenous languages by the state. In 1986 it participated in the Fourth Meeting of Bolivian Studies and succeeded in bringing to the attention of national researchers the issues of cultural oppression of the indigenous peoples of the Oriente for the first time (Zolezzi, 1989).

The 1980s, then, were years of recognizing contradictions and finding ways to overcome them. The structural adjustment policies managed to curb inflation but did not succeed in attracting investment, new industry and growth to the highlands. Yet the drug-trafficking proceeded and while bringing in sorely needed foreign exchange it threatened to undermine international political support for the whole reform process and destabilize the country (Erdinger, 1997). While the highland area stagnated, the lowland area around Santa Cruz flourished with new industry and the Amazon was subjected to unregulated exploitation of natural resources.

In 1991 the growth rate of 4.1 per cent was inadequate to compensate for the growing poverty and the government recognized that the state must take a more active role to combat poverty in the poorest sectors (Barríos, 1995). This state intervention included a protagonist role in the design and implementation of a reform of the education system to 'improve the quality of education for the future of the country' (Ministry of Planning and Coordination, in Barríos, 1995, pp 20ff.). The 1955 Education Code was now out of alignment with the changes which society was undergoing and 'responding to a different mentality, and above all a different emergency, responding to the possibility of united action against depredation and colonialism... and says nothing about education pluricultural and bilingual but rather tries to form a homogeneous nation'.

Following the mood of discussion and debate on education as promoted through UNESCO's Major Project in Education for Latin America and the Caribbean, the 1955 Education Code was excessively Westernized, homogenizing, vertical and ethnocentric (CENDES, 1994).

Educational reform: new proposals and old objections

Estenssoro's government put forward a proposal for education reform in 1986 which the unions strongly opposed. Strikes were called and COB decried the reform as a step back from the democratic precepts of the 1955 Code. COB presented an alternative proposal, the Popular Education Project (Proyecto Educativo Popular, 1989) which was rejected by government as being 'a repetition of its revolutionary axioms rather than a technical proposal to deal with education under new conditions' (Rivera, 1992). Throughout the 1980s the teachers' unions fought to maintain their position of control and decision-making over the planning of the school system and resorted to strike action as and when they felt necessary. However, not all the member organizations of COB were hostile to change and by the late 1980s the Church, the Urban Teachers' Union, the Rural Teachers' Union, the CSUTCB and the universities had all drawn up proposals for reform. The most powerful sectors that controlled La Paz teachers' union were outmanoeuvred by this alliance of the organizations and at the 1992 National Education Congress a set of recommendations was produced on the basis of which the reform law was drafted (Camacho, 1995).

Rivera, writing at the end of the 1980s, argues that in the 1980s Bolivia faced a vacuum of social and educational theory to deal with the challenges posed by a new educational reform due to an almost complete absence of educational research and an educational model still based on anti-imperialist, anti-feudal principles laid down in the 1950s (Rivera, 1992). But if we look beyond the strikes and consider the loosening of grip by the unions which allowed the voices of other sectors of society to be heard and their presence felt, we find a very different situation. The mid-1980s were a time of growing confidence after years of dictatorship, the last two of which were particularly brutal. This was also a time of growing confidence among indigenous organizations and NGOs that their commitment to a culturally and linguistically diverse Bolivia would lead discussion and reform in a politically, socially and theoretically sound direction. Alfonso Camacho, Director of the Association of Promotion and Education Institution of Bolivia, argues that one may not understand the logic of the social and political processes in Bolivia over this period which could be construed as being confused or chaotic but, he argues (and thus implicitly explains) that the organizations involved were all committed to ensuring that the education system did not become fragmented (Camacho, 1995).

In terms of finding a structure and logic to the transitions and changes of the 1980s, two phases have been identified in the development of intercultural and bilingual education: pre-1983 when there were some isolated projects with no consistent proposals, no institutional support and in an unpropitious climate; and post-1983 when the new political and economic climate provided openings and new perspective but few concrete or sustained initiatives (L D'Emilio and X Albó, in Muñoz, 1997). In 1983 the National Service for Literacy and Popular Education (SENALEP) was set up and immediately set to work to produce a national literacy plan. This National Literacy Plan is widely recognized as diverging from a 'national revolutionary' line and called for the reconstruction of the cultural identity of the indigenous peoples and communities and the importance of the defence of their autonomy and participation in the life of the nation (Moscoso, 1989). The Confederation of Rural Teachers (CONMERB) included proposals for intercultural bilingual education in its plans and the Confederation of Urban Teachers talked in terms of training for 'pluricultural man' (Muñoz, 1997)). The COB education proposal, the Popular Education Project, though rejected in the main, stated that there was a need for the maintenance and permanent development of native languages and cultures as well as learning and using the national language of communication, Spanish (ibid).

The government of Sanchez de Losada which came to power in 1993 appears as yet another paradox. Hailed as an ultra-neo-liberal President, it was his government that made changes to the Constitution and passed a package of reform laws before its term ended in 1997. The Sanchez de Losada government was in fact a unique alliance between the neo-liberal President, and the Katarista (MRTK) Vice-President Victor Hugo Cardenas, who between them brought on board populist and left-wing support (Camacho, 1995). The coalition was able to capitalize on the consultations set up by the previous regimes, and pass legislation for the Law of Popular Participation (1994), the Education Reform Law (1994) and the Law on Administrative Decentralisation (1995). The Law of Popular Participation and the Education Reform Law were envisaged as important means of carrying out a profound restructuring of the nation and establishing a new multi-ethnic and multilingual Bolivia. Subsequently in 1996, after CIDOB with support from the CSUTSB and other organizations, brought the country to a halt with a second march to La Paz, a land reform law was passed (Ley INRA).

The Education Reform Law

The Education Reform Law builds on the 1955 Code in recognizing the responsibility of the state for education, that it is universal, free and obligatory at primary level. Moreover, it is democratic because society actively participates in its planning, organization, implementation and evaluation (Article 1). Taking on board the debates of the 1980s it emphasized it was 'intercultural and bilingual because it recognizes the socio-cultural heterogeneity of the country in an environment of respect between all Bolivians, men and women' (Article 1). It is also 'a right and duty of all Bolivians because it is organized and developed with the participation of all society without restriction or discrimination by ethnicity, culture, region, social, physical, mental or sensory condition, by gender, creed or age' (Articles 1.6).

Interculturalism and bilingualism are established as key components of the reform because, as Avalos (1997) points out, interculturalism is not just a methodological device but rests on the recognition that cultural diversity is needed to create a liveable social integration and that this must be at the top of the agenda. Interculturalism is therefore a conceptual framework, a principle, a philosophy which arises from the recognition of a culturally and ethnically diverse society and bilingualism (or plurilingualism) as the linguistic expression of this society (Chávez, cited in Camacho, 1995, p 155).

Interculturalism as a conceptual framework for society in general and education in particular is encompassed within a process of popular participation. The Law of Popular Participation created 311 municipalities within the nine

departments that comprise Bolivia, which every four years elect a district
board and mayor. The districts' main function is to draw up a yearly development plan which includes physical infrastructure, potable water, building
and maintenance of schools and health posts. The district receives a block
budget from the central government (Erdinger, 1997). For participation in the
education system the Law established seven levels of participation from the
school level up through the school cluster, district, municipality, department
and national level. The cluster school becomes an important centre for teaching resources and groups 6–8 schools under a director and a pedagogic adviser who is responsible for professional development activities. Each cluster is
administered by a council including representatives from the communities,
parents, teachers and students. This structure is intended to allow civil society
to participate in the formulation of policies including areas such as curriculum, rather than being limited to providing school buildings.

When combined with an intercultural and bilingual dimension the participation of community and parents alongside teachers and students becomes
crucial in ensuring that the education being provided really reflects the
intercultural and bilingual context of the students. To support this process the
Education Reform requires that pedagogy is renewed through organizational
change, in which the classroom is reconfigured as a learning environment.
There is thus a transformation of the role of the teacher and the active and
on-going participation of pupils and the community in general (supreme de-
cree 23950, cited in Barríos, 1995).

The Education Reform Law implements these new dimensions to education through four pillars: popular participation which determines the levels of
community organization for their participation in education; curricular reorganization which defines areas, levels and modalities of education; curricular
administration which determines the degrees of responsibility in the administration of educational activities; and teaching and resource administration.
Basic and primary education is organized in eight-year cycles with automatic
promotion between grades. New curricula are structured around the core curriculum with exhortations to teachers to make the curriculum relevant to local
conditions.

The bilingual dimension to the Reform has prioritized the four main languages of Bolivia: Spanish, Aymaran, Quechua and Guaraní, and educational
materials have been produced in these languages. UNICEF has been working
closely with the Ministry of Education to produce language, maths, social science textbooks and workbooks in these languages according to the new curriculum and pedagogy. Indigenous organizations and other NGOs have been
collaborating with the Ministry of Education to consolidate linguistic work on
unifying alphabets and grammars for Aymara, Quechua and the
Tupi-Guaraní language group, work which has been taking place throughout
the 1980s (Amadio and Zuñiga, 1990).

Avalos (1997) notes that one of the novelties of the Bolivian reform is the recognition that the change in learning and teaching styles and classroom organization implies a huge change from the previous 'frontal' delivery system to facilitating children's learning through their own construction of the learning on the basis of their existent knowledge and experience. Change at the classroom level also implies change in pre-service training, and includes proposals for universities to become the sites of teacher education. A system to monitor and evaluate the results of the system is being set up, though it is still early to judge the results of the reform.

In short, a participatory intercultural bilingual education implies radical change in the conceptualization of school–community relations, in the nature of educational knowledge and in conceptualization of teaching and learning. It is demanding of parents and the community in terms of their participation and of teachers in terms of their ability to take on profound changes in their practice. With a few examples of intercultural and bilingual programmes from the 1970s and 1980s as resources,[1] educational administrators, teachers, trainers and local communities alike are faced with translating the aims and rhetoric of the Reform into a practice which is meaningful and satisfactory for them. Two critiques of the Education Reform have been made which merit some attention here in order to evaluate the nature of the challenge: one is that the Reform was designed by external consultants from international agencies such as the World Bank (strongly rejected by the Technical Support Team for Educational Reform, ETARE) and the other is that from a bottom-up perspective the Reform, for all its popular participation, and perhaps because of its Law of Popular Participation, is very top-down (Erdinger, 1997). The next section considers the international dimension to the Reform and its discourse while the following section takes a look at the Reform from the margins.

Global transitions

When the Bolivian government called in the IMF, followed later by the World Bank, it did so to achieve 'integration with the rest of the world' which implied a desire to be part of a wider agenda. This section investigates the wider agenda within which the Bolivian reform process has taken its own shape and form, given that it has been based on a long and complex process of national consensus-building lasting some 10 years. Whether this is seen as a distinctly Bolivian process resulting from a 'lack of social and educational theory' (Rivera, 1992) or 'organised chaos' (Camacho, 1995), as Shiefelbein (1995) reminds us, it did not happen in a vacuum.

UNESCO's Latin American and the Caribbean office project, the 'Major Project', which was launched in 1979, ran a series of seminars and publications that illustrated that unequal access, low achievement rates and high wastage in basic education were huge problems in most Latin American countries. This critique of education began a process of reconceptualization of education in relation to development. High on the regional agenda were issues of equity, quality, efficiency and effectiveness, issues also high on the agenda for educational reform of international organizations such as UNESCO and the World Bank. The Bolivian transition from a Marxist centralist state, via military dictatorships through hyperinflation, budget deficits and import substitution, to a neo-liberal model of international competition, deregulation of the economy and labour market was not an isolated process but part of a transition taking place in many Latin America countries. The transition has also been accompanied by a greater concern for democratic governance and reduced inequalities (Shiefelbein, 1995).

The Major Project focused its efforts through bi-annual meetings of Ministers of Education to introduce new themes into the political agenda. Initially it encouraged the meeting of targets such as a minimum of 8–10 years basic education, the elimination of illiteracy and the improvement of the quality and efficiency of educational systems through necessary reforms (Rodriguez *et al*, 1983; UNESCO-OREALC, 1990). The 1989 meeting of Ministers was an important turning point in a time of acknowledged general crisis, not only in Bolivian education but in Latin American education in general. At a time of strikes and uproar in Bolivia, the regional forum recognized the need for medium- and long-term policies based on social pacts and national consensus that rose above the daily urgent and immediate problems of strikes and demands (Cassasus, 1995).

The 1990 Jomtien Declaration Education for All supported by the World Bank, UNESCO, UNICEF and UNDP, had put meeting basic education needs as a top priority on most reform agendas so that all children left school with a minimum of learning that would allow them to make the most of their environment and their lives. It also focused the aid agencies and donors on the need for social sector loans to education and health and encouraged a new focus on basic education. The impact of the EFA Declaration cannot be ignored in the overwhelming emphasis on basic education given to the Bolivian Reform Law, which universities saw as threatening (Erdinger, 1997).

The conference also had the result of focusing donor agencies such as the World Bank on education in general and basic education in particular, which in turn emphasized the impact of structural adjustment programmes on the poorest in society. The World Bank began to take a wider view of adjustment and to consider the need to invest in education and health reforms that would put the population in the best possible position to take advantage of reviving economic conditions by having the skills and knowledge that the economy needed. Concerns of equity and parental participation (at least in terms of choosing schools) became important links between education and poverty elimination. So the World Bank made loans available for educational reform in Bolivia, on the condition that it was more than a curriculum reform and was not initially put in the hands of the Ministry of Education, still closely controlled by the unions. It funded the Technical Support Team for Educational

Reform (ETARE) set up by the President in 1990 to develop a proposal for educational reform. The Reform itself received its major loans from the World Bank and the Interamerican Development Bank while UNICEF contributed substantially to materials production and other bilateral donors supported specific areas (for details, see Camacho, 1995).

Another meeting of significance for the process and nature of the reform in Bolivia was the Meeting of Ministers of Economics of the Region in 1992 organized by UNESCO and the Economic Commission for Latin America (CEPAL) and its report *Education and Knowledge: Basic Pillars of Changing Production Patterns with Equality*. This document underlined the poor learning achievement of school leavers and laid the cornerstones of education reform: education for equity and quality based on the training of human resources in the areas of skills, aptitudes, information networks and capacity to innovate and create, among others (CEPAL-UNESCO, 1995). It proposed a strategy for transforming the education systems of Latin American countries by emphasizing education for modern citizenship and international competitiveness by linking education closely with sustained economic development and participation, together with a careful evaluation of the efficiency of the system. To achieve this, institutional reform would be key, as well as decentralization to give schools more autonomy to become more locally relevant and responsible for their own results and efficient use of resources (ibid, pp 59–60). Much of this discourse is echoed by the World Bank and stresses the importance of measurement: of results using cost-benefit analysis and through monitoring and evaluation (Pisani, 1995). Privatization and alternative sources of funding for education are strongly recommended.

In these international and regional fora we find the discourse and rhetoric of much of the Bolivian Education Reform Law. Of two main pillars – participation and interculturalism – we find participation and decentralization deeply embedded in these developments. Interculturalism, on the other hand, emerges as a more indigenous characteristic. In Bolivia in the late 1980s and early 1990s, any discussion of quality and equity in society and in education in particular could no longer ignore the ethnic and linguistic diversity of society. Throughout the Andean region, and the countries with large indigenous populations in both South and Central America, indigenous peoples' rights had been put firmly on national and international agendas, including the right of indigenous peoples to intercultural bilingual education. What the transition in Bolivia signified was the coming together of certain conditions – democracy, indigenous organization, social and linguistic research, experimental projects – that allowed interculturalism and bilingualism to achieve the position and prominence they gained in the 1994 Reform. The Major Project as well as indigenous organizations such as the Coordinadora for the Amazon Basin (COICA) were leading protagonists in the regional discussions on indigenous peoples and education, while the United Nations Working Group on Indigenous Populations which began in 1982 has been a catalyst for the recognition of indigenous self-determination and interculturalism on a global level (see Aikman, 1997). While other countries made changes within the state structure for indigenous ministries (Ecuador) or directorates within the Ministry of Education (Peru), Bolivia established interculturalism and bilingualism as the cornerstone of educational reform for the whole society.

In 1997 Hugo Banzer, former military dictator of the 1970s, was elected president. Fears for the continuity of the Education Reform were allayed when he vouched that he would respect the process and rose above the short-termism of earlier regimes and other countries such as Peru which has been undermined by reversals of policy and legislation (Aikman, 1997). Instead, in his 'Operational Plan for 1997–2000' Banzer states that three years on, more effort must be made to overcome the structural problems which are still an obstacle to satisfactory implementation (Banzer, 1997).

A view from the Lowlands

The Education Reform Law gave priority to intercultural bilingual education for three ethnic groups: the Quechua, Aymara and Guaraní, the three largest groups in the country. The Amazon region was to be included in the Reform in its second phase. The relegation of the Lowlands reflected its lack of importance in national terms which has resulted in a lack of investment in infrastructure and resources as well as a lack of studies, both linguistic and educational, on which to form a basis for the implementation. At the time of the National Revolution in the 1950s the Summer Institute of Linguistics, a North American Protestant Sect working on Bible translation, entered Bolivia and established its base at Tumichucua in the Riberalta region of the north east. It worked on language transcription and translation until in 1984 it left the country but its work was not subject to wider scrutiny or wider availability. Few, if any, other studies have been carried out into the 30 or so languages and ethno-linguistic groups living in the vast Amazon region.

The implementation of the Education Reform, nevertheless, was given a rapid start by DANIDA through its Sectoral Programme for Support to Indigenous Peoples. The DANIDA Programme has taken great care to work closely with CIDOB and the indigenous peoples' organizations as well as the Ministry of Education and the Ministry of Indigenous Affairs. The particular characteristics of this region highlight the complexity of the reform and its interrelationship with other fundamental rights for the indigenous peoples, in particular, land rights and the Ley INRA.

While the Law of Popular Participation has established a few indigenous municipal districts in areas with a majority indigenous population, many indigenous peoples find themselves minorities within municipalities dominated by Spanish-speaking colonists which severely restricts their representation and participation. The organizations also had to lobby for a re-clustering of schools in the region because the Law of Popular Participation had ignored ethnic group boundaries and produced a very disjointed and problematic organization of schools and clusters according to districts but not according to ethno-linguistic group.

Despite the draft agrarian reform law, there was a lack of commitment by the government to a land reform that recognizes indigenous ancestral rights and control over the natural resources (Ley INRA). There were also fears among the indigenous peoples that business interests would simply ignore it so when the government gave way to business interests over indigenous rights in the draft consensual agreements in 1996, CIDOB called for a National Mobilization and Indigenous March together with *campesino* and colonist organizations and support of CSUTSB. As a result of the March, the Ley INRA was approved which was only the beginning of the demarcation process (CIDOB, n.d.).

If we look at the radical changes implied in the Education Reform, we can see that in terms of school–community/parental relationships a huge change has taken place. Bilingual intercultural education means a shift from non-indigenous Spanish-speaking teachers to local indigenous teachers, a shift which has been difficult to make in other Amazon areas where expectations of what a school should be, what it should teach and who should do the teaching are quite clear – questions that many parents and communities have been led to believe by government and union-appointed teachers are not their concern.[2] A participatory intercultural bilingual education implies radical change in the conceptualization of school–community relations but this is a region where there has been little information or discussion on the nature of the Education Reform and its associated laws.

The Education Reform Law demands that teachers work closely with other members of the community, such as elders and leaders, to develop collaboratively a curriculum which in the Lowlands will respond to the often politically tense local conditions because of unresolved issues over land and resource ownership. It demands that teachers have an adequate knowledge of not only their indigenous language but Spanish, and that they have the skills and ability to be able to adapt local issues to the national core subjects.

With almost no written materials in many languages, and no alphabet and orthography in many others, the first task is to train teams from each ethno-linguistic group to develop teaching materials. Pedagogical advisers have been put under contract and trained in La Paz but find their task of co-ordinating between schools quite daunting in many regions given the days of travel by canoe between villages and the need for expensive air transport to bring teachers together for training. Training of indigenous peoples for intercultural bilingual education is also a long-term task. Because of the very low completion rate for secondary education in the region, a new interim teacher training qualification has been introduced in the last two years of secondary schooling – *bachillerato pedagógico*. It is hoped that this qualification will encourage more indigenous youths into teaching and will provide a cadre of trained teachers to implement bilingual intercultural education.

While the reform process tackles these problems, the discrimination against the indigenous peoples of the Amazon continues unabated and their everyday situation remains largely unaltered. Despite the Law of Popular Participation, discrimination and political paternalism continue to thrive in the townships, while the local centres of power continue to underlie the control of the traditionally dominant urban groups, who do their utmost to prevent any real participation by indigenous people in political life and participative planning in municipal management (IWGIA, 1997).

This is not to say that the indigenous peoples of the Amazon region do not welcome the Education Reform. On the contrary, they have been lobbying for state recognition of their languages through CIDOB and local federations because of the intimate relationship between them and their culture and way of life. CIDOB has always been committed to the development of the way of life and values of the indigenous peoples and communities of Eastern Bolivia and promoting the maintenance, study and analysis of their culture. What is needed is a coming together of state and indigenous agendas in a dialogue that recognizes that the reform is not a blueprint to be replicated throughout the country but that its strength lies in not only supporting popular participation but the state's ability to listen to the priorities of the populace in different parts of the country. In a region as ethnically and linguistically diverse as the Oriente, where tensions over control of land and resources run high, indigenous peoples' own organizations and NGOs have an important role to play in ensuring the rights to democratic participation and 'respect for all Bolivians' enshrined in the Constitution. Reiterated in the Education Reform Law, democracy, equity, quality, interculturalism, bilingualism and participation are common goals for government, NGOs and indigenous peoples of the Lowlands alike. The challenge now is finding a common means of expressing these through educational practice.

Conclusion

The Education Reform Law in Bolivia was the outcome of a profound transition encompassing all of society and ways of life. That the Education Reform and its associated package of reforms have achieved legal status implies that the beginning of the transition from the state capitalist model prior to 1985 has been superseded by a neo-liberal market economy. But it is also only a beginning. The transition has been made in the statue books but in practice the process is still tentative.

Avalos draws our attention to the scope and pace of the reforms and the apparent political urgency to get things done soon. She indicates that the cultural change required in reforms resting on a different view of learning, different learner–teacher relationships and school management is huge and can result in too much pressure on teachers (1997, p 21). The Lowlands example above also provides reason for caution. The haste to develop orthographies and educational materials in indigenous languages for bilingual education leaves little space for considering that indigenous language maintenance may take many forms and depend on the local circumstances and needs of the people. For example, a school-based mother-tongue literacy may be of no use to students on leaving school but the ability to read and write well in Spanish may, paradoxically, provide the means of maintaining the indigenous language and culture because it provides the ability to fight for self-determination through the courts (in Spanish). For peoples with an oral tradition, biliteracy taught in the very literate environment of the formal education system may not be the best option for language maintenance.[3]

The long-term success of the reforms, as Avalos (1997) suggests, depends on the extent to which those with political clout within and outside Bolivian society question their human capitalist model and recognize its limitations. What of the inequalities and poverty and the need for a more humanitarian focus? As Juan Carlos Tedesco stated recently, educational reform 'is not merely a matter of what contribution is made by education to social equity but rather how much social equity is needed for education to be successful' (1998, p 1). It took a decade for the transition process to arrive at new legislation and principles for Bolivian society for the 21st century. The complexity of change inherent in the package of reform laws, including the Education Reform Law, suggests that the negotiation and the contestation process will continue as different sectors of society jostle for power and real participation in the new democracy.

Notes

1. Amadio and Zuñiga (1990) discuss the Proyecto Educativo Rural I, the Proyecto Educativo Integrado del Altiplano and the Proyecto Texto Rural Bilingüe, while Muñoz (1997) provides a detailed analysis of the Proyecto de Educación Intercultural Bilingüe PEIB.
2. My research with the Harakmbut peoples of the south-eastern Peruvian Amazon, bordering with the Riberalta area confirm this. Brief conversations with representatives of indigenous organizations at Tumichucua, Riberalta suggest the situation is similar.
3. Examples of this discussion are provided in more detail in Aikman (1997).

References

Aikman, S (1997) *Intercultural Education and Literacy: An ethnographic study of indigenous knowledge and learning in the Peruvian Amazon*, John Benjamins, Amsterdam

Amadio, M and Zuñiga, M (1990) Bolivia, in *La Educación Indígena en América Latina: Mexico, Guatemala, Ecuador, Peru, Bolivia*, ed F Chiodi, pp 227–319, Abya-Yala, Quito

Avalos, B (1997) The modernisation of educational systems: contents and issues as seen in the case of Chilean and Bolivian reforms, paper presented at the Oxford International Conference, 11–13 September

Banzer, H Suárez (1997) *Para Vivir Mejor: Plan operativo de acción 1997–2002*, Government of Bolivia, La Paz

Berríos, M Gosález (1995) *Quién le teme a la Reforma Educativa¿* Centro de Documentación e Información, La Paz

Brysk, A *et al* (1995*) Economic Adjustment and Ethnic Conflict in Bolivia, Peru, and Mexico*,Paper no. 216, Latin America Program, Woodrow Wilson International Center for Scholars

Camacho, A (1995) Intervención, in *La Construcción de las Políticas Educativas en América Latina*, ed V R Edwards and J V Osorio, pp 147–57, CEAAL/ Tarea, Lima

Cassasus, J (1995) Intervención, in *La Construcción de las Políticas Educativas en América Latina*, ed V R Edwards and J V Osorio, pp 71–78, CEAAL/ Tarea, Lima

CEDOIN (1996) *XI congreso: Tiempos difíciles para la COB*, Centro de Documentación e Información, La Paz

CENDES (Centro de Estudios Sociales) (1994) *La Alfabetización en Boliva: Situación actual y perspectivas*, Embajada de España, ILDIS, La Paz

CEPAL-UNESCO (1995) *Education and Knowledge: Basic pillars of changing production patterns with equality*, UNESCO

CIDOB (n.d.) Balance de la Marcha Indígena y la Proyección al Trabajo en 1997, unpublished report

Erdinger, K (1997) Oprindelgie folk og Modernisaeringsprocesser: En analyse af uddannelsesreformen I Bolivia, special paper for Institute of Philosophy, Copenhagen University, April

Green, D (1995) *Silent Revolution: The rise of market economics in Latin America*, Latin American Bureau, London

IWGIA (1990) *Yearbook 1990*, International Work Group for Indigenous Affairs, Copenhagen

IWGIA (1997) *The Indigenous World*, International Work Group for Indigenous Affairs, Copenhagen

Moscoso, A (1989) Plan nacional de alfabetización y educación popular: estrategia de interculturalidad y bilingüismo, in *Identidad Cultural y Lengua: La experiencia guaraní en Bolivia*, ed J Riester and G Zolezzi, Abya-Yala, Quito

Muñoz, H Cruz (1997) *De Proyecto a Política de Estado: La educación intercultural bilingüe en Bolivia, 1993*, Maestría en Sociolingüistica de la Educación Básica y Bilingüe/GTZ/ UNICEF, La Paz

Pike, F (1973) *Spanish America 1900–1970*, Thames and Hudson, London

Pisani, L (1995) Intervención: políticas del Banco Mundial en el campo de la

educación, in *La Construcción de las Políticas Educativas en América Latina*, ed V
R Edwards and J V Osorio, pp 55–60, CEAAL/ Tarea, Lima

Rivera, J P (1992) Bolivia: Society, state and education in crisis, in *Education,
Policy and Social Change: Experiences from Latin America*, ed C Alberto Torres,
pp 23–33

Rodriguez, N, Masferrer, E and Vargas, R (eds) (1983) *Educación, Etnias y
Descolonización en América Latina*, UNESCO/Instituto Indigenista
Interamericana, Mexico

Shiefelbein, E (1995) Education reform in Latin America and the Caribbean,
Major Project Bulletin, **37**, pp 4–23

Tedesco, J C (1998) Challenges facing education reforms in Latin America, *IIEP
Newsletter*, **XVI** (4), pp 1–2

Ticona, E Alejo (1996) *SCUTCB: Trayectoria y desafíos*, Centro de
Documentación e Información, La Paz

UNESCO/OREALC (1990*) The State of Education in Latin America and the Caribbean 1980–1987*, Major Project of Education, Santiago de Chile

Zolezzi, G (1989) La recuperación de contactos entre pueblos nativos, in
Identidad Cultural y Lengua: La experiencia guaraní en Bolivia, ed J Reister and G
Zolezzi, Abya-Yala, Quito

4.   Brazil: an incomplete transition

Candido Alberto Gomes

Brazil's incomplete transition is that of a former agrarian country, the industrialization of which started in the 1930s, based on import substitution. This model moved the country onto the development process, but has declined from the 1960s onwards. The country then looked for partnerships with international industrial and financial capital, while keeping its economy closed and tied to relatively low levels of competitiveness. This happened because entrenched interests were opposed to any structural change. Thus the major changes have been:

- a predominantly neo-liberal agenda was offered in the 1980s in the political arena (competitiveness, privatization, cost reduction were the key expressions);
- its partial implementation since 1990, with some discontinuity, by means of opening up the economy; redefining the state's role, and privatizing most state-owned companies;
- the improvement of the representativeness of the regime;
- structuring an open, internationally competitive economy;
- the creation of a modern, more equal society.

Educational modernization, marked by substantially improved quality, equality and efficiency, particularly at the first level of education, and based on a loosely articulated movement, started to be practised by some state administrations after the mid-1980s and especially after 1991. This process in Brazil occurred slowly. Of course, as expected, the most resistant area was the aspiration for a more equal society. Political speeches are one thing; practice has been as problematic as in previous decades. There have been slow steps towards the reform of state apparatuses. However, the emphasis is often on things like payroll reduction (especially in many states and counties), whereas the state requires profound changes to increase its effectiveness and efficiency, particularly in education, health and public safety.

Fearing Pandora's box

A basic feature of Brazil's five-century history is conservatism, in society, in the economy and in education. Firmly entrenched power elites and an asymmetrical class society have made important negotiations difficult which has often led to compromise and a little lack of clarity, particularly in crucial matters such as the opening up of the economy, political liberalization, and educational modernization. Sluggish change is a socio-historical consequence of such a *status quo*.

Early in this century, Brazil was an agrarian society that exported coffee and other primary products. This exogenous economy, however, was dismantled by the crisis of coffee export, triggered by the Great Depression and the Second World War. As in other Latin American countries, the decrease in the prices of export commodities prevented Brazil from being able to pay for the manufactured goods necessary for its survival. The response to this challenge was industrialization based on import substitution. Economic growth was predominantly grounded in the development of internal markets, some of which were later sophisticated enough to support multinational manufacturers. In such an inward-oriented model, the state played an active role by providing economic and technological support to business and industry. Furthermore, foreign savings were a powerful means of accelerating expansion, not only through investment in infrastructure but also through direct productive activities (see, eg Furtado, 1976, 1977).

In the 1980s, however, after two oil shocks, this sort of introverted economic model was spent. In spite of its commercial introversion, with its overprotected and non-competitive manufactures, such a model was financially dependent upon international savings. Although in the 1970s the flow of foreign capital was assured by an abundance of petrodollars, interest rates in the international market rose again during the 1980s dramatically increasing the foreign debt of developing countries. Brazil then became a net capital exporter at the same time as it lost its external sources for financing economic growth (net foreign savings in 1985 were -2.27 per cent of the GDP). Fiscal crisis and domestic debt were added to this nightmare. High inflation, recession and decreasing salaries eroded the state's capacity to implement public policies. There was also violence and the widening gap between the haves and the have nots (see, eg Gomes, 1993).

In a few years, the economic crisis helped bring the military regime to an end. In 1985 re-democratization was the beginning of the transition. Social demands were liberated so that the public deficit increased and, consequently, inflation rose from 110.2 per cent in 1980 to 235.1 per cent in 1985 and 1,782.9 per cent in 1989. The reaction to this crisis took such a long time that the country almost reached hyperinflation. In fact, business, political and union leaders feared opening Pandora's box of reforms. To achieve the goals of fiscal equilibrium, state modernization and an increase in domestic savings would imply renouncing import-substitution industrialization, as well as exposing the economy to international market forces. This would mean massive loss of jobs to unionists, loss of profits to business and loss of votes to politicians.

After the failure of seven stabilization plans after 1979, a successful one defeated inflation in 1994. A new currency, initially linked to US dollar parity, along with other reforms, resulted in an inflation decrease from 1,093.8 per cent in 1994 to 14.8 per cent in 1995 (see Carneiro, 1994).

Nevertheless, optimism about stabilization slowly gave way to expected and, to some extent, unavoidable evils. The income redistribution effect provided by the end of high inflation which had particularly benefited the lower income brackets petered out in a couple of years. Modernization led to an increase in overt unemployment from 4.6 per cent in 1995 to 7.7 per cent in January 1999, according to conservative criteria. Another source reveals that overt and hidden unemployment in the metropolitan area of São Paulo, the most populous and significant economy in the country, rose from 13.2 to 17.2 per cent in the same period. The reason is the same as in the rest of the world: new technologies and management methods increased productivity at the expense of labour. Furthermore, high interest rates, resulting from the need to finance the public deficit, did not encourage investment and economic expansion. What makes the difference between a developed and a developing country is that, in the latter, there is not sufficient protection against economic shocks and unemployment, so that the effects of a 7.4 per cent rate may be devastating to some groups. Perhaps the most tragic impact of this economic opening was on agriculture. While the government spent about US $4 billion on agrarian reform in 1985–95, over 3 million workers lost their jobs during the same period. People migrated to cities and/or participated in social movements, wandering throughout entire regions, occupying farms and claiming land and assistance. The worst problem, which makes it an explosive force, is that this relatively irreversible loss of jobs is a consequence of lower productivity levels, resulting from the use of unqualified labour-intensive technologies.

Despite being trapped by the constraints of economic expansion, the current economic plan withstood the devaluation of the Mexican peso in 1995 and the Asian crisis (1997) but not the Russian moratorium. The government devalued the currency in January 1999, thereby aggravating the markets' pessimistic expectations, so that the devaluation, as in several Asian countries, was dangerously higher than intended. An agreement with the International Monetary Fund was unavoidable as a result of the weaknesses in the economic policies: the lack of sound fiscal adjustment; high interest rates, that contributed to the growth of domestic debt; the negative trade balance; low levels of internal savings and reliance on volatile foreign savings, which are, to a large extent, of a short-run and speculative nature. In fact, the public deficit, an astonishing 59.1 per cent in 1993, decreased to 4.2 per cent in 1997. Further reduction is difficult, it being easier to increase fiscal receipts than to control expenditure and indebtedness. Although these are serious problems, the main obstacle is the late reforms and the lack of a new, sound and reliable social pact. Four long years (1995–98) were necessary to approve the guidelines of state and social security reforms, but insufficient to obtain relative consensus on other crucial reforms, like that of the tax system. The waste of time can be attributed not to a large opposition group in the National Congress, but to the lack of political unity among those who formally support the government. Many politicians at that time seemed to fear the consequences of reform and assumed that political losses would follow. They wished to rely on the important but insufficient political asset of economic stabilization.

The risk in extending the agony is that the result may be the opposite of Pandora's story. Whereas in mythology, despite the liberation of evils, Hope remained inside the jar, the lid having been shut down before she escaped, in Brazil the jar may have been open for such a long time that it may be completely empty.

Education: a hard transition

As a mirror of the social structure, education in the beginning of the so-called 'lost decade' (the 1980s) was dramatically varied. In spite of some islands of excellence, there were problems with efficiency, quality and equality. The gross and net enrolment ratios were 99 and 81 per cent (1980), but the percentage of repeaters was 20 per cent and their absolute number, 4.6 million, was the highest in the world. People who had access to the second and third levels of education were a small minority: the gross and net enrolment ratios for second levels of education were 34 and 14 per cent, whereas the gross ratio for third level education was 11.1 per cent.

The 1980s was a decade of severe budget cuts and neglect. In fact, despite the crisis, the number of teachers increased faster than the number of students in the first and second levels of education. Teachers' salaries, as a consequence, dropped in real terms, leading to numerous strikes and extremely low levels of satisfaction. Positive signs, however, were the decentralization and the constitutional earmarking of a percentage of tax revenues for education. The end of two decades of a military regime led to new solutions to old problems, although management discontinuity and populism plagued public education (Plank, 1996).

Some of the main innovations in this new era of political liberalization were:

- the democratization of school management – based on the choice of principals by teachers, aides, students (over 14 years of age), and parents (they were previously appointed on the basis of political criteria most of the time);
- the creation of school boards, with a consultative or deliberative role, to share management with the community;
- the allocation of financial resources directly to schools to cover current expenditure (with the exception of personnel);

- the automatic promotion of pupils in basic education or integration of the first and second grades to avoid high repetition ratios at the end of the initial year of schooling.

The public choice of principals (as well as universities' presidents, deans and heads of departments) often had populist tones, occasionally sacrificing competence to political expediency. In some school systems this was a means of decentralizing management rapidly, transferring the problems, formerly dealt with by central administration, to principals with few resources. Once power was asymmetrically distributed, the democratization process often favoured the schoolteachers rather than the community, as has also happened in other countries. Nevertheless, these were the earliest steps of the educational transition.

After the political hangover that followed the authoritarian regime, a new stage of innovations was introduced. Economic stabilization brought new challenges, since the labour force was clearly underqualified for the difficulties of economic modernization. Economic competitiveness, citizenship, equality, efficiency, and evaluation have been the common refrains since the early 1990s. Yet, educational change, as already mentioned, is slow and far from being complete. Reforms have been negotiated stage by stage, counting on some important actors, most of them recently mobilized. Groups of businessmen, some intellectuals, some non-governmental organizations and sectors of the press have demanded educational change according to diverse values and ideals. Teachers' unions played a somewhat ambiguous role, as a result of low salaries and social prestige during many years (although the job losses of schoolteachers were less significant than those of other occupations). Relative aloofness has distinguished the typical behaviour of parents and students in basic education. In general, they have been a silent majority in an undereducated population. This does not prevent hot discussions in areas where community mobilization has not only been attempted but has also been successful.

Despite all these obstacles, since the early 1990s, or even the late 1980s, a new generation of innovations has been implemented by federal and many state and municipal governments. In fact, the educational transition is close to adulthood. The search for quality, equality and efficiency has reached some important benchmarks. The perspective of decentralization and school relative autonomy has progressed. Financial resources transferred directly to schools are already significant. About US $10.5 billion in 1998 (or about 1.2 per cent of the GDP) was being used to decentralize the first level of education and management to counties and to assure a minimum of resources per pupil. Its impact on equality is highly likely to be significant, at least within each state in its first full year of implementation. There is evidence that the enrolment rate has increased, as well as the average salary of teachers, particularly inland.

In several state school systems the emphasis on qualified school management has led to the selection of principals by means of technical certification criteria, followed by public choice of the eligible candidates. At the same time that federal and state governments pursue efficiency and quality by means of decentralization, evaluation systems, based on achievement, facilities and other inputs, have been expanded. Disseminated by the media and mobilizing different public sectors, their results have had increasing political effects which renew the transition process.

Research has found that most of the improvement in the first level of education in the 1990s, measured by achievement scores and drop-out and repetition ratios, was largely a result of three institutional innovations mentioned earlier: the direct transfer of financial resources to schools, the public choice of principals, and the creation of school boards, consisting of faculty, parents and pupils over 14 years of age (Barros and Mendonça, 1998).

In fact, pupil cohorts progressed faster in the 1990s. The age distortion ratio in the first level of education was reduced from 76.2 in 1982 to 47.0 in 1996, whereas the number of pupils who finished the same level of education increased 125.1 per cent in 1991–98. However, the repetition ratio reduction has been more a result of the systems' new rules and regulations than pedagogy and teachers' attitudes and behaviour. In fact, after numerous attempts to face the problems with the co-operation of teachers and principals, the school systems seemed exhausted and prone to choose other alternatives. Communication between governments and bitter teachers and principals is a delicate problem. Furthermore, teacher training is still old-fashioned and so are educational programmes for graduate principals, supervisors and counsellors. Mostly provided by the third level of educational institutions, these areas are not used to innovations.

Nevertheless, national achievement scores show that the repetition ratio has not decreased at the expense of pupils' proficiency in national language and mathematics. An interpretation of this finding is that an educational transition overcame its populist stage and is in progress.

In sum, numerous innovations have been implemented by most of the state secretariats of education (see Table 4.1). Innovation occurs at that level because Brazil is a huge territory of 5,313 square miles. It has federal, state and local levels of government. This complex structure includes 26 states and one federal district, as well as over 5,000 counties. States are legally responsible for the first and second levels of education, although most of them provide higher education, in particular teacher education. Counties are expected to offer, mainly, the first level of education and education preceding the first level. The federal government is informally charged with higher education and is constitutionally responsible for supporting the sub-national governments in general.

As in other reform movements, educational practice is distinguished by the contradiction between claimed and actual values, one of which is decentralization. As in earlier decades, the law and policies have stressed school autonomy.

Table 4.1 Innovations in educational decentralization adopted by state secretariats of education at the first level of education, 1997

Innovations	No of secretariats
School management	
School boards	13
Parents and teachers associations	17
Other participatory school management processes	7
Choice of school principals by teachers, aides, students and parents	8
Selection of school principals	
By exams and public choice	6
By technical critieria only	1
By teachers, aides, students and parents	8
School planning	
School projects, often developed through participatory processes	23
Other processes	3
School funds and materials	
Direct delivery of state governmental funds to schools	18
Direct delivery of federal governmental funds to schools	14
Direct delivery of other public funds to schools	7
Decentralization of the school lunch programme: at the county level	22
Decentralization of the school lunch programme: at the school level	13
Decentralization of the textbook programme (at the state level)	6
Decentralization of the textbook programme (at the school level)	11

Note: The total number of State and Federal District Secretariats is 27.
Source of the original data: Parente and Lück (1999)

This means that schools are henceforth responsible for drafting and implementing their own plans and exercise more independence in managing their personnel, facilities, equipment, and financial resources. Nevertheless, in most state and municipal systems, curricula and programmes should comply with detailed guidelines established by traditional bureaucracies at diverse governmental levels. Furthermore, the introduction of evaluation based on paper and pencil tests, notwithstanding its powerful incentive to quality, may lead to standardized practices in the classroom, in particular training the pupils in the ability to take tests. Progress toward financial autonomy is remarkable, although most schools do not handle more than 5 or 10 per cent of their budget. In some cases, for instance, except by informal means, schools and communities are unable to select their teachers or influence salary policies.

On the other hand, higher education institutions are still over-regulated centrally, whether they are private or public. As the rules are too detailed, their enforcement is problematic. In a difficult political arena, the recent Law of Policies and Bases of Education missed some important opportunities to liberalize this field. At least curricular prescriptions will be more flexible, while another reform achievement is the attribution of some autonomy to clusters of colleges and highly reputed research institutions. Institutional evaluation advanced in the 1990s. The programme aims at reviewing and strengthening each institution, as well as stimulating the constant improvement of academic activities. Over two-thirds of the Brazilian universities have participated in this programme (see Figueiredo and Sobreira, 1996). Since the Ministry of Education regarded it as necessary but insufficient, it instituted an external evaluation system, based on inputs in general and the graduates' achievement in their exams as outputs. In spite of resistance, once publicized, the results have stimulated competition among institutions, producing an impact on the finance of private universities and colleges.

The Gordian knot, however, remains in public higher education, particularly in the sensitive areas of management and finance. Governments often complain of high expenditure and low responsiveness in public universities and colleges. A dream for several decades has been less financial dependence on the public budget and more reliance on fund-raising. Since legal restraints and market forces impose severe limits on the universities' own financial capacity, most sectors in the academy suspect that the government is, in fact, interested in a serious cutting of funds or even privatization. In some state universities substantial progress has been attained, once they have been assured of earmarked resources from tax revenues. Research found significant achievements in efficiency, but the model – suitable in the richest state in the Federation – is probably not generalizable.

Despite mutual suspicion, the federal government and its institutions recently had some successes. After a four-year freeze on faculty salaries, at least a significant percentage of any increase will be on the basis of academic performance criteria, defined by institutions. However, agreement has not been reached on constitutional and legal constraints to university autonomy, as well as assurances of public funding and accountability. It is more likely that neither the governmental nor the radical academic positions will prevail. A third position, perhaps open to agreement, has at least been outlined.

Some effects of this long and unfinished transition are reflected in the net enrolment ratio at the first level of education (95.8 per cent in 1998), the percentage of repeaters at the same level (11.4 per cent in 1997), and the net enrolment ratio at the second level of education (24.4 per cent in 1996). These numbers suggest not only a quantitative change, but also a qualitative one, expressed, in particular, by the dramatic reduction of failure at the first level of education. As a result, a great number of pupils have become eligible for the second level of education, and this expansion, also stimulated by the demands of economic competition and rising unemployment, has been the most re-markable one in the educational system. This upsurge, formerly restricted to the first grades, will soon reach higher education. The top of the pyramid has successfully withstood change: the gross enrolment ratio increased from 11.1 to only 14.4 per cent in 1980–94. However, it is expected that new wine in old bottles will soon make the latter break, thus motivating re-structuring of tradi-tional undergraduate and graduate programmes. It is likely that such contra-dictions will lead to new changes to overcome clientelism and government over-regulation of the public and private sectors. A test of persistence of the main actors, educational change in Brazil, as stated at the beginning of this text, is slow, and subject to complex negotiations.

Conclusion

Monetary stability (1994–98) raised expectations that employment and eco-nomic growth would contribute to more equal income distribution and im-proved public health and educational services. However, the economic crisis in a certain sense puts back the clock to the pre-stabilization period. Although economic recovery is highly likely, the issue now is not only to overcome the crisis, but also to move to an open, internationally competitive economy. As usual, social policies may be the preferential targets of budget cuts. It is too early to predict to what extent social contradictions will grow worse and if the transition will be interrupted. In spite of a general shortage of financial re-sources, it will not be easy to move backwards, especially in schools and com-munities that increased their participation in decision-making processes.

Although it is not wise to expect too much from education, the economics of education has a lesson: no nation has attained socio-economic development without providing universal, basic education. Research findings in relation to other levels of schooling are debatable or, at least, less widely agreed. As is rec-ognized internationally, Brazil has been an under-educated country in rela-tion to its level of economic development. To overcome this gap, besides encouraging a reduction in demographic growth, present trends in public ed-ucation are promising.

Access to the first eight years of education improved as much in the last few decades in Brazil as it did in the industrialized countries in a century. Effec-tively, the enrolment ratio in that level of schooling increased 390.9 per cent in 1950–80, and the net enrolment ratio has more than doubled in the same three decades (36.2 to 80.4 per cent). Therefore, school building (not necessarily equipment), as well as school lunch and textbook programmes were the main priorities at all government levels. Less visible and more complex areas, such as curricula, evaluation, school and educational system management, teacher education, and the improvement of instructional materials, are likely to cause problems to public administrators, and have systematically received less money and attention. Politicians have responded to strong demands for massive expansion and, consequently, weaker demands from an under-educated population for efficiency, quality, and equality. The acceptance of these priorities is strictly rational from a political point of view – accepting the preferences produces votes, prestige, and power.

As pointed out, new winds have stimulated changes. However, one cannot be certain whether this is still the dominant trend. The move to modernization and the likely impact of education on income distribution may strengthen the forces favourable to change. This margin of uncertainty is a result of the unsteady relationship of social, economic and cultural forces in the framework of an unfinished transition. In this, the Brazilian case is not unique in the world today.

Sources of statistical data

Economic and financial data: Getúlio Vargas Foundation; demographic data: IBGE Foundation (Ministry of Planning); educational data: Ministry of Education and Sports (1996) *Development of Education in Brazil*; international comparisons of educational data: *UNESCO Statistical Yearbook, 1996*, and *World Education Report* (1998) UNESCO.

References

Barros, R Paes de and Mendonça, R (1998) *O Impacto de Três Inovações Institucionais na Educação Brasileira* [The impact of three institutional innovations on Brazilian education], Brasília, IPEA

Carneiro, D D (1994) Growth prospects after stabilization: issues and challenges, *Revista Brasileira de Economia*, **48** (4), pp 505–18

Figueiredo, M C M and Sobreira, M I F (1996) The evaluation of higher education systems in Brazil, in *World Yearbook of Education*, ed R Cowen, pp 34–50, Kogan Page, London and Philadelphia

Furtado, C (1976) *Economic Development of Latin America: Historical background and contemporary problems*, Cambridge University Press, Cambridge

Furtado, C (1977) *Formação Econômica do Brasil* [Brazil's economic background], 17th edn, Nacional, São Paulo

Gomes, C A (1993) Education, democracy and development in Latin America, *International Review of Education*, **39** (6), pp 531–40

Parente, M M de A and Lück, H (1999) *Mapeamento da Descentralização da Educação Brasileira nas Redes Estaduais do Ensino Fundamental* [Mapping Brazilian education: decentralization at the first level of education], Brasília, IPEA

Plank, D (1996) *The Means of our Salvation: Public education in Brazil, 1930–1995*, Boulder, CO and Oxford, Westview Press

5. Education in transition: Canada

Jon Young and Ben Levin

Introduction

Canadian provinces[1] have not stood aloof from efforts at large-scale education reform – defined here as 'programs of educational change that are government directed, initiated on an explicitly political analysis (that is, one driven primarily by the political apparatus of government rather than by educators or professional bureaucrats) and justified on the basis of the need for a radical break with existing practice' (Levin and Young, 1997, p 3). Echoing, in part, broader international trends, school reform in the 1990s in Canada has seen an increasingly managerialist focus on curriculum standardization, testing, accountability and control, a centralizing reduction in the number and authority of local school boards, along with some attention to giving parents a greater say in which schools their children will attend and in select aspects of local school governance. Associated with these developments has been a stalling or reorientation of many of the egalitarian initiatives in education that had begun to take root in the 1970s and 1980s (Moodley, 1995; Ng *et al*, 1995).

These changes tend to reflect the influence of neo-liberal views that promote the inevitability of a corporate-dominated global economy in informing educational policy-making across the country. Nevertheless, this ideology has not gone unchallenged (Barlow and Robertson, 1994; Dehli, 1998; Kozolanka, 1998), and in comparison to many other countries, we would argue that Canadian educational reform has generally been, to date, less radical in terms of its rhetoric (Levin and Young, 1997) and its changes less firmly entrenched than in many other jurisdictions.[2]

School reform in Canada

Establishing a start date

The more large-scale, ideologically consistent, and radical a shift in educational policy and the more homogeneous the education system, the easier it is to trace the origins of reform and establish some sort of a 'beginning' or 'start date' for the change. Given the diversity of Canadian public schooling, any designation of a pivotal 'start date' for current reform initiatives is essentially arbitrary.

In Canada one could point to the federal Liberal Government's 1969 White Paper on Indian policy (Canada, 1969), its rebuttal by the National Indian Brotherhood, and the publication in 1972 of the Brotherhood's policy document *Indian_Control of Indian Education* (National Indian Brotherhood, 1972) as pivotal points in the radical restructuring of First Nations' education. Similarly, the repatriation of the Canadian Constitution and the passage of the Canadian Charter of Rights and Freedoms in 1982 proved a significant juncture in federal–provincial relationships, particularly in relation to the province of Quebec and in Canadian schooling with regard to minority (official) language education as well as the rights of students and teachers. At a provincial level, British Columbia's Royal Commission on Education which reported in 1988 provided an early attempt to rethink schooling. Conversely, it might be possible, given the literature on 'policy borrowing' (Halpin and Troyna, 1995) and the deterministic impact of 'global restructuring' (Brown *et al*, 1997) to talk of international 'start dates' for Canadian reform initiatives such as 1973 (the OPEC oil crisis) or 1979 (the election of a Conservative Government in the United Kingdom under Margaret Thatcher).

Rather, we choose to talk of the mid-1990s (1993–97) as the period in which school reform initiatives were begun in earnest across many, but not all, of Canada's provinces. It was, for example, early in this period, in 1994, that the province of Alberta released a three-year plan for education entitled *Key Directions for Education in Alberta* and the province of Manitoba introduced its policy document, *Renewing Education: New Directions, A Blueprint for Action*, while the end of this period saw the province of Ontario embark on its restructuring offensive with documents such as *Putting Students First: Ontario's Plan for Educational Reform* and its far-reaching and controversial Education Improvement Act (Bill 160).

The public rhetoric of reform

Public debate about education in the early 1990s across Canada was vigorous, and, in marked contrast to the earlier decade, saw powerful business-supported organizations such as The Conference Board of Canada and the Fraser Institute as well as the Federal Government playing a leading role. These debates served to shatter any public consensus on education that had previously existed and increasingly saw government and business organizations pitted against teacher unions and organizations such as The Canadian Centre for Policy Alternatives in a struggle over the agenda for public education (Taylor, 1996, pp 50–124).

Taylor (1996) characterizes the business-led debate on Canadian school reform, which she argues had come to exert a dominating role on educational policy decisions in the 1990s, as being centred on three main discourses; those of 1) 'the fiscal crisis of the state'; 2) 'education for economic prosperity'; and 3) 'the dissatisfied parent' (pp 50–82). The first of these held that by the 1990s the size of federal and provincial deficits and debts constituted a critical threat to the well-being of the country that could not be addressed through increased taxation but rather had to be tackled by a combination of reduced government spending and the 're-inventing' of government.[3] The dominance of this view was evidenced in the overwhelming concern of all governments in the country, at this time, with the reduction and elimination of budget deficits. In this regard, the federal government led the way with sharp reductions in almost all areas of spending, including transfer payments to the provinces. However, provincial governments of all political stripes – Liberal, Conservative and New Democrat – also implemented severe austerity measures, and many provinces passed legislation prohibiting themselves from running operating deficits in the future. The impact on education was that 1993–94 heralded the beginning of a period of sustained cutbacks to educational funding and represented the first time in more than 20 years that actual expenditures on public elementary-secondary education declined in some provinces (see Table 5.1).

Table 5.1 Expenditures on public elementary–secondary education for selected provinces, 1970–71 to 1995–96

Year	Province							
	Newfoundland		Quebec		Ontario		Alberta	
	Actual $	Change* %	Actual $	Change* %	Actual $	Change* %	Actual $	Change* %
1970–1971	77.2	-	1,368.9	-	1,825.8	-	365.5	-
1975–1976	182.4	9.2	2,314.2	1.9	2,872.1	3.0	659.6	4.2
1980–1981	303.9	0.5	4,143.2	2.1	4,882.0	1.0	1,189.3	3.2
1985–1986	466.8	2.1	5,156.0	-1.7	7,687.2	1.2	2,108.0	4.0
1990–1991	603.0	1.0	6,457.0	0.1	12,216.7	4.6	2,663.7	1.2
1991–1992	623.7	-1.1	6,858.5	1.8	13,680.0	5.8	2,880.3	2.9
1992–1993	648.9	1.9	7,276.1	3.5	13,933.7	-2.5	3,054.7	1.6
1993–1994	650.2	-5.2	7,107.4	-4.8	14,373.9	1.3	3,132.9	0.1
1994–1995	618.4	-6.1	7,320.1	4.4	13,840.7	-3.8	3,083.1	-3.0
1995–1996	585.1	-6.8	7,256.7	-2.5	14,080.3	-0.7	3,000.6	-4.9

Note: Actual dollars and average annual rates of change in constant dollars (1986 = 100).
Source: Canadian Teachers' Federation (1998, pp 12–13)

The second element of this discourse – 'education for economic prosperity' – argued for much closer links between the worlds of school and work, a greater emphasis on science and technology, and 'raising standards' through more clearly stated goals and outcomes, greater external accountability for students and teachers, and greater educational choice for parents. Within this framework of discussion the role of public schooling in the development of citizenship was generally under-developed and given a particularly corporate orientation (Osborne, 1996).

Furthermore, issues of equity and social justice that had achieved significant prominence in the 1980s became recast into the rubrics of 'success for all' and 'equality of educational opportunity' – a reform rhetoric that has been critiqued in another context as 'neither orientated towards issues of equality and social justice nor equipped to address them effectively' (Hatcher, 1998, p 268).

The third element that Taylor (1996) argues has come to characterize this discourse on school reform is that of 'the dissatisfied parent' – the claim that parents generally have lost confidence in Canadian schools to provide their children with the knowledge, skills and values deemed necessary for the perceived challenges of the 21st century, and the need, therefore, to reclaim a larger parental role in school-based decision-making. Despite the critiques of this position as ideologically constructed (Barlow and Robertson, 1994) and of the role of the media in constructing a so-called crisis in public education, this discourse of 'user dissatisfaction' has been influential in informing 'common-sense' reforms in education and initiatives to involve parents or their representatives more in school level educational decision-making.

The elements of reform in Canada: some specifics

The debates of the early 1990s represented a shift away from public orientations to education in the previous two decades. While we believe that the reforms that have actually been implemented in Canada to date have been generally less dramatic than in many other jurisdictions, this has been a period of significant changes to the structure of public education and, notwithstanding our arguments as to the importance of understanding the unique circumstances of school reform within each province, it is possible to point to a degree of commonality in rhetoric and the practice of reform across the provinces.

In all provinces some attention has been given to most if not all of the elements listed below:

1. Curriculum centralization and standards testing.
2. Changes in the roles of school boards.
3. School-based management and parental involvement.
4. School choice.

As points of focus in the rhetoric of Canadian school reform, these elements reflect a level of similarity across the country and with international reform initiatives. However, this similarity in terms of a language of reform (both in terms of the areas of school life warranting particular attention – eg testing – and in terms of the justifications for specific proposals for change – eg standards, accountability, global competition) does not translate very well into common educational structures and responses across jurisdictions when the specificities of the local provincial context (political, cultural, economic and educational) assert their mediating influences.

A fifth area of Canadian school reform that warrants particular attention is that of Aboriginal/First Nations education, calling into play a unique and complex political web of Aboriginal peoples' inherent rights to self-determination (Canada, 1996), the federal government's constitutional responsibilities for Indian education, and the provincial governments' provisions for the education of 'off-reserve' and 'non-status' Indians.[4] These changes are given added significance in light of the fact that, in general, school reform in Canada in the 1990s appears to have stalled many of the egalitarian and multicultural reforms of the previous decade (Graham and Young, 1999).

Curriculum centralization and standards testing

Across the country curriculum centralization has found expression in the establishment of inter-provincial curriculum frameworks, single year or multi-year performance outcomes, and province-wide testing (most often at grades 3, 6, 9 and 12). No longer the prerogative of local school divisions and teachers informed by provincial *curriculum guidelines*, curriculum content is now more closely prescribed via *curriculum frameworks* and *standards or performance outcomes*, and monitored by way of *provincial examinations*.

The emergence of Pan-Canadian and regional curriculum development collaboration in the 1990s was a new phenomenon in Canadian education. The provinces and territories now constitute four regional curriculum development units – The Western Canadian Protocol for Collaboration on Basic Education (Manitoba, Saskatchewan, Alberta, British Columbia, North West Territories and The Yukon), Ontario, Quebec, and The Atlantic Provinces Education Foundation (New Brunswick, Nova Scotia, Newfoundland and Labrador, and Prince Edward Island) – as well as participating, through The Council of Ministers of Education in Canada (CMEC), in a single Pan-Canadian curriculum development consortium for Science.

The justification for more centrally developed curriculum frameworks is threefold: 1) 'rigour': that in a context of 'global competitiveness' Canadian students could and should be presented with a more challenging and relevant curriculum; 2) efficiency: that curriculum development could be better carried out through inter-provincial collaboration without undermining provincial autonomy; and 3) accountability or 'system control': a desire to ensure that 'educational systems are both more responsive to public policy goals and more effective in achieving them' (Mawhinney, 1998, p 95). In this regard, Manitoba's reform documents talk of defining essential or basic learning for all grade levels and the development of rigorous and relevant content. The Ontario government, similarly, talks of 'a new and rigorous curriculum' and states:

In recent years these [provincial curriculum] requirements were not rigorous or demanding enough, and they were vague... The new curriculum describes in detail what students should learn in each grade.

It also sets new, high standards of achievement for every student in the province. (Ontario Ministry of Education and Training, 1997, p 4)

The most controversial aspect of these reforms has generally been the intensification of assessment activity associated with a return to provincial and national assessment practices. In contrast to the decentralized practices of the 1960s and 1970s, today almost all Canadian provinces participate in some form of province-wide and national assessment. McEwen (1995, pp 10–11) reported that in 1993–94 all but two jurisdictions – Prince Edward Island and The North West Territories – had some kind of provincial assessment programme in place. Assessments tend to focus on core subjects – Language, Arts and Mathematics – with some provinces also including other subjects; results are usually published on a school-by-school basis; and most provinces have high school exit examinations for graduating students that constitute between 30 per cent and 50 per cent of the students' final mark in exam courses.

Changes in the roles of school boards

The emphasis on centralization of authority in education in the 1990s has seen a changing role for local school boards across the country. Originally forming a patchwork of local public authority, often around a single one-room school (Young and Levin, 1998), school boards by the 1980s had evolved into much larger administrative units, governed by locally elected school trustees who were generally responsible for the day-to-day management of the school system, who had the power to set property taxes in support of public schools, and who would negotiate collective agreements locally with their teachers. In virtually every province the 1990s have seen the provincial government consolidate and reduce the number of school boards, resulting in a reduction of some 45 per cent nationally (Peters, 1997).

Consolidation constitutes a common theme across Canadian provinces. However, major differences exist between provinces in terms of:

1. the pre-existing size and responsibilities of boards;
2. the justifications that accompanied consolidation;
3. the processes of consolidation; and
4. the new configuration and roles of boards.

Towards one end of this continuum the government of Manitoba, after commissioning a substantial review of existing school board boundaries and then rejecting its recommendations to consolidate, decided not to mandate any changes to school board boundaries but rather to encourage voluntary mergers and inter-divisional collaboration. Elsewhere, the province of Alberta reduced the number of school boards from 141 to about 60 in 1994 (Peters, 1997) and Ontario from 129 to 66 in 1997, leaving, in the case of Ontario, one of the new school districts 'the size of France' (Kozolanka, 1998, p 47). In New Brunswick school boards were abolished completely in 1996 and replaced by a system of school councils, although administrative control reverted primarily to the provincial Department of Education.[5]

The consolidation of school boards has generally been justified by governments as a mechanism for increasing system efficiency and for asserting provincial control over educational spending. At the same time that consolidation has been taking place the functions of boards has also been changing with the majority of Canadian provinces moving to a model of 100 per cent provincial funding for public education and removing from school boards the power to raise taxes locally in support of education.

In some jurisdictions this consolidation has been achieved voluntarily but in others it has been vigorously contested both politically (Kozolanka, 1998) and legally (Green, 1999; King, 1999) as an unacceptable and unconstitutional attack on the tradition of local autonomy. Regardless of the outcome of the challenges to their legality, these developments collectively have amounted to a very significant centralization of control of education to the provincial level at the expense of local authority previously exercised by school boards and by teachers.

School-based management and parental involvement

The other side of this pattern of centralization has been policies designed to strengthen parental and public involvement at the school level, primarily through the giving of legal status to some form of Parent Councils or School Advisory Councils and through expanding parents' choice of schools that their children may attend.

All provinces have, in the 1980s and 1990s, provided legal status to some form of local school councils. In some provinces, such as British Columbia, these committees are composed only of parents with children attending the school but the more common model is for them to consist of a majority of parents but also to include teachers, community members, and, at the high school level, students. Within and across provinces there is considerable variation as to the enthusiasm with which parents have responded to the legal status of these new bodies (Parent–Teacher Associations as informal structures have a long history in Canada). While they have generally contributed to a more open climate of local school administration these councils all serve in a consultative and advisory role that falls far short of the powers given to similar bodies in, for example, England or New Zealand.

School choice

As has already been noted, Canadian school systems have always been characterized by a considerable degree of diversity which, in some jurisdictions at least, has provided certain parents with considerable levels of choice as to the school their children attend. In addition to publicly funded denominational schools and partially funded private schools, large urban school divisions had by the 1980s already developed school systems that offered students a range of programmes – French Immersion schools, Bilingual Education schools, Aboriginal Focus schools, Technical–Vocational schools. School reform in the 1980s and 1990s has seen some slight extension of this parental choice – normally in the form of allowing parents to enrol their children in school outside of their local school district without being charged extra fees. However, these changes have not seen very much in the way of aggressive campaigns by schools or school divisions to recruit students from other jurisdictions nor a large-scale shift of students from school to school.

Alberta is the only province to date to move beyond this level of parental involvement to provide for the establishment of a few 'Charter Schools'. Under the School Amendment Act passed in 1994, provision was made for the establishment of up to 15 Charter Schools or autonomous public schools. These schools would be governed by an agreement between a school board or the Minister of Education and the individual or group setting up the schools. Under the agreement Charter Schools would be given 'flexibility and autonomy to implement innovative or enhanced educational services which will broaden the range of educational opportunities and enhance student learning' (Alberta Education, 1995, p 1). This initiative has generated considerable attention and debate within the education community (Robertson *et al*, 1995; Dobbin, 1997) and has stimulated public schools and school boards to be more attentive to community interests, but to date the charter school movement has generated little enthusiasm in Alberta and has not been taken up in other provinces in Canada.

Aboriginal education

As a federal rather than provincial responsibility, the education of registered Indian students in First Nations communities across Canada has largely stood apart from the school reform initiatives within provincial jurisdictions. Nevertheless, it is perhaps within Aboriginal education that some of the most striking reforms have begun to take place.

For most of Canada's history, Aboriginal education, controlled by the federal government and delegated to the churches, was shaped by policies and practices designed to assimilate Aboriginal youth into the lower strata of the dominant society. A number of different institutional forms were experimented with over the years but by almost any indicators of educational well-being, the schools served Canada's Aboriginal students dramatically less well than every other segment of the Canadian population (Mallea and Young, 1997).

Since the early 1970s substantial changes have taken place in Indian education, driven by the principles of autonomy and self-determination, laid out first in the seminal policy document *Indian Control of Indian Education*, published by the National Indian Brotherhood in 1972 and repeated subsequently in such documents as *Tradition and Education: Towards a Vision for our Future* produced by The Assembly of First Nations in 1998 and *The Royal Commission on Aboriginal Peoples* (Canada, 1996).

Guided by these principles, virtually all First Nations schools are now operated locally, governed by the First Nations government structures and educational authorities while still funded through the federal government, and the nature of schooling has changed significantly. At the heart of the issue of self-determination has been a struggle for control of the curriculum and for curriculum relevance and change. For Aboriginal people self-government in education has provided the opportunity (although not always the resources) to develop new curricula that provide a balance between Aboriginal and non-Aboriginal languages, content, and experiences. Driving this curriculum change has been the growth over the last 20 years in the number of Aboriginal teachers graduating from Faculties of Education – often but not exclusively from one of some 20 Native/Indian/First Nations Teacher Education Programs in operation across the country – and working, particularly at the early and middle years, in First Nations schools.

In Canada's urban centres, Aboriginal control of education is evolving in a variety of different ways that have seen the establishment of separate Aboriginal Focused schools as well as efforts within the existing multicultural urban school system to create a much stronger Aboriginal presence in all aspects of curriculum, staffing and governance.

The outcome of these changes has been higher retention rates in Aboriginal schools, higher graduation rates, and higher participation rates in post-secondary institutions. These rates are still disappointingly far below the national average but the changes have none the less been substantial. A detailed and critical analysis of these developments within the broader discourse of school reform and within the context of a general reorientation to issues of equality in education lies outside of the scope of this chapter, nevertheless, it is possible to argue that Aboriginal education constitutes one of the primary areas of significant school change in Canada over the last two decades.

Discussion: when the dust has settled

The 1990s were, without doubt, a period of political turmoil over education in Canada. This was a decade that witnessed the demise of a pre-existing public consensus that had supported increases in the funding of schooling for some 20 years, left educational decision-making largely in the hands of the profession, supported a liberal arts curriculum with relatively loose connections between the worlds of school and work, and generally expressed positive attitudes towards the quality of Canadian schools and the work of their teachers (Livingstone and Hart, 1995). At the end of the decade there was little left of this consensus and the arena of public education remains contested. Governments have talked the language of massive restructuring, and significant changes, described above, have taken place centralizing authority with provincial governments, tightening the links between school and work, and requiring that teachers' and students' work be much more open and accountable to the schools' various 'publics'. It is unlikely that many of these changes will be substantially reversed in the near future. Yet, with the federal and provincial deficits generally eliminated, few governments seem committed to pursuing further the radical restructuring efforts that have been seen elsewhere.

At a time when reforms are promoted in the name of preparing students for a changing world, it is paradoxical that the action in Canadian education reform may actually be missing the really important issues. The real drivers of educational change historically have been outside the school system, in changes in families, patterns of work, income distribution, knowledge production, legal requirements, demographics, and changes in the prevailing currents of opinion (Levin and Riffel, 1997). School systems face demands from more educated parents, and from a more diverse population that is more aware of its rights. Patterns of knowledge production and dissemination are shifting in important ways, generally reducing the power of many traditional knowledge providers. The advent of the Canadian Charter of Rights and Freedoms has changed the way public institutions relate to their clients. A declining proportion of the population with direct contact with schools has made it harder for schools to command the same share of public resources. Growing immigration from different parts of the world has led to new challenges in accommodating diversity. Changes in the labour market have made the completion of high school almost useless as a labour market credential, thus reducing the legitimacy of secondary education for many students. High levels of family poverty mean that many children come to school with serious disadvantages. These are the real changes that affect the process of education, yet they have not been an important part of the reform process in Canada to date. When we look at recent events with the advantage of hindsight, we are likely to focus on the tasks that were either not seen or avoided rather than on the powerful impact of what has passed for reform.

Notes

1. Public education in Canada, with the important exception of First Nations' education, is a constitutional responsibility of the country's 10 provinces – a responsibility that historically has been jealously and successfully guarded. There is no federal office or department of education, and while the federal government

does have a significant involvement in education in a variety of different areas, this involvement is spread among many government ministries, usually without any direct links to what occurs in schools. Across, as well as within, provinces historical, cultural, political and economic differences abound. Any reform project in Canada must take into account the complex legal, organizational and political considerations that result from these arrangements. This is a large part of the reason why it is so difficult to speak of educational reform at the national level. The Council of Ministers of Education in Canada (CMEC) is a creation of the provincial governments that plays an inter-provincial co-ordinating role in education, but it has no jurisdictional powers over any of the provinces.

2. At the time of writing this chapter (spring, 1999) two provincial election campaigns (most significantly in the influential province of Ontario) are underway and others are on the brink of being called. Schooling is a primary and contested issue in all of these jurisdictions and it is therefore likely that the year 2000 will be a crucial one in establishing the eventual parameters of reform in Canada.

3. As governments have succeeded in balancing their operating budgets these debates tend to become refocused between continuing to reduce the role of government and 'reinvesting' in the social services that bore the brunt of prior funding cuts.

4. Aboriginal peoples of Canada are defined in the Canadian Charter of Rights and Freedoms as including Indian, Inuit, and Metis people of Canada. *The Report of the Royal Commission on Aboriginal Peoples* (Canada, 1996), estimated the Aboriginal population of Canada in 1991 to be some 727,700 people of whom 438,000 were registered North American Indian, 139,000 Metis, and 38,000 Inuit. The funding of education for registered/status Indians on reserves is a constitutional responsibility of the federal government. The provision of education for the children of non-status/non-registered, off-reserve Indians and Metis people is normally a provincial responsibility. (See *The Report of the Royal Commission on Aboriginal Peoples*, Vol. 3 for a detailed discussion of Aboriginal education in Canada.)

5. New Brunswick has two provincial Departments of Education, one Anglophone and one Francophone.

References

Alberta Education (1995) *Charter School Handbook*, Alberta Education, Edmonton

Barlow, M and Robertson, H-J (1994) *Class Warfare*, Key Porter, Toronto

Brown, P *et al* (1997) The transformation of education and society, in *Education, Culture, Economy and Society*, ed P Brown *et al*, Oxford University Press, Oxford

Canada (1969) *Statement of the Government of Canada on Indian Policy*, Queen's Printers, Ottawa

Canada (1996) *The Report of the Royal Commission on Aboriginal Peoples*, vols 1–5, Minister of Supply and Services, Ottawa

Canadian Teachers' Federation (1998) *School Finance Statistics, ESN, January 1996–7*, Canadian Teachers' Federation, Ottawa

Dehli, K (1998) What lies beyond Ontario's Bill 160: The policy and practice of education markets, *Our Schools/Our Selves*, **9** (4), pp 59–78

Dobbin, M (1997) Charting a course for social division: The Charter School threat to public education in Canada, *Our Schools/Our Selves*, **8** (3), pp 48–82

Graham, R and Young, J (1999) School and curriculum reform: Manitoba frameworks, equity and teacher education, paper presented at the annual Canadian Society for the Study of Education conference, Sherbrook, Quebec, June

Green, M (1999) The future of Bill 160: life after the Court of Appeal's decision, paper presented at the Canadian Association for the Practical Study of Law in Education conference, Toronto, Ontario

Halpin, D and Troyna, B (1995) The politics of policy borrowing, *Comparative Education*, **31** (3), pp 303–10

Hatcher, R (1998) Social justice and the politics of school effectiveness and improvement, *Race, Ethnicity and Education*, **1** (2), pp 267–90

King, D (1999) Achieving balance: the province, school boards and school councils, in *Reaching for Reasonableness: The educator as lawful decision-maker: the proceedings of the 1998 conference of the Canadian Association for the Practical Study of Law in Education*, ed W Foster and W Smith, pp 13–18

Kozolanka, K (1998) Ten weeks that shook the province: the fight for public education in Ontario, *Our Schools/Our Selves*, **9** (4), pp 43–58

Levin, B and Riffel, J (1997) *Schools and the Changing World: Struggling towards the future*, Falmer Press, London

Levin, B and Young, J (1997) The origins of educational reform: a comparative perspective, paper presented at the annual Canadian Society for the Study of Education conference, St John's, Newfoundland, June

Livingstone, D and Hart, D (1995) Popular beliefs about Canadian schools, in *Social Change and Education in Canada*, 3rd edn, ed R Ghosh and D Ray, pp 16–44, Harcourt Brace, Toronto

McEwen, N (1995) Accountability in education in Canada, *Canadian Journal of Education*, **20** (1), pp 1–7

Mallea, J and Young, J (1997) Intercultural education in Canada, in *World Yearbook of Education, 1997: Intercultural Education*, ed D Coulby, J Gundara and C Jones, Kogan Page, London

Mawhinney, H (1998) Patterns of social control in assessment practices in Canadian frameworks for accountability in education, in *The Politics of Accountability: Educative and international perspectives: The 1997 Yearbook of the Politics of Education Association*, ed R Macpherson, Corwin Press, Thousand Oaks, CA

Moodley, K (1995) Multicultural education in Canada: historical development and current status, in *Handbook of Research on Multicultural Education*, ed J Banks and C Banks, Macmillan, Berkeley, CA

National Indian Brotherhood (1972) *Indian Control of Indian Education*, The National Indian Brotherhood, Ottawa

62 JON YOUNG AND BEN LEVIN

Ng, R, Staton, P and Scance, J (1995) *Anti-Racism, Feminism, and Critical Approaches to Education*, Bergin and Garvey, Westport, CT

Ontario Ministry of Education and Training (1997) *Putting Students First: Ontario's plan for education reform*, http://www.edu.gov.on.ca/

Osborne, K (1996) Education is the best national insurance: Citizenship education in Canadian schools, past and present, *Canadian and International Education*, **25** (2), pp 31–57

Peters, F (1997) Government-driven educational reform: reaping what we sow, paper presented at the Annual Conference of the Canadian Education Association, Toronto, September

Robertson, S *et al* (1995) 'Chartering' new waters: the Klein revolution and the privatization of education in Alberta, *Our Schools/Our Selves*, **7** (2), pp 80–106

Taylor, A (1996) Education for 'post-industrial' purposes: understanding the context of change in Alberta schools, unpublished Ed D thesis OISE/UT, University of Toronto

Young, J and Levin, B (1998) *Understanding Canadian Schools: An introduction to educational administration*, Harcourt Brace, Toronto

6.   Greece: the lack of modernity and educational transitions

Evie Zambeta

Introduction

The decade of the 1980s represented a transitional period in Greek society. In 1981 Greece joined the European Community as a full member state, while at the same time the Greek socialist party came to power, facts that have effected major transitions in political and socio-economic structures. Tensions between the impact of globalization and modernization strategies, on the one hand, and established traditional interests, on the other, form the main context of the social conflicts that outline the limits, as well as the dynamic of transition. Undoubtedly this tendency has its roots in the past. Nevertheless, major shifts in the political discourse and the state–civil society relationship, expressed more clearly after 1985, converge on the elaboration of a consensus towards modernization of the Greek society.

These tendencies have been made explicit in the educational discourse and reform policies adopted since the early 1980s. This chapter argues that the process of transition in state apparatus and social stratification is related to educational structures, though not in a linear way. The ways educational institutions respond to socio-economic and political change do not follow any sort of direct correspondence principle. Education is perhaps one of the least flexible state apparatuses, reflecting tradition and resistance to change. Educational transition is readable, but eclectic and provisional. The main features of educational transition are identified in a trend towards democratization and modernization of educational structures and contents. At the same time though, continuities, regarding the ethnocentric character of knowledge and traditional forms of educational policy formation and control still persist.

Sovereignty and democracy under construction: the lack of modernity

The concepts of democracy, national sovereignty and socio-economic development constitute dominant subjects of the political discourse in the Greek historical trajectory. The element of crisis forms the intrinsic connecting saga of this discourse. Lack of political and social democracy, or features of under-development, have been confronted as side effects of a continuing sover-eignty crisis which determines the main priorities of Greek politics.

It could be argued that since the foundation of the new Greek state, in the early 19th century, there has been a continuing process of constructing de-mocracy, sovereignty and development. This has not been an evolutionary process. Contradictions and conflict have produced discontinuities in the pro-cess of the new Greek state formation that have been expressed by a succes-sion of overthrows of parliamentary democracy and totalitarian regimes as well as by civil war.

The third Greek republic, established after the fall of the totalitarian regime in 1974, was a period of stabilization of the Western-type parliamentary de-mocracy. Nevertheless, certain features of the pre-modern era are still visible in the Greek polity. If a modernist polity, derived from the enlightenment pro-ject, were defined as a type of governance accountable to the citizen, either through a social contract or through forms of representative democracy (though this has not been universally the case in the modernist regimes), it could be argued that in Greece the modernist project has not yet been fully im-plemented and fulfilled. Clientelism as a form of mediation of interests through the political parties (Mouzelis, 1993) and the pre-modern extended family, which acts as a compensatory mechanism to the lack of welfare poli-cies, constitute perhaps the most illustrative features of the modernity gap in the Greek society (Charalambis, 1996). Moreover, the elaboration of Greek identity which draws upon ancient Greece, Orthodox Christianity and histor-ical memories of the Byzantine empire constantly tends to refer to lost imagi-nary homelands. In this respect nationalism has not only been an ideological construction towards the formation of Greek identity, but an intrinsic charac-teristic of the Greek polity as well. Nationalism was the ideological compensa-tion for the lack of democracy and a key feature of the unfinished Greek modernity project. As has been argued (Doxiades, 1996), nationalism is the way in which Greek late modernity reconciles itself to its pre-modern, pre-industrial, socio-economic and political structures. In this process, educa-tion has been a critical institution in the construction of the Greek identity and state formation. Furthermore, the history of the Greek educational system's formation and change throws the modernity gap into relief.

The emerging narrative

In the general elections of 1981 PASOK, the Greek 'socialist' party, came to power. This was a major change for Greece, which, with very few exceptions, throughout its history, has been governed by right-wing parties. It was in the same year that Greece became a full member of the European Community.

These events triggered a long process of adaptation of the Greek economy. In 1981 PASOK promised social change, redistribution of wealth and power in favour of the 'non-privileged' and a foreign policy that would ensure national sovereignty and independence. Furthermore, PASOK professed the abolition of the centralist authoritarian regime established by the Right, decentralization of power and the introduction of participatory institutions. The discourse was presented as both radical and focused upon the major problems of the Greek polity, namely lack of democracy and sovereignty. Memories of the to-talitarian regime of 1967–74 and unresolved issues in the country's foreign af-fairs, such as the case of Cyprus and the controversy over the exploitation of the Aegean's natural resources, had been internalized in a populist nationalist discourse that was presented as anti-imperialistic, anti-American, anti-European and anti-Turkish. What was rejected was the policy of the Right, as being unjustifiably authoritarian and too submissive in important national is-sues. The new government was expected to accomplish two main tasks. First, to restore the 'nation's dignity' within the international community. Second, to end the post-civil war political climate and to promote social cohesion by providing equal access to the state machinery to those who had till then been excluded, mainly the left-wing citizens. In PASOK's words, the fundamentals of democracy would be the parliament, trade unionism and local govern-ment.

After 1985 the discourse and the actual policies adopted by PASOK under-went a dramatic change. In fact this change had been underway since the early 1980s. While in 1981 there was a clear ideological and political barrier be-tween Right and Left, during the following four years the traditional barriers became less visible, a process that was made more explicit after 1985. The hard core of the nationalistic discourse gave place to more realistic politics. The so-cialist slogan of 1981 'Europe of the monopolies' was no longer an anathema, but the only available and definitely unavoidable route that would ensure socio-economic development and democracy (Soteropoulos *et al*, 1996, p 20). The aims of social equality and redistribution of income gradually gave way to that of the stabilization of economic indicators. Since 1989, the main focus of Greek politics has been economic convergence with the aim of the inclusion of Greece within the European Monetary Union. The borderline between Right and Left has become practically invisible in the fields of fiscal policy and la-bour relations. For example, in 1984 PASOK introduced 'Article four', a regula-tion that declared nearly all strikes illegal.

During this process the opposition political parties were facing a continu-ing identity crisis. The Right was arguing that PASOK had developed by adopting the policies of the Right, but without efficiency. The traditional Greek Left, the Communist Party and the pro-European Left, after going through a period of political embarrassment in the early 1980s, presented an introversion towards redefining their own political identity. The collapse of the Eastern European Communist regimes had critically affected their political profiles. In fact, no viable political alternative was present in the Greek polity. A conservative consensus stressing efficiency rather than equality emerged during the 1980s aiming at bridging the Greek modernity gap.

Politics, economy and civil society: changing relationships

The process of globalization has strongly influenced Greek society since the 1980s. Not only European integration, but more global trends regarding flows of capital, products, people, cultures, symbols and meanings were also at work exercising their impact (Harvey, 1989; Giddens, 1990; Featherstone *et al*, 1995; Oncu and Weyland, 1997). During these years Greek society witnessed a range of dramatic changes in production and social stratification. The traditionally extended agricultural sector was facing a serious decline, being unable to change its modes of production and types of cultivation in order to compete effectively in the international market. This fact led to new urbanization waves. Furthermore, a polarization has been observed in the secondary sector. On the one hand, massive de-industrialization processes in key sectors led to the increase of unemployment rates, while on the other, dynamic industrial sectors emerged in certain fields (Getimis and Economou, 1992). The new areas of intense capital accumulation in the fields of banking and services, information and communication technologies in particular, led to considerable redistribution of income in favour of new emerging elites. Moreover, massive waves of economic immigrants (mostly coming from the Far East during the 1980s and from the Balkans and Eastern European countries in the 1990s) provided a cheap labour force occupied mainly in construction and auxiliary services. This 'grey labour' increased the already substantial informal sector of the Greek economy, which co-exists with a particularly extended public sector.

In this context a peculiar shift can be identified in the relations between politics and the economy. While evolving globalization tends to diminish the role of the central state, through the establishment of transnational networks that bypass it and adapt to local interests producing 'glocalities' (Kafkalas and Komninos, 1993; Luke, 1997), it seems that the central state is still strong. By important decision-making processes held at a supranational level, the state continues to be strong, but in different terms than before. One example would be the case of the distribution of resources coming from the European Union Support Framework. Perhaps the most interesting aspect of this process is that, though the central state achieved a new challenging field of intervention and power, at the same time it became more 'sensitive' to particular pressures exercised by certain economic interests either at the central or local level. As long as the limits of the state are declining, new social borders emerge in terms of wealth and power acquisition. New elites and interweaving interests that perform a wide spectrum of interrelated economic activities, ranging from international trade and construction to banking services, telecommunication industries and mass media, tend to concentrate control over the formation of public opinion, culture and ideologies. In this respect their influence over the political realm becomes much more intensive. Not surprisingly, by the end of the decade, two governments had fallen. Prime Minister Papandreou, in 1989, blames the 'new elites' for this, while the Prime Minister in 1993 (Metsotakis) blames the 'interweaving interests'.

By the end of the decade the political enthusiasm of the early 1980s for 'social change' and 'social participation' seemed to be lost, while the interest of the individual citizen in politics was reduced, a trend more explicitly identified after 1985 (Kyprianos, 1997). At the same time the parliament and other forms of participatory bodies lost power in favour of the central government. Nevertheless, during the same period an expansion of social policies was being promoted in the Greek society.

It seems though that this was a conflicting process that has not led to the strengthening of civil society (Getimis and Gravaris, 1993). As has been argued, one of the historical characteristics of the Greek state is that it has not been used as a vehicle to accomplish collective ends, but rather as means of establishing clientelist networks (Mouzelis, 1993). This particularistic logic in social development, which lately has been transformed into corporate clientelism, is legitimized and reproduced by populism (Charalambis, 1996; Mavrokordatos, 1988). While in 19th- and early 20th-century Greece, the state apparatuses used to treat the individual citizen as a political client, nowadays the state performs a parallel political manipulation with regard to organized corporate interests. This political process is not based on transparent forms of dialogue that could promote social consensus, but it does lead to mutual dependence between the state apparatus and the respective interests. In various cases during the 1980s, the government promoted fragmented policies in favour of certain corporate interests. These policies could be opposed to a long-term perspective on political and socio-economic development. Educational policies, in particular, not only follow the same pattern of political construction, but also present an example of its contradictory content.

Educational images

In the early 1980s the new government expressed its commitment to changing the structures and objectives of the educational system. PASOK's programme in the 1981 elections, the so-called 'Contract with the People', identified education as 'the keystone of change'. The educational system was to serve as a main agent for the country's 'self-sufficient development' and was to cultivate the spoken Greek language and civilization. Furthermore, education would be a critical agent of social change by promoting the principles of democracy, national sovereignty, social equality and equality of opportunities.

The term 'educational reform' was rejected as referring to a modernization strategy that corresponded to the Right's way of governance that was incapable of changing both the structures and the rationale of educational institutions. The new government declared its political will towards the 'real change' of education. The 'real change' would involve a serious restructuring in power relations and devolution to decentralized institutions and participatory mechanisms. The highly centralized, bureaucratic, authoritarian education system would be transformed into a democratic system, accountable to Greek society, that would serve the 'needs of the people and the country'.

During this period PASOK was using an ethnocentric, populist discourse accompanied by a general rejection of the policy of the Right. The new foreign affairs dogma assumed that Greece was part of Europe, the Balkans and the Mediterranean rim, while the 'danger' would not come from the North and the Warsaw Pact, but from the East, Turkey, which means from another NATO member state. This was in sharp contrast to some parts of the traditional Greek education curriculum and rituals. Consequently, the curriculum should redefine 'who the others were' as well as promote 'critical knowledge' and cultivate the Greek identity, re-conceptualized as a 'crossroads' of eastern and western cultures. The evident self-contradictory character of the above argument – suggesting both ethnocentrism and internationalism, reflected the multiplicity of cultures, ideologies and interests that were supporting PASOK's educational policy. The hard core of PASOK's political strategy was the attempt to put under the same roof the various interests that were traditionally excluded from power mechanisms and decision-making processes. Those interests, which were politically addressed by PASOK as the 'non-privileged social strata', had conflicting ideologies and objectives. This partly explains the ambiguity of political language and educational policy of this period.

The educational reform law, introduced in 1985, constitutes the main legislation that regulates primary and secondary education and reflects the contradictory concept of the reform. According to the law, education should promote 'creative and critical thinking', while at the same time it should 'encourage the student's loyalty to the country and faithfulness to the authentic elements of the Orthodox Christian tradition' (Law 1566/85, art. 1, par. 1). The historically complex relations between the church and the state (Soterelis, 1998) and their impact on education policy in Greece was made even more evident when the government resisted any amendments to the above article, despite harsh criticism. Interestingly, the criticism, that was clearly expressed in the press as well as in parliament, did not come from the teachers, but mainly from the Left and intellectuals. The dispute regarding the strictly denominational character of education obliged the government to add in the same article that 'the freedom of religious consciousness is inviolable'. This type of conflicting discourse is found throughout the law and the educational policies during the 1980s (Zambeta, 1994). The so-called 'social participation' defines teachers, parents, students and local government as being the new social partners in education governance and policy making. Nevertheless, the hierarchical structure as well as the centralized and rigidly controlled, bureaucratic character of the Greek education system did not change, despite the alleged decentralization strategy of the reform (Kazamias, 1990). The introduction of 'democratic educational planning' and the introduction of participatory institutions both at the central and local levels, were not followed by the devolution of actual responsibilities and real power in decision-making processes. Moreover, the reference in the law to the concept of 'social humanitarianism' was not accompanied by any visible regulation regarding recognition of minority rights in education. The humanistic aspect of the rhetoric of the reform was restricted to the democratization and expansion of the egalitarian character of the educational system, on the one hand, and to the traditional prevalence of ancient Greek studies in the curriculum, on the other.

It should be recognized that during the 1980s certain regulations showed a tendency towards improvement of quality and democratization of education, such as the upgrading of primary teachers' education or the introduction of the 'Polykladiko' (multi-branch) Lyceum (a type of a comprehensive school at the upper secondary level). However, structural features of the democratic deficit in education still persist and continue to characterize the Greek educational system (Zambeta, 1994). These features include phenomena such as:

- drop-outs from compulsory schooling;
- functional illiteracy;
- uneven development of educational institutions and infrastructure;
- considerable inequalities between urban and rural areas, as well as within inner city areas;
- high private educational expenditures despite the allegedly public character of the educational system;
- helenocentrism and exclusion of others.

The use of this awkward concept of 'social humanitarianism' is an example of the shift in PASOK's political discourse. While in the early 1980s the government think tanks were referring to dependence and semi-periphery theories, presenting a politically radical rhetoric, some years later the aim of 'social transformation' favoured more realistic politics and Greece's accession to the European unification process. By the end of the decade the European Community Support Framework had become a major component of education funding. Thus, to a certain extent, it exercises an indirect influence on the redefinition of educational objectives. Gradually but steadily education finds itself under siege.

Education as the 'keystone of change' became equally, if not less, important to training. Education lacks flexibility in relation to market needs. Moreover, it is considered responsible for the increasing rates of unemployment, which is defined as structural unemployment. Throughout this period there was a visible shift in the orientation of education politics, as well as in government discourse and practices. This process became more intensive in the 1990s. Education was to be modernized in order to become more effective and responsive to the new challenges of the increasingly globalizing economic, social and knowledge systems. More specifically, education was to be definitely readjusted in order to converge with trends in the European Union. It was not the processes that mattered, but only the outcomes. Consequently, it was efficiency rather than equality that was at issue. In spite of the fact that there was a governmental change in 1989, when, after a period of political instability, the Right came to power for three years, the modernization process was not suspended. It would be an oversimplification to assume that the modernization project started in Greece during the 1990s, when the so-called modernization wing of PASOK came into power. In fact, this process started in the 1980s despite its many contradictions and discontinuities.

Education in transition

The main focus of education politics in the early 1980s did not differ from that maintained in other state apparatuses, such as the army or the police. What actually was at stake was the political control of the state. One of the intrinsic characteristics of the Greek state was not only its bureaucratic structure, but one-party control over the state bureaucracy, a feature reproduced through clientelism. In this respect, the major concern of the new government was to replace the existing control mechanisms of the Right. In the case of education, PASOK's rhetoric of an education system 'accountable to the Greek society' was not only a political response to the widely accepted need for educational democratization. Above all, it was expressing a political strategy towards the erosion of the control over education as a state apparatus exercised by the Right. The professed aims of democratization, decentralization and 'social participation' in educational planning and decision-making were also an attempt to change the power mechanisms in education. The question whether there was any real change regarding power mechanisms within the state as a whole is rather complicated.

In the early 1980s there was a wider social consensus on educational democratization, which was expressed in particular in the demands made by the teachers' and students' unions. In the case of primary and secondary education the teachers' unions had to be, and were, the key agents of reform. PASOK had incorporated in its programme all the demands expressed by the unions. The teaching profession, not well paid, with low socio-economic status, depressed by the Right's authoritarian, bureaucratic statism, was one of the aspiring components of the so-called 'social block of change', since it belonged to the 'non-privileged social strata'.

The concept of educational democratization and accountability was placed in this context. Education was to be accountable to society and responsive to its needs. Accomplishment of this ambitious goal would involve the abolition of the authoritarian centralist educational structures and the introduction of new institutions in educational management and evaluation processes. One of the most intense and urgent demands of the teachers' unions was the abolition of the inspection system. Until 1981 the inspectors, appointed by the Ministry of Education, had administrative as well as inspection responsibilities at the regional level. They were the key agents in monitoring education and exercising control over school governance and teachers' performance, as well as professional and social behaviour. Not surprisingly, the new government's first political inclination in education was to abolish the regime of the inspectors, well before being ready to introduce any sort of reform measures.

Certainly the rationale for this action was not restricted to the political pressure exercised by the unions. It was the political and ideological control over the state apparatus that was at stake. The introduction of the dichotomy between educational administrators and school advisers offered the opportunity to satisfy the unions' interests, on one hand, and to change the top educational executives on the other. Central committees, loyal to the Ministry of Education, were appointed to select the new administrative personnel. Among the main criteria for selection was conclusive evidence of the candidate's 'democratic ethos'. In fact, the power mechanisms within the state or the centralist character of education monitoring did not change. The introduction, in 1985, of 'democratic planning' through participatory institutions which assumed 'advisory' responsibilities made even more evident the main strategy of the new government: to establish its own political regime within education institutions, legitimized and reproduced through a new clientelist network.

Ironically, it was this process of political legitimization that suspended the attempt at reform. The highly publicized new institution of the School Advisers, who were expected to become agents of reform at the regional level, did not enjoy the professional status that would allow them to attain this goal. The questionable procedures of their selection along with resistance expressed by the teachers' unions with regard to the Advisers' domain, were the crucial factors that led to the undermining of reform from within. During the 1990s the legislation of a complicated, multilevel hierarchy of educational evaluation, though not yet fully implemented, illustrates the intensification of the modernization project, as well as its convergence with global trends.

A parallel process can be identified at the level of university education. Until 1981 the Greek universities had a notoriously strict hierarchical structure based on the regime of the professorial Chair. While the university enjoyed 'self-management' and 'academic freedom', the overall management, curriculum control and appointment of the teaching staff rested with the powerful body of a limited number of professors. At the same time almost 80 per cent of the teaching staff was of assistant teaching personnel (ATP) status who had extremely restricted possibilities for promotion and no chance to participate in university decision-making. The ATP, though recruited by the professors, was the main pressure group for reform. In fact, it was a highly influential group since it could be argued that many of its members were the organic intellectuals of PASOK's government, or the intellectuals of the left-wing political parties. Moreover, the ATP had kept close links with the student unions, a fact even more obviously demonstrated through the process of mediation of interests within the political parties.

The attempt of the new government to attain power over the statutory, traditionally conservative, educational apparatus was securely based on the ATP and the student unions. The rhetoric was that the university should be the fundamental source of the country's self-sufficient development. Changes in university structures and devolution of power to new participatory mechanisms were perceived as the vehicles for the necessary transformation of its orientation. Above all, the main task was to be the abolition of the so-called 'establishment of the professors'. The abolition of the regime of the Chair, the introduction of a four-level academic staff hierarchy and student participation in university management were some of the most important measures of the reform. The ATP, PhD holders, gained automatically most of the new posts in the academic hierarchy without open procedures. In fact, no other candidates were eligible to apply for these posts. Moreover, while the ATP had acquired tenure, irrespective of their position in the hierarchy, by contrast any 'outsider' entering the university teaching profession at the level of the lecturer had to wait at least seven years and be evaluated at least three times, through open procedures, in order to be promoted and get tenure. As a result, university teaching posts were mainly accessible to those who were already within institutions at the beginning of the 1980s. Nevertheless, the 1982 university reform policy was a major restructuring that changed the power relationships, while it formed a basis for university modernization. This was not a linear process and certain features of the past, especially regarding transmission of knowledge, still persist.

During the 1980s the professed goals of democratization of educational structures had been accompanied by a public discourse on 'critical thinking and knowledge'. Till then, certain aspects of the cultural heritage were excluded from school knowledge. The history of the country needed to be rewritten to incorporate also the recent period, which had been taboo, since it involved, at least, the highly controversial issue of the civil war and the roles of both the Right and the Left. Language teaching also needed to include 'progressive' literature and poetry. Certainly, curriculum reform and control do not take place in a vacuum. It is perhaps the most controversial aspect of reform in that it tends to present continuities as well as discontinuities regarding the definition of Greek identity and culture. Though certain attempts towards curriculum modernization have taken place, such as more emphasis on modern foreign language teaching or information and communication technologies, the ethnocentric and traditional aspects of the curriculum still persist. In fact, what was taught in the past continues to be the key determinant of curriculum reform, which of course is not a Greek peculiarity (Coulby, 1989). Despite the central control over the Greek curriculum, what is actually taught is not always in line with the rhetoric of the reform. The new and allegedly 'progressive' subjects were of marginal influence in the hard core of the curriculum. In many cases the issues that have been 'bypassed' due to the lack of time are exactly these new subjects, such as art education or contemporary history, and of course not the strongholds of Greek identity such as religion or ancient Greek history. In this respect, 'critical knowledge' is far from being an accomplished task.

Continuities and change

A lot of things have been written on 'the reform that never took place' in Greece (Dimaras, 1987–88; *Comparative Education Review*, 1978). It is true that throughout the history of the Greek educational system many attempts at reform have been suspended. On the other hand, most of the literature on the Greek educational system is focused on an analysis of its 'over-centralized' structure, while education policy formation is defined as a 'top-down' process. This type of argument could be seen as inconsistent, since it raises the question: why in such a centralized system can 'reform' not be implemented? If the reform is suspended due to the resistance expressed by the social actors who are excluded from power mechanisms, then why should education politics be defined as a top-down process? Education politics is a much more complicated process than an 'authoritarian' legislation promoted by the central state. This process involves mediation between the state apparatus and the various corporate interests that seek power and it is also interrelated to global impacts.

Assessing educational reform in terms of its ability to respond to processes identified in the fields of the economy and social stratification could lead to simplistic, if not short-sighted, approaches. As has been argued earlier in this chapter, the case of Greek education indicates that in many cases tradition and change coexist in a strenuous symbiotic relationship. Any attempt to interpret the educational present exclusively through its contemporary political and socio-economic context could lead to serious misunderstanding. It is this tendency behind the discourse on reform that always stresses its 'delay'. Education is in a process of transition between past and present. As Cowen (1996, 1998) suggests, it is the concept of sociological time that would allow a more comprehensive interpretation of educational transition. It is perhaps through this concept that educational transition in Greece could be understood and gain meaning.

In the educational reform promoted during the 1980s, the links between education policy and political change are far more readable than the links to socio-economic change. The attempt to implement educational democratization, modernization and redefinition of school knowledge, though not always successful, reflects the transition in the political culture of the period. At the same time, continuities regarding the structural and cultural characteristics of the Greek polity, such as clientelism, ideologies of nationalism and sovereignty crisis tend to set the limits of transition. The point that educational reforms in Greece have failed to contribute to socio-economic development (Pesmazoglou, 1987) is placed within the same context, thus emphasizing the discontinuities between the political, economic and cultural spheres in Greek society.

Nevertheless, looking at educational reform in the long term, the 1980s represent a transitional period, when the main impetus towards modernization was taking place while Greek education became more open to global, European in particular, influences. This process should not be considered as linear, however. It was rather conflicted and provisional.

References

Charalambis, D (1996) Irrational contents of a typically rational system, in *Society and Politics: Aspects of the 3rd Greek Republic 1974–1994*, ed C Lyrintzis *et al*, Themelio, Athens (in Greek)

Comparative Education Review (1978) Featuring educational reform: Greece, *Comparative Education Review*, **22** (1)

Coulby, D (1989) The National Curriculum, in *The Education Reform Act: Competition and Control*, ed L Bash and D Coulby, pp 100–09, Cassell, London

Cowen, R (1996) Last past the post: comparative education, modernity and perhaps post-modernity, *Comparative Education*, **32** (2), pp 151–70

Cowen, R (1998) Thinking comparatively about space, education and time: an approach to the Mediterranean rim, in *Education and the Structuring of the European Space: North–south, centre–periphery, identity–otherness*, ed A Kazamias and M Spilane, pp 61–72, Seirios, Athens

Dimaras, A (1987–88) *The Reform that Never Took Place*, Ermes, Athens, vols I, II (in Greek)

Doxiades, K (1996) In the Greek ideology the 1974 Referendum has not been done yet, in *Society and Politics: Aspects of the 3rd Greek Republic 1974–1994*, ed C Lyrintzis *et al*, Themelio, Athens (in Greek)

Featherstone, M *et al* (eds) (1995) *Global Modernities*, Sage, London

Getimis, P and Economou, D (1992) New geographic inequalities and spatial policies in Greece, *Topos*, **4**, pp 3–44 (in Greek)

Getimis, P and Gravaris, D (eds) (1993) *Welfare State and Social Policy*, Themelio, Athens (in Greek)

Giddens, A (1990) *The Consequences of Modernity*, Polity Press, Cambridge

Harvey, D (1989) *The Condition of Postmodernity*, Blackwell, Oxford

Kafkalas, G and Komninos, N (1993) Strategies of local development and the new role of state policies, in *Welfare State and Social Policy*, ed P Getimis and D Gravaris, pp 203–21, Themelio, Athens (in Greek)

Kazamias, A (1990) The curse of Sisyphus in Greek educational reform: a socio-political and cultural interpretation, *Modern Greek Studies Yearbook*, **6**, pp 33–53

Kyprianos, P (1997) The formation and performance of the party field in Greece, *Greek Political Science Review*, **9**, pp 102–37 (in Greek)

Luke, T H (1995) New world or neo-world orders: power, politics and ideology in informationalizing glocalities, in *Global Modernities*, ed M Featherstone *et al*, pp 91–107, Sage, London

Mavrokordatos, T (1988) *Between Pityokamptie and Prokroustie: Corporate organisations in contemporary Greece*, Odysseas, Athens (in Greek)

Mouzelis, N (1993) The state in late development, *Greek Political Science Review*, **1**, pp 53–89 (in Greek)

Oncu, A and Weyland, P (eds) (1997) *Space, Culture and Power: New identities in globalizing cities*, Zed Books, London

Pesmazoglou, S (1987) *Education and Development in Greece 1948–1985*, Themelio, Athens (in Greek)

Soterelis, G (1998) *Religion and Education: The constitution and the European convention. From catechism to pluralism*, Sakkoulas, Athens (in Greek)

Soteropoulos, A *et al* (1996) Quality and functions of the third Greek Republic, in *Society and Politics: Aspects of the 3rd Greek Republic 1974–1994*, ed C Lyrintzis, pp 19–42, Themelio, Athens (in Greek)

Zambeta, E (1994) *Education Policy in the Greek Primary Education (1974–1989)*, Themelio, Athens (in Greek)

7. Transitions in Hungary

Katalin Kovacs

A co-ordinated political transition

In 1989–90 rapid, profound and unexpected changes swept over the countries of the Soviet bloc, and among them Hungary. In a few months the constitutional state system was completely transformed and the political institutions of the new parliamentary democracy came into being. Private property was liberated from its previous restrictions and the legal foundations for a capitalist economy were laid down. No revolution in the history of the country has achieved more in the transformation of the economy and the society in such a short time. Yet the progressive changes that happened in Hungary have not been called a revolution.

The transformation of society and the economy was revolutionary in content but not in its modality. By the late 1980s it was becoming obvious that the one-party state was facing a crisis of legitimacy. The position of the state-party, the Hungarian Socialist Workers' Party, was no longer strong enough to stand in the way of the demand for political change. Yet the forces of the democratic opposition, who were not yet strong and organized enough, could not be sure of the steps the ruling party and the Soviet Union might take (remembering Hungary in 1956, Prague in 1968) if they felt threatened. So – caution, daring, and the mutual willingness to compromise, led to co-operation between the political forces within and outside the institutionalized authority and prevented the collapse of political co-ordination. It was Hungary that opened its western borders to make it possible for the fleeing East Germans to leave for the West, and it was Hungary that made history by cutting the first opening into the iron curtain. These two steps – real but fast acquiring a symbolic meaning – show that Hungary, unlike most other countries of the bloc, took an active role in initiating the changes that led to the dismantling of the political–economic system of Communism.

The transformation of society that quickly unfolded in 1989–90 was the result of negotiations between the state party and the democratic opposition. A national roundtable was formed with the participation of the ruling party and the representatives of the opposition, and their proposals for the way transition in Hungary should be orchestrated were approved by a referendum. The legislative acts that opened the way to the first free elections since 1948 were passed by the parliament of the old regime. In Hungary, law and order were never suspended or violated. No alternative centres of power came into being. The changes that took place were more like measures of a top-down, overall reform and were institutionalized by the political power that was itself under transformation. Thus the events that happened in Hungary in 1989 and 1990 showed the characteristics of both a revolution and a reform. Strangely, the word 'reform' is rarely heard within the country. In Hungary, the alienation from the concept of reform can be explained by the legacy of the state socialist system, which regularly launched new reforms but was unable to, and did not even aspire to, win the approval of the general or the professional public. What is called a 'revolution', or 'co-ordinated transition', by political analysts is generally referred to in Hungary as 'the change of the regime'.

The Hungarian economy started the transformation into a market economy with a fairly mixed legacy. Compared to the other countries of the region the Hungarian circumstances could be perceived as being more advantageous: a gradual process of democratization and economic liberalization was initiated as early as the 1960s, and was carried further at the beginning of the 1980s, when Hungary joined the World Bank and the IMF. So people in Hungary had relatively wider and longer experience of markets and enterprises, and the transition was helped by the presence of an educated and well-trained labour force. All this led to a higher degree of consensus on the direction of reform in the 1990s. But the basic condition at the beginning of the 1990s was the deep and prolonged economic crisis: a sharp decline in the GDP, high inflation, a soaring public deficit, the collapse of the large industrial facilities, mass unemployment and growing poverty. By 1994 the deficit in the total governmental expenditure amounted to 84 per cent of the GDP. In 1995 the government responded with severe austerity measures to raise the revenues of the state and cut public welfare spending, which had serious implications for education as well. Yet the traditional institutions of a market economy – capital market, stock exchange, two-tier banking system – gradually came into being and have become more and more active. The far-reaching transformation of the macro-economic infrastructure has meant the privatization of the state properties and the mushrooming of small enterprises. Foreign investment in Hungary during the 1990s has been considerably larger than in other Central European countries. By the mid-1990s the number of companies with majority public ownership gradually diminished and the number of, and the added value produced by, the majority foreign owned companies increased considerably. The economic stabilization programme managed to restore the macro-economic balance by 1997 and accelerated the pace of economic reform. Nevertheless, while the fundamental political and legal reforms were carried out fairly smoothly, the management of the economic crisis is taking longer.

At the beginning of the transitional period there was consensus among the political actors on the political and economic orientation the country should

take. Hungary was turning its back unhesitatingly on state socialism, on the
COMECON and the Warsaw Pact, and was to be part of 'Europe', meaning
Western Europe or the European Union. The vast majority of parties and civic
organizations that were formed and facilitated the changes – though engaged
in fierce ideological debates with one another – saw no alternative to the orientation towards Europe. Even the former political elite, the reorganized reform Communists, were more than eager to embrace Western-style capitalism
and social order.

The general feeling at the new millennium, when Hungary is celebrating
the one-thousandth anniversary of its conversion to Christianity and its statehood in Europe, is that the Yalta Agreement of the Second World War had
forced Hungary into a politically and culturally alien sphere. The events of
1989 are seen to have restored the country's organic position. They also
showed that Hungarians were willing to take risks and make sacrifices to
restabilize ties with Europe, where they felt their country belonged. The general will to catch up with the West, and the obstacles that lie in the way of accession to the European Union, have practically silenced the critique of
capitalism and suppressed the demand for new outlooks. Finding a 'third
way' remains the dream of a few. After decades of deprivations and unful-
filled promises people now want to be left alone to live their lives and want to
see social progress and prosperity.

At the end of the 1990s the country is a member of the Council of Europe,
the OECD, NATO, and is an aspirant for membership in the European Union.
The prospect of accession to the EU has influenced every piece of legislation
that has been passed. The adaptation to European norms, and more recently
the gradual adoption of the *acquis communautaire* of the European Union, has
been carried out by every government coalition since 1990, irrespective of the
political orientation of the constituting parties.

Systemic change in education

After the first free elections in 1990 the parties coming to power could be characterized by a sharp opposition to the previous Communist regime. They
were determined to carry through a radical political and economic transformation. Due to the way and to the speed these parties had to be organized
they did not have, and could not have, a detailed and well-formulated plan of
how to lead the country out of its deep economic and social crisis. They did not
have an elaborate educational policy either. They could, however, build on
the educational reform that was launched by the Education Act as early as
1985. The decentralization of the education system started before the change
of the regime, as did experimentation, for example, with alternative curricula.
Thus, in Hungary, some signs of transition could be identified in education
before 1989. The transformation of the education system was not initiated but

accelerated by the political events. The direction of the change has brought about an education system where pluralism has become the most characteristic feature: pluralism in ownership and administration, in structural and curricular matters, and in ideology and educational philosophy.

After 1989 the first measures relating to education served the purpose of reinstating freedom of learning, freedom of conscience and freedom of religion. The foundation of non-state educational institutions was authorized by the 1990 Amendment to the 1985 Education Act. Another 1990 parliamentary act recognized the right of the historical churches to education and charitable activities and the right of citizens to education at institutions of religious commitment. With reference to this act the churches, which had maintained 60 per cent of all educational institutions until 1948, could reclaim part of their property expropriated by the Communist State.

Probably the most important piece of legislation affecting the education system was the parliamentary act in 1990 that conferred the responsibility to provide education upon the municipalities, the local governments of the settlements, and to that end, also transferred to them the ownership rights of the formerly state-owned institutions of public education. This was the first step in the creation of a four-level system of educational administration, in which the central, the regional, the local and the institutional levels share the responsibility for the provision of educational services. As a result, the formerly centralized education system of Hungary became decentralized. The school structure also underwent significant changes. The formerly unified structure of 8 years general schooling followed by 3 or 4 years of secondary education was broken by the appearance of 6- or 8-year-long secondary schools (taken as 6+6 and 4+8 structures) and by the appearance of mixed-type schools (offering both general and vocational education, for example).

The new Education Act of 1993 codified the steps of the reform process of the previous years. The pace of reform is shown by the fact that it was necessary as early as 1995, and again in 1996, to amend the new Education Act. Certain restrictions had to be introduced into the exceedingly liberal structural regulation so that the transferability of the education system could be maintained. As well as stabilizing the education infrastructure, the main aims of the 1996 Amendment to the Public Education Act were to make the school system more transparent, to increase the system's accountability, and to implement the modernization of educational contents. The main elements of modernization were the new National Core Curriculum (adopted in 1995 and introduced in schools in 1998), the elaboration of a new examination system (coming into force in 2002), and the development of a quality assurance system. With the former restrictions on enrolments lifted in higher education, the expansion of the sector has taken place on an unprecedented scale. Not only are the traditional institutions of higher education undergoing a transformation but the infrastructure of a new institutional sphere, that of post-secondary education, is emerging fast.

Shifts in education policy

While some of the results of the educational reform – new legislative acts, freedom of education, expansion, the system of shared responsibilities created in
educational management – are impressive, the process itself that has brought
them about has been conflict-laden and dramatic. Education, which had been
a highly ideological field during state-socialism, especially in its first decades,
almost immediately became one of the most important battlegrounds for the
political parties and the various forms of professional groups and civil organizations that came into being. There were conflicts between the representatives of conservative, liberal or socialist values, of the public, private or church
spheres, groups were arguing for the rights of the local or the central level in
educational administration, and some protected professional arguments
while others insisted on the politics of everything. The various platforms obviously could not stabilize in the short time given. Since all three elections in the
1990s resulted in the victory of opposition parties, the following overview of
the education policies of the three coalition governments may cast a light on
the areas of conflict of interests.

The first coalition government of 1990–94 consisted of parties with Christian, national and conservative orientation. They were heavily influenced by
the historical traditions of the pre-Communist period; several parties even
bore the name of their predecessors that had operated in Hungary between
the world wars. These parties expected schools to strengthen the national culture and national identity, to represent and instil civic-bourgeois ethics and
values, and most of all to carry out the rehabilitation of religion. For them the
change of the regime partly meant the restoration of the ideology of an earlier
era, so they were shocked to realize that those pre-war traditions and values
no longer survived as vividly as they had imagined. They failed to win majority support for compulsory confessional education and did not manage to
adapt the National Core Curriculum to ensure that its requirements were
based on the ideological principles of Christianity and conservatism. The dis-
appointed government did not attempt to reconsider the basic questions and
their own attitude but tried to find scapegoats. Consequently what was called
a 'media war' or a 'cultural war' was started and teachers were blamed for having taken part in the corruption of the nation. But, unlike during the previous
changes of the political regime in the history of the country, there were no re-
taliations. What is more, the rhetoric of the government alienated the majority
of the people from the resurgent nationalism. Debates focused more on the
development of the economy, on raising living standards, and on the prospect
of integration with Europe, than on national glory lost and to be restored.
Ideological pluralism remained a protected achievement of the transitional
period, and ideological neutrality remained a respected value in schools.

By the mid-1990s the major structural and administrative changes in the
education system had taken place. Thus one of the key slogans of the central

educational administration operating between 1994 and 1998 was modernization which, as a political objective, characterized the whole of the new Socialist-Liberal government coalition. Their educational policy aimed at the modernization of the contents of education and at the thorough reform of content regulation. A large-scale government project was launched to develop the schools' information technologies and to connect them to global telecommunication networks. The Socialist-Liberal government also laid special emphasis on the introduction of a new in-service training system that would ensure the constant development of the professional competencies of teachers and in so doing would realize, in the long run, the objective of lifelong learning within the teaching profession.

However, the new objective of modernization was closely tied up with the signs of crisis and the ensuing need to adapt. Stabilization and modernization had to be carried out amidst the dramatic deterioration of the external conditions of education, such as economic recession, the huge deficit in public finance, and the consequent austerity measures. The main period of fiscal restrictions, 1995 and 1996, brought school closures, the discontinuation of certain services, teacher dismissals, and a lot of local and institutional level conflicts revolving around these events. It was in 1995 that the formerly unbroken trend in which public education received a growing share of the gross domestic product was halted, and, for the first time, the rate of the support for education sank below the officially published rate of inflation. In 1995 and 1996 the real value of teachers' salaries decreased to an unprecedented extent. (The crisis in school education provoked by the austerity measures was amplified by the parallel change in another important external condition, in the continued severe decline in the birth rate.)

The ongoing educational reform has to reconcile two seemingly incompatible aims: educational modernization and fiscal restrictions. Modernization and restriction together are by no means a unique pair. In Hungary, however, there have been serious concerns voiced about whether the modernization of educational contents, following years of change and instability, is viable in a prolonged crisis situation, where resources, as well as teachers, are exhausted. Based partly on this view the conservative government coalition that came into power in 1998 has decided to repeal some of the radicalism of the National Core Curriculum and to introduce so-called 'frame curricula' developed centrally for each school type. A further recent change is that by re-structuring educational management at the central level (the whole of vocational education, formerly the responsibility of various sectoral ministries, has come under the auspices of the Ministry of Education), the conditions have been created for the elaboration and implementation of a coherent, all-encompassing education policy that may be able to respond well to the new challenges, such as creating the conditions for lifelong learning. Yet while the education system as a whole has become more flexible, and more responsive to change in general, it has become more difficult to implement a top-down reform. Because of the extreme decentralization of the administration of public education and the extended autonomy of educational institutions, the government and the Ministry of Education can only use indirect methods, such as legislation and financial incentives, to influence educational processes at the local and institutional levels, where most decisions on educational matters are made.

Focus on the details: equality and quality

The quality of general schooling and higher education has traditionally been regarded as good in Hungary. This may be explained not only by the value attached to education but also more objective factors, such as the widespread development of early childhood education, a rather high level of teachers' qualifications, and – until recently – a very favourable teacher/student ratio. According to public opinion polls the level of satisfaction with the educational services has not decreased since 1990.

However, the macro-level analyses of the education system often voice concerns about the realization of the two basic values of education: equality and quality. As a consequence of the reform of the school infrastructure and of content regulation, the system has not only become multi-coloured but also less transparent, making it much more difficult to judge and control the realization of these two values. There are reasons for concern, for example, concerning the transferability of the system. The achievements and higher educational chances of students and student groups in different secondary schools have begun to show characteristic deviations.

Measuring of educational achievements in subjects by standardized tests has been carried out in Hungary since the 1970s. The achievements of Hungarian students at International Student Olympics, especially in the sciences, has been outstanding. However, the National Assessment Surveys of Student Achievement show, for example, a decline of 12 per cent in grade 8 reading performance and a 3 per cent fall in mathematics performance. Most of this decline has occurred in small towns and villages, calling attention to problems of educational quality in smaller settlements and to the growing performance gap between urban and rural areas. Striking differences emerge between different types of schools, with performance lagging behind in lower vocational schools. Taking into account both the regional disparities and the difficult situation of less-educated youth in a labour market that is becoming more highly selective, there seems to be an increasing risk of economic and social exclusion for a growing proportion of disadvantaged young people. Many of these risks are concentrated in the lower vocational and special vocational schools and affect the children of manual workers, whose employment prospects were once secure but who have been hardest hit by the impoverishment that accompanies large-scale unemployment. The Romani population is also heavily concentrated among the disadvantaged. In view of their higher birth rates, the magnitude of the problem is likely to increase unless their relative situation in education and on the labour market improves and is addressed by more coherent and effective policies.

It is still hard to judge what role is played in the deterioration of educational achievements and in the widening of gaps between various population groups by the social and economic transformation, by the different economic situation of the different settlements and regions, by individual choices, and by the conditions provided by public education. It is recognized that schools alone cannot compensate for the unfavourable effects of the social and economic processes. More publicity and support can be expected to be given in the coming years to the programmes that may compensate for these disadvantages.

New solutions for quality assurance in general are required both by the decentralization and the ongoing modernization of education. The system of quality assurance is undergoing changes and could be characterized as State in flux. The institutions of input control, such as the school inspectorate, were abolished in the second half of the 1980s but the institutions of output control have not yet been stabilized. The development of the mechanisms of quality assurance has been accelerated by the recognition that the Hungarian system in its rapid transition does not yet have enough guarantees built in to the system to ensure that schools follow curricular programmes and textbooks of proper quality.

The Act on Public Education is fairly clear in stating the responsibilities of the various actors in education for assessment. According to the Act the national or regional level assessment of pupils' performance takes place through nationwide measuring assignments or surveys, which do not aim at the assessment of institutions. The latter task is the responsibility of the maintainers, who, in turn, cannot assess the work of individual teachers. This is the task of the employers of the teachers, ie the school heads. The reorganized institutions of the national pedagogical services can be assigned by the Ministry of Education to carry out the nationwide assessment tasks. There are two national centres involved in the development of the item bank of standard assignments, which are adjusted to the requirements of the National Core Curriculum: the new fundamental knowledge examinations (to be taken optionally at the age of 16), and the new secondary school-leaving examinations. The experts who are entitled to chair the examinations are listed in a national register but the definition of conditions to be registered and the standard preparation of the examiners are still under development. Administrative responsibility for the quality of textbooks and teaching aids is assigned to the national level, the Ministry of Education. There is a National Textbook Council to assess and recommend new textbooks but much of the responsibility for educational contents lies with market forces (the textbook and curricular supply). Competition between them is expected to bring about more even and better quality only in the long term.

To ensure that schools developed their new pedagogical programmes and local curricula by 1998, in line with the requirements of the National Core Curriculum, a completely novel form of content regulation in Hungary, the development of a national curricular databank was started in 1996. (Direct reliance on the tools of modern informatics and telecommunications in a nationwide curriculum reform is a unique phenomenon internationally.) Curriculum developers were asked to adjust their proposed curricula to a standardized format and each curriculum was evaluated by an expert before being added to the databank. The new pedagogical programmes and local curricula of schools have been adopted by their maintainers. As a majority of school maintainers, especially in small settlements, do not possess the ability and means that permit the assessment of the institutions and thus quality assurance, it is necessary to develop these abilities. It is also intended to explore the local institutional aspirations for quality assurance and to publicize the best models. To enhance this process and to protect the interests of young people in school today, the methods of quality assurance in educational management training and the possible ways of rewarding and supporting quality work programme accreditation systems, forms of self-development and self-evaluation for schools are being rapidly developed. In this field there seems to be a need for further government-led influence at the system level, though preferably by preserving the advantages of autonomy at the local and institutional levels.

Knowledge

The 'dictatorship of the proletariat' established in Hungary from 1948 made its own curriculum and educational contents exclusive, and determined what knowledge was valid at school, for two main reasons. One of them was the highly important ideological control; the other was the intention to break the educational monopoly of the former ruling classes. Teachers in the 1950s could only pass on knowledge that was printed in the new textbooks and pupils could only be assessed in what had been learnt in class. Later on, among the political conditions of the 'soft dictatorship' of Hungary, these requirements and expectations softened as well. Curricula continued to be issued centrally, the system of inspection ensured that they were followed, and there was practically one textbook for each grade and subject until the mid-1980s. However, teachers from the 1970s onwards were no longer required to testify that they believed in the official ideology. Many of them did, at least for a time, but those who could not identify with the one world-view offered did not necessarily have to suffer a conflict of conscience. There was a tacit understanding that truth could have several versions and interpretations and that the official version of truth did not necessarily coincide with what was truth for an individual.

The change of regime in 1989–90 replaced the unified and official ideology with pluralism, which was uncontested in the wider political context, but there were fierce battles fought about whether schools should become ideologically neutral or committed, and about whether confessional religious education should again be made compulsory. This controversy was reassuringly settled by the declaration that it was the parents' right to decide what kind of moral or religious education their children should receive. There was, however, no controversy over the abolition of the Russian language as a compulsory subject. The passive resistance to compulsory Russian during the 40 years of the Soviet-bloc era, together with the limitations on travel, have resulted in a very low level of foreign language knowledge among the adult population of Hungary. Schools continue to be under enormous pressure from parents to provide high quality language teaching – in modern Western European languages, especially English and German – for the pupils in school today.

When it comes to deciding what is good and useful knowledge today it has to be taken into account that Hungary has not only witnessed the end of a political era. The political changes and the educational reform process are taking place on the threshold of the new millennium, among the conditions of late modernity, or post-modernity, ie they coincide with the perceived end of an era in world history. The change in the status of science in general does affect the way education can be carried out in schools. Pluralism has reached Hungarian schools with respect to the sources of knowledge acquisition as well. It is gradually being recognized that the traditionally highly valued factual knowledge is less enduring than the tools and methods of selecting, analysing and criticizing knowledge and information. The Hungarian National Core Curriculum is up-to-date by international standards. It is, furthermore, revolutionary in the history of Hungarian education, in approaching and organizing educational contents in general knowledge or culture areas, rather than in individual subjects, in encouraging a variety of methodologies for the organization of learning, rather than teaching, and in emphasizing the importance of helping pupils acquire a broader range of general skills.

However, there may still be a strong opposition at school level or by teachers to the National Core Curriculum. It is not at all certain whether, and actually how, the 'post-modernization' of Hungarian education – envisaged by some policy-makers – will take place. The Ministry of Education under the Socialist-Liberal coalition faced strong opposition when it declared its intention to make the choice of the subject of history optional at the school-leaving examination. This was strongly criticized, even in parliamentary addresses, so history has remained a compulsory examination subject. Much of the conservative education and cultural policy discourse continues to revolve around the re-creation of the lost or injured national identity and around the necessity to reinstate the traditional moral values and the authority of teachers. It is yet to be seen whether the new fundamental knowledge examination from 2002 will follow the approach dictated by the traditional organization of science or will concentrate, in line with the requirements of a new era, on basic skills. The Hungarian school system, like other school systems, has to break the tradition of handing down closed knowledge packages because these packages can no longer satisfy the demands of the consumers and the market economy. But consumer and market tastes and demands are themselves currently under development. It is somewhat reassuring, however, that these epistemological challenges, unlike a large number of country-specific problems that Hungary has to solve by itself, can expect global responses besides the national ones.

Conclusion

One of the most powerful metaphors ever used to describe Hungary was that written by the poet, Endre Ady almost 100 years ago: the 'ferry country': 'Ferry country, ferry country, ferry country. Even in its ablest dreams it just comes and goes between east and west, mostly back to east.' Hungary entered the 20th century as part of a middle-size European empire (the Austro-Hungarian dual monarchy) and lived through not only the two world wars (like the rest of Europe) but, as a consequence of the wars, it lost some two-thirds of its territory and population. The 'ferrying' in this landlocked country continued all through the short 20th century: the population has witnessed a change, and mostly violent change, in the political regime on eight occasions. It is no wonder that there is very little feeling of continuity.

After 10 years of the most recent of social transitions the hopes are high that stabilization can finally settle down. But stabilization in the given socio-economic context has to mean the stabilization of transition, ie the acceptance that the reform of the society has to be continued. The fairly swift completion of the most significant stages of the transformation of society has resulted in exciting new developments but also in the emergence of new problems. While the country had great expectations for the new society, the difficulties involved in its transformation and in its integration with the international economy have been underestimated. It is now realized that changing the organization and the management of a society, and especially changing the attitudes of its citizens, takes a very long time.

For the past 10 years the transformation of the Hungarian education system has proceeded in parallel with the modernization of the economy and the change in political regime. First, systemic changes had to be implemented, creating the new legislative framework and aiming at the transformation of the formal school infrastructure. Having completed most of these tasks reformers can now concentrate on further important issues, both within and outside the formal education system (such as quality and equality, or lifelong learning). The direction of the reform at the end of the 1990s seems to show fewer and fewer regional characteristics: educational change in Hungary is less and less directed by the country's geopolitical position in Central Europe.

There are a large number of specific national problems and a variety of global challenges to further the cause of reform in Hungarian education.

Further reading

Featherstone, M *et al* (eds) (1995) *Global Modernities*, Sage, London

Garton Ash, T (1990) *We The People: The revolution of 89*, Granta Books, Penguin, Cambridge

Halasz, G and Lannert, J (eds) (1998) *Jelentes magyar kozoktatasrol, 1997* (Report on Hungarian Public Education, 1997), OKI, Budapest

Halasz, G *et al* (1998) *Inter-governmental Roles in the Delivery of Educational Services*, manuscript, OKI, Budapest

Kis, J (1997) Reform es forradalom kozt (Between reform and revolution), *Kritika*, 1997, Budapest

Nagy, M (ed) (1998) *Report: Education in Hungary, 1997*, National Institute of Public Education (OKI), Budapest

Setenyi, J (1996) Az oktataspohtika europai vizioja (The European vision of education policy), *Educatio*, Tel, Budapest

Suranyi, B (1997) Kicsoda a pedagogus, es miert jelenthet ez problemat? (Who is a teacher and why can that be a problem?), *Iskolakultura*, 2 (3)

8. Iran

Jan Derry

The 1979 Iranian Revolution came as a surprise to the majority of analysts and commentators who were following the development of Iran. Even more unexpectedly, it swept to power a theocracy (which has variously been labelled backward, medieval and populist). The Islamic Republic appeared an anomaly in the evolving modernization of Iranian society.

Yet at the time of the revolution, the political rhetoric recruited from an Islam embodied in popular culture found a language to articulate dissent. This Islamic rhetoric attracted the implicit sympathy, if not the active support, of the majority of Leftist groups and secular nationalists in Iran and a variety of academics and commentators in the West. The Mullahs possessed in their Islam what Fischer described as 'a reservoir of symbolic terms people could use to create a meaningful world' (Fischer, 1980, p 46). Importantly, in a country that had not fully established civil society, the historically institutionalized role of the Mullah provided stability at a time when the more contemporary edifice of the monarchy had fallen.

Leftist groups had understood their struggle against the Shah's modernizing regime via a 'third worldist' focus using broad unspecified categories such as 'exploitation' and 'dependency' (Moghadem, 1987). Oil revenues had helped perpetuate the fragile basis of the power of the Shah, diminishing the urgency of building a strong civic base and leaving a vacuum that the Mullahs with their local bases of power could fill.

What was later called a 'fundamentalist reaction' grew out of dissatisfaction with the forces of modernization as they had been experienced under the Shah. Those forces made Iran try to function as if it were a modern nation–state.

Fundamentalism as a term has been used to capture the character of the transition that occurred, post-1979, but the term itself hides what has more appropriately been called 'political Islam'. David Menashri in his book, *Education and the Making of Modern Iran*, describes how in many ways 'the Islamic revolution presented a new prototype of power seizure… its new ideology was actually the return to a glorious old one: Islam in its pristine form' (Menashri, 1992, p 1). But the claims to an authentic Islam can interestingly be considered against Khomeini's doctrine of government (*velayet-i faqih*). This doctrine, which has provided the ideological base for the Islamic Republic, has also been a source of ongoing tension.

Rhetoric

It was the Islamic theory of political and spiritual leadership (*velayet-i faqih*) developed by Khomeini that provided the rationale for operating an Islamic Republic and for religion to be at the heart of the state and government. The theory places the leader of the Republic in a position of authority to interpret God's will. The status of Imam (supreme spiritual leader) goes beyond mere mortal qualities and the doctrine of *velayet-i faqih* created powerful support for political authority to be vested in one person. The extent to which a notion of 'pristine Islam' may be applied to the rule by clerics is controversial. Zubaida has argued that the terms that characterized the rhetoric and claims for authenticity in Khomeini's speeches rely on highly modern notions of state, nation and people and are in many respects modern constructions. This is a departure from historical Islamic thought and practice (Zubaida, 1997, pp 104–05).

The particular interpretation of rule by *faqih* (jurisprudent, one who has total knowledge of the law and can apply it in a just way) does not counter the possibility of challengers. It also provided the source of authority behind the fervour with which the regime set about the Islamization of society, with the education system as a central means to this end. The problems of rapid and uneven development prior to the revolution were understood as resulting from the negative influence of the West and the eradication of such influence was central to the project to Islamisize.

Islamization

In its rhetoric the changes made to the education system appeared to express a Fundamentalist determination to make society Islamic. The confidence with which the project was instituted was derived partly from the knowledge of failure of either capitalism or socialism to attend to humanity, and partly a belief in the righteousness of purpose and special role of guidance secured by the doctrine of leadership (*velayat-i faqih*). However, there was much pragmatic implementation of policies framed in such rhetoric.

The project of Islamization was built upon the foundations of a history of struggle against the Shah. A range of revolutionary forces had provided a culturally familiar language, making the project meaningful (Moghadem, 1987). A significant shared ground dealt with 'Westoxification' (*gharbzadeh* – serving the interests of the West), 'dependency', 'opposition to imperialism', and 'purification of the ideological contamination of the Iranian people'. These were to be broached in schooling, higher education and literacy initiatives in rural areas. As Vakily emphasizes, freeing the minds of Iranian youth and intellectuals from imported ideologies characterizes Iranian education policy (Vakily, 1992, p 45).

The anti-Western rhetoric was expressed in different ways at different levels of the education system. Islamization of schooling took place through a revision of textbooks which were seen as a key medium for the transmission of values. Higgins notes the key role given to the textbook revisions is indicated by the speed at which changes were made as well as by the importance given to education by the Islamic Republic (Higgins and Shoar-Ghattari, 1994, p 36).

Mosenpour (a Director of the Bureau of Research on International Education Systems of the Ministry of Education in Iran) identifies areas where Westernization or Westoxification occurred in the education system. From games used in kindergarten to an approach to sporting activities – emphasizing the need to win rather than encouraging discipline and order – Western cultural patterns and value systems were seen as the basis on which pupils were socialized into a materialist existence. In the view of Khomeini's government, this included a subtle mixture of Marxist and atheist ideas underlying the content of what was to be studied. Sociology books dealing with secularization as an outcome of industrialization demeaned Islamic values, mathematics books used as examples calculations of usury as a means of accumulating wealth, history textbooks ignored the history of Muslim nations. Adjustments to textbooks were made accordingly. Among the major goals approved by the Higher Council of Education was the need to strengthen the belief in the leadership of the pure Imams via *velayet-i faqih*. This would confirm the authority of the political leadership of Iran. The sovereignty of God to rule over human beings was linked to obedience to the prophet of God and in turn to the leadership of religious jurisprudents with the argument that 'instead of the shah, only the Almighty God has the right to rule over human beings' (Mohsenpour, 1988, p 83).

Textbooks have been considered to have an important socializing function and much analysis of the Iranian education system deals with this aspect (Matini, 1989; Mehran, 1989; Nafisi, 1992; Shorish, 1988; Vakily, 1992). Overtly and implicitly, textbooks counter what were seen as the Shah's imposition of Western values, the presentation of a solely Persian heritage and what was taken as the earlier censorship of religious texts. In addition to the substitution of an Islamic history, texts encourage a modest Islamic, traditional dress, including the veiling of women. The West is presented as responsible for family breakdown, psychological alienation, delinquency and drug addiction. Martyrdom and sacrifice for the republic are emphasized, as is a global Islamic community (Mehran, 1989; Vakily, 1992).

Shorish makes a further point that textbooks were seen as 'guides for the realization of the new Islamic society' and that this accounts for the investment in the production of books and the training of teachers for this crucial task. The role played by the teacher was critical if Khomeini's doctrine of government (*velayet-i faqih*) was to be fulfilled.

Nothing less than an inner revolution was called for in those to be educated, with major emphasis on moral and spiritual development. Knowledge, expertise and skill were to be part of the process of inner revolution and carried by it. The process was to be carried out under the guidance of teachers who had been selected and trained for their role by commitment to the concept of *velayet-i faqih* and by following courses in religion, the Holy Qur'an and ethics. Teachers involved in the literacy campaign, which was seen as having a crucial role in the transformation of values, went through the same selection process (Mehran, 1989).

The notion of 'guidance' gives a special meaning for the idea of a teacher (leader, *imam*) making teachers central to the process of value transformation but also enabling this 'inner revolution'. The teacher's role is to make sure children see 'not only their goal and their mission but also their dependency on a leader to guide them, further demonstrating to them the inseparability of the leadership in Iran from Allah and His Way, the *Shari'ah'* (Shorish, 1988, p 71). The idea of guidance seeks to confirm the authority with which 'rule by *faqih'* is endowed – the authority comes from God and the will of God.

Shorish emphasizes the idea of inner revolution and self-control, learnt by following a guide, as the rationale for the rejection of alternative political formations, 'capitalism and socialism are unable to provide the mechanism through which man is able to control himself from within' (1988, p 69). He argues that what people lack and need most is guidance and that the notion of guidance is crucially important for Islam. The development of character involves an emphasis on discipline and orderliness and 'training and purification'. An implication of the philosophy of education is the priority given to moral development of ideal citizens as good Muslims, over and above the development of a trained workforce (Higgins and Shoar-Ghattari, 1994, p 20).

The emphasis on guidance and training suggests a particular conception of pedagogy containing a model of learning that depends solely on absorbing the correct knowledge. However, a more recent document issued by the Ministry of Education in 1993 suggests a different emphasis. Their publication, *Education in the Islamic Republic of Iran*, documents changes in the system of secondary education and lists deficiencies and problems of the present system. One major problem is described as follows: 'The curriculum in this level is extremely subject matter centered, emphasizing memorization rather than developing skills for critical and analytical thinking' (Ministry of Education, 1993, p 60).

Where textbooks had been presented as indicative of the ideological values of the Pahlavi regime, the whole education system under the monarchy was seen to harbour the supremacy of Western values. As with schools, universities were to be reconstructed to rid them of 'Westoxification'. At the start of the revolution this entailed their closure. However, it would be wrong to see the moves made against the universities as merely an attack on Western values. Menashri comments that although Western educated intellectuals came under Khomeini's direct fire, 'apparently his opposition to them was not merely due to their educational policy but also their political rivalry' (1992, p 311).

Serious struggles took place to establish the theocracy as a state at the beginning of the post-revolutionary period. Universities, as the centre of political activism and more importantly as an alternative power base, were a focus of this move to consolidate power. Expressed as a need to purify and purge the values brought in by Western educated and influenced intellectuals, the universities became a focus of political struggle and the source of what was to be announced as the Cultural Revolution. During a three-year period, there was a purging, in the universities, of anyone who failed to believe in, that is support, Islamic government (Matini, 1989, p 51).

But this expulsion had consequences that were to prove serious in terms of shortages of professionals. The dogma was adjusted. By 1984 Khomeini was advising restraint and a balance was sought between the drive to Islamisize and reality. The need to recruit professionals with expertise was an important example of this adjustment (Menashri, 1992, p 313).

Political rivalry did not disappear with the elimination of opposition forces that had been in control of the universities immediately after the revolution and prior to the Cultural Revolution. Education policy served as a focus of dispute between rival forces within the clergy. By the late 1980s pragmatism was the order of the day when serious shortages of professional labour and a stricken economy modified some of the strictures of the Cultural Revolution. The Revolution, its after-effects and the war had created a serious drain of professional expertise from Iran. That expertise could not readily be replaced by an education system that was emphasizing commitment more than competence. Speeches were made advocating tolerance towards professionals and those in charge of education policy were encouraged to practise moderation (Menashri, 1992).

A number of pronouncements illustrate that the education system, like other areas of government policy, was a source of dispute and power struggles between different sections of the government. There was concern about the esoteric slogans that had attempted to prescribe what were understood as anti-Western policies. Menashri quotes Rafsanjani: 'For the reconstruction, one cannot work with slogans, commotion and sentiments.' Iran cannot live in today's world without the 'material capabilities and the advancement of science and technology'. Khamene'i similarly stated that Iran needed 'the assistance and co-operation of others... Domestic resources and expertise are not enough' (Menashri, 1992, p 316).

Surveillance of the education system to ensure the success of Islamization took varied forms but was adapted in response to pressure and, given the various loci of power, was often arbitrary in its application. Initially 'ideological tests' were instituted to establish 'moral competency', defined as being a Muslim, or member of an officially recognized religion, but also entailing having no links with opposition movements or the East or West. Enquiries were made of the applicant's neighbours and this could mean that applications took two years. Universities were monitored by disciplinary committees checking for deviance from norms of behaviour defined by the regime (Menashri, 1992, p 317). Menashri describes the move to regularize what was an arbitrary process so that information could only be obtained from official bodies rather than via neighbours or informants. The practice of monitoring students during their time at university has had the undesired effect of creating a depoliticized student body. This political apathy is at odds with the aim to develop active Islamic citizens and as such is considered to be a form of struggle against the regime and is a matter of concern (Mojab, 1991, p 203).

Tensions and pragmatism

The policy changes have left their mark in exposing tensions intrinsic to the notion of rule by *faqih* and the idea of an Islamic practical politics. These tensions expose conflicts within the Islamic Republic, but also highlight the pragmatic response when issues of principle conflicted with practicality or utility.

The regime's aims were Islamization of schooling and higher education, that is the development of Islamic personality. This was to occur through the eradication of Western intellectual thought, the eradication of 'Westoxification' in Western-dominated textbooks such as social science books and even co-education. Access to universities and teacher training was to rely on commitment rather than competency. Quotas provided differential access for war veterans or their families.

The pragmatic consequences of coming to power and having to govern rather than make esoteric pronouncements contained contradictions. The heavy opposition to experts who had been educated in a Western milieu decreased as shortages became evident. Doubts were cast on the idea that access to universities should depend more on commitment than competence. The ruling on co-education was relaxed for rural areas and the position on access of families of war veterans was not clarified. There was a complete reversal in family planning policy given the pressure on the education system from a population growth rate that was among the highest in the world and where 50 per cent of the population was under the age of 17. These turns – the lessons of practical politics – meant a change in constitution of the Majlis incorporating some Western-educated academics. Rafsanjani selected a government of religious technocrats, rather than revolutionary ideologues. He made it clear that he wanted a government of experts, not of politicians. As he said in response to critics, 'Studying in American universities was not and is not a negative point' (Menashri, 1992, p 328).

Purification and ridding Iran of 'Westoxification' was seen as a major issue for education policy in the early years following the revolution, yet the unease about the policy 'commitment rather than expertise' emerged in various disputes and pronouncements on the universities. Even in the early days of the Republic warnings were made. Khosrow Sobhe, Director of the Office of

Planning in the Iranian Research Organization of Science and Technology, in an article comparing the Chinese Cultural Revolution with that of Iran, made a plea against 'mere sloganizing to gain political ends'. He saw similarities between the potential outcomes of the Iranian Cultural Revolution and those of the Chinese. He argued that in the case of China, 'mere political consideration and putting politics in command retarded the development of the country... personal wills and idealism of the authorities shifted education from one extreme to another' (Sobhe, 1982, p 279). Costs were great and did not outweigh benefits. Writing at the start of the 1980s he was concerned about the closure of the universities and the long-term consequences for the supply of skilled manpower. Sobhe cautioned against the view of post-revolution Iranian authorities that if an expert is not a devout and orthodox Muslim he or she is of little worth to the country. He stated: 'The Chinese case teaches us that mere commitment to ideas does not make a difference. The real commitment should be to the people. The message is clear: Iran needs experts first to reduce and then eliminate dependence on foreign countries' (ibid, p 279).

Continued disputes took place among those lobbying for influence and the adoption of 'their' strategy for Higher Education. The haphazard character of the rhetoric and its mediation for political purposes give some indication of the strangely plural character of Iranian politics but also of its opportunism and tactical shifts. This was evident in the regime's ruthless moves to rid the universities of opposition to the theocratic oligarchy as it consolidated its power in the early post-revolution years.

The contradictions in policy are also illustrated by Mojab's description of the struggle about the role of universities either for sufficient manpower development or for ideological commitment, 'in 1984, the Prime Minister called for increasing the capacity of the universities by 150% in order to solve the problem of manpower shortage which he said would be one of the main problems of Iran's development in the next five years... A few months later he argued that emphasis on expertise and manpower was a Western value and should be avoided' (Mojab, 1989, p 45).

The issue of nationalism was a further area of tension. One of the social goals of the school curriculum was 'extending and strengthening Islamic brotherhood and cooperation as well as strengthening national unity' (Mohsenpour, 1988, p 85). Nationalism was even embodied in the constitution where Article 115 states that the President must be Iranian both by origin and nationality (Zubaida, 1997, p 105). Nationalism is seen as a source of opposition to Islamic ideals, yet the Islamic Republic 'has been unable to remove the feeling of nationalism from the average Iranian and from some of those in the leadership itself' (Shorish, 1988, p 72). Shorish argues that this will act as a divisive factor which may prevent the revolution from growing.

The difficulty of maintaining the education system under economic pressures and an expanding and youthful population led to a revision of the expectation that all universities were to be 'guided', ie under government control. Before 1989 no private universities were permitted to operate but a change in policy occurred in 1989 when the first application for a private university was approved. By 1992–93 there were 372,445 students in public universities and higher education institutes and approximately 350,000 students enrolled in the non-profit universities (Vakily, 1992). The Ministry of Education states in its own publication 'there are also a number of non-profit universities offering both medical and non-medical programs, which are not under the supervision of either of these ministries' (Ministry of Education, 1993, p 71). Necessity had overcome the concern to limit access to those with greatest commitment.

In relation to the role of women, other contradictions and tensions were visible. Zubaida comments:

> The compulsory veiling of women has been, to international public opinion, the hallmark of the revolution. The paradox of veiled women holding up machine guns… has not brought home to most observers the contradictory implications of the revolution for women. In mobilizing and politicizing the women, the revolution gave them sources of ideological and political powers which have prevented their complete subjugation. (Zubaida, 1997, p 114)

The attitude of the radicals and conservatives towards women stressed their traditional role and imposed various severe restrictions on their movement and dress. Again the rhetoric of Islamization led to its own contradictions. Various commentators note that despite what might be expected due to various limitations imposed on women by the Islamic Republic, available data do not suggest a fall in educational enrolment or access and in certain cases figures show an increase in achievement (Mehran, 1991; Higgins and Shoar-Ghattari, 1994; Zubaida, 1997). The pressures of the war and the exodus of expertise placed demands on women to fill government positions and to provide medical and teaching services for women to comply with the demands of Islamization. Mehran notes some improvements in literacy for women and a narrowing of the gap between the genders.

Hafisi argues the quota system offered some possibility of social mobility to women in the lower strata and Higgins notes that women in less developed rural regions had increased access to education (even assisted by veiling). Higgins states that: 'If we compare the number of graduates from each of the academic fields in 1989–90 with 1975–76, we see that the proportion of females has increased in every academic field' (Higgins and Shoar-Ghattari, 1994, p 30). She suggests that it would seem to be due to the lobbying of the Women's Cultural and Social Council that most of the restrictions and quotas on women were lifted in 1989. Zubaida explains how the continued contentious question of women and the family are exemplified by opposing forces:

> On one side are conservative forces, led by many Mullahs, who want to limit women to the domestic sphere and to impose traditional interpretations of sha'ria provisions. On the other are women activists and their liberal

supporters, leading a vocal constituency of women and exploiting the am-
bivalence of the government ideology to push their definitions of the appropriate 'Islamic' roles for women. In this conflict socioeconomic forces have
been on the side of the liberationists. (Zubaida, 1997, p 116)

One way of understanding the changes in the education system may be
through its centralized, authoritarian prescriptions. A return to the essential
principles of the Qur'an apparently entailed segregated education, censored
and revised textbooks, the monitoring of student eligibility for higher education and purging of any non-Muslims. However, another way of understanding the changes in the education system is to see policies as an expression of
wider struggles in a country managed by an oligarchy, struggling to resolve
various countervailing forces while maintaining the rhetoric which played a
role in its coming to power. With this latter reading, contradictory forces are
evident, producing tensions which required the pragmatic responses.

Conclusion

Thus, the Iranian transition and its processes suggest that the Qur'an as a set of
statements cannot simply be applied to the task of government. The statements have to be interpreted in specific conditions and cannot merely follow
the model of the just *faqih*. The Mullahs, who might be seen to exemplify what
has been understood as 'Fundamentalist Islam', were unable to make their
project of Islamization succeed. Some commentators see this failure as due to
an excess of emotionalism, over the intellectual emphasis necessary to develop a political form capable of responding to what was seen as a traditionally religious population and the inappropriateness of western models of
government (Vakily, 1992, p 54).

The original dominance of the impetus to rid Iran of all that was Western is
now facing new difficulties of expression. Khatemi, the current president of
Iran, notes the lack of political foundations intrinsic to Islam to strengthen the
basis of the rhetoric of the revolution. Saul Bakhash, in reviewing Khatemi's
book *From the World of the City to the City of the World*, states: 'he seems to be saying that his own country and the Islamic world itself need powerful and imag-
inative thinkers (like Locke, like Hobbes) who will engage in far-reaching
interpretation of Islamic political thought and create political institutions adequate to the present time' (Bakhash, 1998, p 47). This point is echoed in com-
mentaries on education policy in Iran – political rhetoric offers a weak basis for
the demands of building an Islamic state (Sobhe, 1982; Vakily, 1992).

The initial rhetoric of rejection of all that was supposed to be of the West,
posed by different sections of the clergy, had an impact only at the level of ideology. The overall structure of the education system remained (Menashri,
1992, p 326). At the university level, radical attempts at modifying courses

failed, resulting only in the addition of Islamic courses (Mojab, 1991, p 169).

How long the social processes of modernity and the need to operate within a global capitalist economy can be resisted remains to be seen. As Abrahamian puts it, a more apt description of the Islamic regime is 'populist' rather than fundamentalist. The pragmatism that has characterized policy including that of education is a response to the attempt of a 'nation state to enter the world'.

References

Abrahamian, E (1993) *Khomeinism*, I B Tauris & Co Ltd, London and New York
Bakhash, S (1998) Iran's unlikely president, *New York Review of Books*, **XLV** (17), pp 47–51
Fischer, M M J (1980) *Iran: From religious dispute to revolution*, Harvard University Press, London
Hafisi, R (1992) Education and the culture of politics in the Islamic Republic of Iran, in *Iran: Political culture in the Islamic Republic*, ed S Farsoun and M Mashayekhi, Routledge, London and New York
Higgins, P J *et al* (1994) Women's education in the Islamic Republic of Iran, in *In the Eye of the Storm: Women in post-revolutionary Iran*, ed M Afkhami and E Friedl, Syracuse University Press, London and New York
Matini, J (1989) The impact of the Islamic revolution on education in Iran, in *At the Crossroads: Education in the Middle East*, ed A Badran, Paragon House, New York
Mehran, G (1989) Cultural revolution and value transformation in post-revolutionary Iranian education, *Muslim Education Quarterly*, **7** (1), pp 20–31
Mehran, G (1991) The education of new Muslim women in post-revolutionary Iran, *Muslim Education Quarterly*, **36** (2), pp 5–12
Menashri, D (1992) *Education and the Making of Modern Iran*, Cornell University Press, New York
Ministry of Education [Ministry of Education, Islamic Republic of Iran] (1993) *Education in the Islamic Republic of Iran*, Ministry of Education, Tehran
Moghadem, V (1987) Socialism or anti-imperialism? The Left and revolution in Iran, *New Left Review*, **166**, pp 5–37
Mohsenpour, B (1988) Philosophy of education in post-revolutionary Iran, *Comparative Education Review*, **32** (1), pp 77–86
Mojab, S (1989) University reform in Iran: the development dimension 1981–89, *Muslim Education Quarterly*, **7** (1), pp 39–46
Mojab, S (1991) *The State and University: The 'Islamic cultural revolution' in the institutions of higher education of Iran, 1980–87*, UMI Dissertation Information Service
Shorish, Mobin, M (1988) The Islamic revolution and education in Iran, *Comparative Education Review*, **32** (1), pp 58–75

Sobhe, K (1982) Education in revolution: is Iran duplicating the Chinese Cultural Revolution?, *Comparative Education*, **18** (3), pp 271–80

Vakily, A (1992) An overview of the education system in the Islamic Republic of Iran, *Muslim Education Quarterly*, **14** (2), pp 37–56

Zubaida, S (1989) *Islam, the People and the State*, Routledge, London and New York

Zubaida, S (1997) Is Iran an Islamic state?, in *Political Islam: Essays from Middle East Report*, ed J Beinin and J Stork, I B Tauris & Co Ltd, London and New York

9. Mexico's difficult double transition

Charles Posner

Introduction

Mexican society has been rapidly moving towards a relatively more demo-cratic internal order and an economy more closely integrated with its immedi-ate neighbours to the north. The aim of this chapter is to describe what effect this difficult double transition may be having on educational institutions and practices.

In 1994 after several years of negotiations the Mexican government took an enormous gamble and joined the North American Free Trade Agreement (NAFTA) as a means of escaping from a severe and seemingly continuous eco-nomic crisis which began as long ago as 1982. Until that time Mexican ideol-ogy, identity and institutions had long been wedded to economic and cultural self-determination, underlined by a fierce nationalism and a related model of autonomous economic development which went far beyond the fashionable leitmotifs of the international organizations of the day. Such a desperate or au-dacious decision was bound to have a profound effect upon the deep social, ethnic and cultural divisions which had been largely controlled until that time by an equally unique political system.

Until recently the entire educational edifice was erected upon the notion of autonomous national development, that is, reliance upon internal material and human resources to build a much more socially cohesive society. As part of their long-time adherence to self-reliance Mexican governments have tradi-tionally placed great store on encouraging the development of elite and/or specialized institutions of higher education, one of whose aims was to reduce its technological dependence on overseas sources. At the same time and possi-bly contradictorily, education has also been seen as the prime instrument to produce a relatively more homogeneous society in order to overcome the large differences typical of many countries in the process of development, where there exist not only social divisions of an hierarchical nature character-istic of European societies but also distinct socio-economic dimensions. In the case of Mexico, social cohesion was even more strongly accented than else-where because it was seen as the only possible means to avoid the type of civil strife that wracked the country between 1910 and the late 1920s when more than 5 per cent of the population died.

From the primary school through to university level and including the myriad of institutions dedicated to literacy programmes and adult education, the educational system was charged with two tasks: 1) an efficient selection of talent, taking into account the voracious needs of a growing middle class; 2) providing social control through the organization of primary education for the large and growing informal sector, that is, small-scale productive units based largely on the labour force of the household and which in its organization of its social division of labour, accounting system and relations with other similar producers and the official market does not operate in accordance with the economic rulebook. Until recently this latter task has been the most important of the two.

In very recent times changes in the ideology buttressing higher education and basic education (education at the primary, secondary and adult levels) seem to be moving in opposite directions. Higher education is increasingly wed to a traditional form of the appropriation of knowledge, similar to Bernstein's notion of a collection code at a time when international bodies are calling for higher education to be both more flexible and creative. On the other hand, the educational codes governing basic educational programmes seem to have been progressively weakened. Why is this the case?

Two examples

In order to try to answer the last question I will present two contrasting examples of recent changes: one in the area of higher education and the other taken from basic education. The first example suggests that the models of education related to a national model of development could well be in the process of being abandoned as a result of the pressures of international labour markets, while the second example suggests that these models of education are not only being maintained but are being expanded.

The Universidad Autónoma Metropolitana – Xochimilco

I have taken the Xochimilco branch of the Universidad Autónoma Metropolitana (UAM) as an example because its structure and curriculum, pedagogy and evaluation are at variance with the mainstream of educational institutions and practices in Mexico and also because it maintains one of the highest rates of completion of first degrees, the measure for evaluating the output of universities. Is the logic of such a switch in educational codes based on the educational usefulness of the model or on a need for standardization and accountability? To what extent can it be related to adjustments that Mexico must make to participate in NAFTA or international educational markets?

The UAM was founded in 1974 at the apogee of the national development model when education was seen as a crucial element in securing the involvement of communities which was considered necessary to underwrite the development of a homogeneous society and a nationally integrated economy. Its Xochimilco campus was important because it was committed to practising an integrated educational code within the university, by providing a common basis for all professional training programmes and by integrating teaching and research as a means of encouraging flexibility and allowing independent thought to develop. Most importantly, it was committed to abandoning the model of the university as some kind of 'ivory tower' by involving communities of small-scale producers in its teaching and research activities, by contextualizing classroom knowledge through students' involvement in projects within communities and by the university staff changing their classroom practices as a result of their research within the communities to help them develop their productive capacity.

From the outset the principle of the organization of curriculum, pedagogy and evaluation at Xochimilco was that learning the principles and content of a profession, whether medicine, animal husbandry or agronomy, required that knowledge be contextualized by community knowledge (local pedagogies) and by testing that knowledge through problem-solving. Such pedagogy is labour-intensive as it involves long hours in workshops, in the field and working with individual students. So long as the national government was willing to provide the extra resources to staff such a mode of learning, Xochimilco could overcome internal and external criticism and maintain its innovative mixture of curriculum, pedagogy and evaluation.

Briefly, we can summarize these principles as follows. The university sought to celebrate a different system of relating knowledge to practice by promoting what we can call 'context-free knowledge' predicated on a close relationship between concepts and application and on concepts being easily modified by the process of application. Learning was seen as based on problem-solving as a group rather than on an individual basis. Learning involved reference to and relating personal experience to knowledge from the field of specialization and, most importantly, to areas outside one's immediate field of study. Knowledge was not to be collected in order to be reproduced but was to be stored as a corpus which could be accessed and adapted to solve problems. In that sense, learning and research were seen as inseparable. The role of the teacher was as facilitator, helping students to work with the context rather than be a transmitter of the text.

The problem with context-free knowledge is that under certain conditions its accumulation can appear to be chaotic and non-systematic and therefore, inferior to a traditional, more context-bound system. From the outset, many parents and potential employers were worried that, for example, the Xochimilco trainee doctors were being educated directly in community clinics rather than in a traditional hospital setting, that the social sciences played a large role in their training and that the process of accumulation of medical knowledge was not as rigorous as the traditional memorization of the

principles of medicine. Many teachers felt that the system requirement of devotion to the mixture of teaching–research–problem-solving meant there was
less time to devote to their own individual research, as each student required
more time than in a more traditional system where the principles and process
of evaluation are also simpler.

So long as demographic factors meant that there was a growing need for
the training of professionals, students from the Xochimilco campus could usually find employment in their chosen fields of study but when after 1982, competition began to be tougher, the situation changed. Employers, whether
private or the state, showed a distinct preference for those trained in a traditional system and according to traditional methods. As state universities could
not cope with the demand, many private universities often sponsored by private firms expanded or were founded to provide these services in the areas of
health, engineering and medicine in particular. While no one openly claimed
that the doctors and agriculturalists etc produced by the Xochimilco system
were less well trained than those being educated in more traditional institutions of higher education research suggests that entrepreneurs and government officials were worried about 'their independence of thought' – a
particularly serious problem in Mexico not only because of its perceived threat
to the system of governance but, also, as we will see, because of changes in the
labour market.

By the early 1990s evidence is found of a growing reluctance to send young
people to the UAM and finally an intervention on the part of government bodies to ease the UAM into a more traditional role so that it would conform to
what was regarded as a more acceptable pattern. Pressures from outside the
immediate sphere of education began to play an important role in legitimizing
the internal criticisms of the model, and practices inimical to the model began
to manifest themselves. First, the model, which had served a national, or, in
the words of Bernstein, the 'new' middle class well, was now criticized as fail-
ing to match knowledge to job opportunities in what was a relatively more restricted labour market. University staff subject to new systems of evaluation
found that their labour-intensive classroom activities were no longer recognized and rewarded, as performance indicators did not take such work into
account. The National Association of Universities (ANUIES), originally
founded as a pressure group to represent individual university interests and
now increasingly serving as a catalyst to reorient university activities to conform to a model in which the throughput of students would be greatly increased, tended to be equally impatient if not suspicious of the Xochimilco
model. A new national system of professional examinations managed by the
National Commission for the Evaluation of Higher Education (CENEVAL)
took no account of the importance of problem-solving as a way of training
professionals and seemed to assume that the role of the university is to slot its
graduates into its own idiosyncratic concept of a labour market. More recently, the Rector of the UAM argued that it was increasingly difficult to justify

such a labour-intensive system and perhaps, more importantly, seemed to insist that the purpose of the university was not as defined by Xochimilco but consisted almost exclusively in training students for the market.

Endogamous factors critical of the model were enfranchised by forces outside the university and, in combination, both seem to be leading towards the adoption of a system of stronger classification and framing within the system of higher education; threatening a successful model which appeared to be training good socially aware professionals with a strong commitment to dealing with the economic and social problems impeding the development of the country. The social climate encouraged a reversion to a more traditional model of curriculum, pedagogy and evaluation hallmarked by context-bound operations. The evocation of the 'market' as the epitome of the unchallengeable hand of inevitability served as sufficient justification for the change in thinking.

This, of course, raises a number of questions: why was a seemingly successful model challenged both from within and outside? What lies behind the justifications for the change? How can we begin to understand the abrupt change in thinking which led to re-emphasizing context-bound thinking? What is the role of the so-called 'market'? To what extent were these internal pressures for change encouraged or conditioned by exogamous factors?

The example of the Coahuila Action-Research Project and primary education

The second example is the strikingly original action-research project conducted in primary schools directed by Silvia Schmelkes that is characterized by close collaboration between a team of researchers, schools, parents and pupils, undertaken on a very large scale, in order to improve the quality of education within a randomly selected group of badly performing schools in the state of Coahuila. The project was sponsored by the newly decentralized state education authority and by the Under-Secretaryship of State for Basic Education. The purpose of the project was to improve the quality of education by strengthening the autonomy of the school and to do so by contextualizing learning through community needs, the involvement of parents, the use of teachers as researchers, using a model close to that developed by John Elliott and Barry MacDonald. The project was based on the premise that this would be a contribution to the economic and social development of the participating localities.

The purpose of the Coahuila experiment was to construct a model of education that allowed community knowledge into the school so that the school would cease to be an interruptor in terms of educational time and space and so that its 'abstract' knowledge would be contextualized by 'local' knowledge. This would increase access to what had previously been perceived as 'foreign' knowledge systems and their incorporation into the corpus of community knowledge and practice. In many aspects the principles, the encouraging of context-free operations, are similar to those practised by the UAM-X.

It was similarly based on the view that much of the potential contribution of the informal sector was lost because the school could not provide time and space so that its knowledge systems could contextualize official knowledge and thereby be translated into relevant actions. Hence, for the project, improving the quality of the school meant mobilizing these forces by developing a contextualizing environment, in Bernstein's terms, a more integrated code.

The group of teachers, parents and researchers defined the specific problems and issues for research within the framework of a shared productive aim. The role of the researcher or facilitator was to help the group to clarify their productive aims by focusing attention on their practices. The process of the research provided theoretical inputs to the problems and issues as they emerged from groups thinking about their concrete problems. They provided opportunities for the groups to render accounts of their reflections to others, and thereby to discover links across individual experiences. They provided opportunities for groups to deepen their own understanding of issues through discussion with each other. They provided opportunities for the reporting of common understandings, developed through collaborative reflection with the other groups. Responsibility for the action rested with participants.

The team found that local needs could contextualize learning and make it more effective and the participation of teachers as creators rather than transmitters of a set curriculum contributed to a sense of enthusiasm, as did the intervention of parents in contextualizing abstract concepts through reference to their own productive activities. Pupils performed better in examinations as well as carrying their knowledge out into the community.

For the professional researcher the action-research project highlighted the need for a number of follow-up studies that will be useful in determining the reasons for its success and its extension to other areas of Mexico and, indeed, other countries with similar problems. These consist of studies whose variables are social position and gender, concerned with the transmission of knowledge within the classroom; studies on the relationship between the home and the school; studies on the effects of the organization of curriculum and pedagogy on the social apprenticeship of children from marginal groups; studies on the forms of the transmission of knowledge within groups of small-scale producers, that is, the forms of social apprenticeship within production; and, above all, studies to provide a greater understanding of the pedagogic practices of the school (official pedagogy) and its effects on local pedagogy (the knowledge systems of small-scale producers); and finally studies contrasting local pedagogic practices within family and domestic productive units of the informal rural and urban sectors.

As opposed to the criticisms of the UAM experiment, no reference was made to the market or market forces in terms of justifying the Coahuila experiment. On the contrary, the project was justified in terms of providing a higher quality of education which would allow pupils to succeed academically as well as their communities to progress. However, this double use of the term 'quality' itself requires more research because, on the one hand, it seems to refer to educational achievement and, on the other, to more effective social control. Such questions deserve further attention.

Context-free and context-bound operations and their social bases

We now find ourselves in the situation of trying to account for the fact that a practice of education to improve educational chances and the possibilities to learn based on the greater involvement of the community and through creating time and space for local knowledge to contextualize learning and make it more effective, is accepted at the level of basic education but rejected as inefficient and chaotic for higher education. How can we account for this apparent paradox?

How can we adequately explain the recent tendencies in Mexico to move towards educational practices within higher education which restrict the creativity and imagination supposedly necessary, as economists and futurologists remind us, for economic and social development? As recent congresses of agriculturalists and animal husbandry practitioners have pointed out, such contextualization is the key to raising production and hence the standard of living as well as providing greater opportunities for research.

On one hand, although the Xochimilco model has proved it is possible to produce more and perhaps better educated professional graduates, it has been ignored and/or rejected. On the other hand, the Coahuila action-research project, operating on similar principles, has been hailed as a major development in and for basic education. On one level the authorities are recommending an integrated code for basic education while trying to influence higher education to adopt a more restricted code, when writers like Reich argue for the opposite in relation to the United States. If educationalists can still argue for the more integrated model, then the pressures for the change seem by and large to have been created by forces outside the sphere of education. We must first look at these by exploring the specificity of educational policy and its roots in the Mexican experience. We must also determine to what extent these pressures are also the product of forces exogamous to Mexico – a theme hitherto explored with recourse to very deterministic arguments. For that reason, restricting myself to the Mexican context, the reasons for such a dichotomy will now be explored, which in turn will allow some further comments about the causes underlying transitions in more general terms.

Elements of a possible explanation

In order to begin to understand the problem we must now look at general trends within the field of education itself in Mexico and those external forces that may have had an influence on its development.

Endogamous factors

We must explore the extent to which the endogamous factors which led to a weakening of the integrated model for the appropriation of knowledge at the university level and to a strengthening of such a model at the level of basic education were related to exogamous factors such as the adjustments which were believed made necessary by NAFTA.

First, the national model of education sought to develop institutions and practices of education which would stimulate the hitherto excluded sectors of society to enter the economy to expand the productive base of the country. And the aim was to develop first-class training of professionals through a greatly expanded system of higher education. Until the 1990s it was felt that higher education had to be based upon a weakening of educational codes, that is, contextualized by national problems and by the need to solve these problems, and this required closer integration between learning and the community.

Second, what makes an explanation difficult is the common practice amongst social scientists to attempt to describe, and, if possible, explain changes in educational institutions and practices by reference to a particular phenomenon or concept recently identified by the field. Currently transitions are looked at through the prism of a list of 'neos' and 'posts'. These terms largely arose in the developed countries and while they might have purchase upon their own internal events, they are difficult to apply to the much more complex social structures of countries like Mexico without distorting that reality, largely because they select what is convenient and neglect what is not. This is compounded by the fact that in countries like Mexico we still lack reliable data, as Carlos Muñoz Izquierdo has argued on many occasions, and socio-historical accounts of the development of education in Mexico, while excellent as in the works of Axel Didrikkson, Hugo Aboites and Patricia de Leonardo amongst others, are still in their infancy. Others try to attribute changes to one single factor. Recently, it has been popular in academic circles to attribute changes to the advent of NAFTA as if endogamous forces counted for nothing.

Hence, an important second question is, what contribution does an examination of recent trends in educational institutions and practices in Mexico make towards the modification of recent theories concerned with the relationship between education and social and economic trends? How can we explain the retreat from a discourse which preached problem-solving to one which preached the need for the training of narrow professionals in the light of these well-established needs?

The salient point about Mexican educational institutions and practices and the often contradictory explanatory discourses which claim to encompass them is that state education was and still is seen as an unalterable accomplishment of the social and political revolution which led to the formation of a relatively more homogeneous society in the 1920s. The expansion of education was originally a unifying if not rallying factor in the forging of the unusual political alliance between the secular middle classes, the rural producers and the military which led to the founding of the political organization that was to dominate all aspects of economic, social and political life until the 1980s.

The modern Mexican state was a creation of the settlement which marked the end of the military revolution and the founding of a single-party state where the role of the party and state was to gather all competing groups into a single organization and actively create a sufficient homogeneity in a multi-dimensional society so that physical conflict would be transformed into negotiations between the elites of these groups. The state created economic, social and political institutions, beautifully satirized by Jorge Ibarguengoita, which were to administer and mediate these conflicts in order to maintain social order, which was the first and overriding priority of the new state.

These managers required special training, as did those entering the professions and sciences who earlier, during the first attempt to create a modern state in the long rule of Porfirio Diáz (1873–1910), had been trained in specialized institutions but with the caveat that even these professions were to be certified by the state and not their own organizations in order to avoid challenging state institutions. At the apex of this complex system were the specialists in administration who dealt with interest groups attempting to maintain a careful balance between groups and also creating a series of links which were over and above those of each interest group.

Higher education was concerned with training these specialists in institutions established or re-established by the government such as the refounded National University in 1917 and later regional universities and polytechnics for the training of scientists. The lawyers, doctors and scientists produced by the system were often more concerned with running agencies of social control than their own professions and moved between the practice of their profession, administrative roles and occasional teaching roles in those institutions designed to train their successors.

In the early days the preparation of such an elite meant that the main institution for their training, the university, had to be relatively autonomous in procedures, regulations and organizations, depending upon the complex web of contacts and interrelations established within the elite groups. Ideological differences counted for little with self-proclaimed Marxists actively working with Catholic traditionalists in the maintenance of the system. Only the natural scientists were opposed to such a system because, in their view, it deadened creativity, but they were powerless to offer what they regarded as a more coherent model until the conjuncture of events some 70 years later permitted such a change.

The main aim of the national and, at the time highly centralized, educational system at all levels was to develop a sufficient level of homogenization within the society to make civil war impossible and to build a society co-extensive with the national frontiers and which overrode the deep chasms between ethnic and social groups. To impose a single national language it was necessary to impose a single national consciousness through a creative re-invention of Mexican history and through the insistence that basic education have as one of its main goals the teaching of civics in one single textbook.

The problem with such a system is that one pays a high price because it allows little room for creative faculties to be developed. Only those with the cultural capital to surmount the one-dimensionality of the educational system could succeed to the few places available in its institutions of higher education.

However, for the mass of the population even down to the informal sector, education was concerned with social incorporation, homogeneity and setting limits to ambition. The absorption of the social codes of control were achieved with stunning efficiency. As Enrique Pieck has demonstrated so eloquently, even state-provided courses for rural sewing-circles operated in such a way.

Primary education was seen as an instrument to lead to literacy for the then majority rural sector and as a means of drawing them into the national economy and consensus. Secondary education was to solidify the progress of the urban working class and lower middle class, providing them with a vehicle to obtain positions as far removed from the productive sphere as possible. Higher education was seen as a means of satisfying the demands of the middle and upper-middle classes to accumulate cultural capital. So long as funding was available, the rhetoric of expansion, similar to that found in the so-called developed countries with their post-war idea of human capital, could match the reality of providing places at all levels leading to economic betterment. As the space provided for economic expansion in so-called developed countries after the war provided the basis for confusing that expansion with the idea that the growth of education was responsible for it in Mexico, the rapid transition from a rural to an urban society and the need to provide a structure which would support that expansion allowed the confusion to continue for an even longer period of time.

However, an important factor in the development of the national model appears to be the rise of a large middle class devoted to administering the system and providing the professional services required by the state. In return for its adherence to the principles of the historical compromise which led to the relative social peace which prevailed for almost 70 years and its relinquishment of its professional independence, the middle class created by the Revolution gained sinecures, the trapping of political power and was endowed with an education system to allow its offspring to accumulate the cultural capital they required. The system worked until the logic of the market and demographic pressure dictated the need to open the university further. With its pre-eminence threatened, the middle class first sought to emigrate to private education and when that proved too costly after the series of economic shocks, to reform the state education system to restrict entry.

Exogamous factors

Many Mexican commentators see NAFTA exerting a determining influence on educational institutions and practices. It is an unusual agreement in several aspects. It represents an attempt to integrate two of the most advanced economies in the world with one that has often been classified as being part of the Third World. For that reason, unlike the treaties produced by European Union countries, labour mobility is an area excluded in the first instance from the integrative process. For obvious reasons the United States, in particular, in the initial phases of integration wished to avoid a still more massive influx of poor, unemployed and underemployed workers from Mexico into its territory. For perhaps very different reasons both the Mexican government and American industry wish to maintain potential Mexican workers within Mexico itself through the development of cheap assembly industries (*maquiladora*) located along the border between the two countries and concentrate on the development of other types of labour-intensive industries in Mexico where, of course, labour is but a fraction of the cost in the United States and little training is required.

In economic terms the jury is still out but it is possible to identify several trends. The *maquiladora* industry has grown enormously and has provided employment usually for young women with little education. While government bodies argue that it can provide the basis for economic development, it can also be argued that the industry is more often than not a foreign enclave in Mexico which contributes little to its own growth. While many US and some Canadian companies have located offices in Mexico, these are staffed by middle-range administrators and other white-collar workers. The tendency has been for higher level posts of authority to emigrate to the United States. In some cases this has meant that large portions of an entire sector of highly skilled and trained people have either left the country or have been deskilled. Are we to conclude that it is no longer necessary for Mexico to train high-level cadres? Is that why curricula and pedagogies based on stimulating the creativity and imagination such as those found in the elite universities in the United States are now frowned upon?

Finally, in opposition to the dominant trend of thought emerging from the World Bank, the Inter-American Development Bank and other international organizations who based their analyses upon a supposedly new international division of labour with its accompanying demands for a new system of education, one can argue as follows: Mexico, in common with many so-called developing countries, must face the problem of its enormous and growing informal sector. Without the redirection of higher education towards solving the problems associated with that sector it will be difficult for Mexico to achieve the kind of homogeneous socio-economic development which is balanced and which will preserve the culture. To do so, as some parts of the Mexican government like Sedesol (responsible for, among other activities, vocational education) recognize, requires education based upon the stimulus of context-free operations and drawn from local practices, problems and conditions rather than the international educational market.

It does appears that influences external to Mexico affect the direction and development of those parts of its educational institutions and practices relevant to wider markets. I write 'influences' because of a tendency of researchers to forget the internal conflicts in society, and, in particular the role of a middle class forced to move from being a middle class dependent on the state to one that must forage for itself and, in some cases, exchange its dependency on national institutions for a less secure dependency on US and/or multinational corporations. As both the author of the educational system and its main beneficiary, it must try to recast education so that it can satisfy its need for the accumulation of exchangeable cultural capital and lifetime security. The national development model provided for such a group, but economic, demographic and political factors have now made this an impossibility. Hence, can one argue that the advent of agreements like NAFTA have provided it with the pretext to push for a more restrictive system of higher education in terms of entry and to redefine the rules of success?

Conclusions: the social bases of educational change

Educational policy and change

I have outlined an apparently contradictory picture: on the one hand, the universities in Mexico have been encouraged to abandon an education code founded on an organic relationship between education and production for one based upon collection while the tendency in basic education – that is, schooling from primary school through to and including educational programmes for children up to the age of 12 and compensatory adult education – has moved largely in the opposite direction. How can we begin to explain a system which practises openness for those entering the system and closure for those at its highest levels, particularly when corresponding levels in European and North American countries celebrate the integrated code?

While the integrated code is clearly more efficient in that it increases the possibilities of flexibility and allows space for innovation in practice it has become restricted rather than abandoned because it is recognized both within and outside the field that without creative thinking a society and culture can only survive with difficulty. What we are seeing evidence of in contemporary Mexico in concrete terms is the growth of a university to train middle-level management and its increased integration into a new international division of labour which seemingly requires that the educational code which marks elite institutions is increasingly absent.

For most of the middle class the need to adapt to a new system and lower one's horizons comes as a severe disappointment if not shock. Their belief in education as a social liberator which would offer responsibility, social promotion and control over the rhythms of labour is shaken. Are we observing how the social pyramid adjusts itself through a process of exclusion in which the victims are as much authors of that exclusion as are outside forces? Given the international division of labour the process of exclusion is most keenly felt in countries like Mexico which have never been able to be part of that elite but have hitherto been able to develop an autonomous system and practice of education. Additionally, international markets have begun to replace the economic functions of the state. Certain socio-economic enclaves in Mexico are clearly more a part of the vaster metropolitan enclaves of the United States than they are related to their own country. The cultural repercussions of this are enormous. The belief in the Mexican state and culture is of little personal consequence for these groups yet is necessary for the maintenance of social and political control. Events in Chiapas have underlined this danger to the social order. It will be surprising if we do not see similar severe reactions to this process sometime in the near future.

On the other hand, perhaps for the reasons cited above, the need to incorporate and, so to speak to homogenize excluded social groups continues unabated, particularly since all else has failed and models likes those proposed by Silvia Schmelkes can be permitted. The vast informal sector and the communities of poor producers continue to be relatively autonomous of world markets and forces largely because, in their terms, this sector is an irrelevancy. However, in terms of the maintenance of social order which is still largely a concern of the territorial state, it is of paramount importance.

In the European setting it is difficult for two such totally different educational codes to co-exist. But in Mexico, as Juan Prawda has recently pointed out, perhaps the very multi-dimensionality of the society requires different codes for different sectors. While it can be argued that in Europe, far from the integrated code disappearing at the higher levels of education, it has merely become the preserve of a few institutions, in Mexico, where important research institutions have been seen as expendable and have closed, the integrated code is in danger of completely disappearing.

It is a widely accepted theoretical proposition that technological innovation and the needs of the market are inevitably responsible for changes in education. Such an argument suits both the needs of those proposing such changes as well as those wedded to a simplistic and deterministic model of social change. At least in Mexico educational reformers have couched their discourse in terms of needing to respond to changes brought about by new technologies and the need for greater regional economic integration. They have not spoken about the need to adjust to new social demands. However, one must stress that these innovations and needs are both socially filtered and conditioned. We have found that change takes place as a result of a conjuncture or coincidence of forces – which themselves are sometimes contradictory – and that the changes that take place may not be what was expected or desired by many of those who have seen them as positive.

Hence we can possibly begin to account for the contradiction between offering an integrated code at the beginning of schooling and an increasingly restricted code at the highest levels, where we already have a proven model which with more resources would allow even more young people from poor backgrounds to compete successfully with young people from the middle class, as well as providing the kind of person supposedly required by new technologies etc. Normally one would expect the private sector of education to operate codes which still allow one to create the limited number of policy-makers etc to manage the system. The private institutions, with one exception, undertake little research and are usually staffed on a part-time basis by teachers from the state universities seeking to supplement their salaries. They are dependent upon the state universities for their staff and for the creation of knowledge.

Hence, are we to conclude that the educational attack upon the UAM in conjunction with the attempted desertion of the state sector by the middle classes is in reaction to the perceived effects of NAFTA on the economic and social structure of Mexico?

Theoretical conclusions

Basil Bernstein suggests that an integrated code is inherently unstable and cannot exist in a society committed to an unintegrated social division of labour. While this is a partial explanation of what happened in the case of the Xochimilco campus, it does not begin to explain the continued popularity of looser or weaker educational codes for basic education.

It can also be argued with some cogency that:

1. The emigration of higher level managerial and professional posts to the United States and the need for greater number of middle-range managers and administrators are having an influence on planning if not policy for higher education; and
2. The development of the new assembly-line industries (*maquiladora*) with their demand for cheap, young female labour has had a different effect upon policy for basic education.

In the case of higher education we find decisions being taken that seem to indicate that there is no longer a need to train creative scientists, managers and thinkers in Mexico. Hence, the integrated code of Xochimilco is superfluous. In the case of basic education, with its need for a pliant labour force, the same argument does not hold. But, as we have seen, these elements are mitigated by a host of others as they are mediated through existing and competing social groups and their perceptions of needs.

This examination of recent changes in educational policy and practices in Mexico suggests that changes in educational institutions and practices are a result of shifting combinations of complex forces internal to education and the social forces from outside which directly and indirectly influence these institutions and practices. In what we call developed countries these shifts are relatively controlled. In countries characterized by weak internal social cohesion and a myriad of internally unrelated economic and cultural dimensions, like Mexico, they are not. Clearly, the evolution of education in Mexico owes as much to the impossibility of achieving a lasting balance between social groups as it does to the sometimes rapid shifts in behaviour of large sections of the indigenous middle class, as a result of their chronically unsuccessful attempts to obtain the right kind of cultural capital to compete first in the internal and now in the international educational market. As the middle class is more often than not the author and chief beneficiary of educational institutions and practices such an instability can have profound and lasting effects.

We have discussed the effects of a double transition on a very complex society which impels us to conclude, like Fernand Braudel, that any event is a very complex one involving a bevy of social forces and a very complex conjuncture of exogamous and endogamous forces.

Further reading

Aboites, H (1991) Tratado de libre comercio y el dilema educativo, *Excelsior*, 2 April

Almeida Armenta, E (1993) Los servicios profesionales ante el TLC, *Carta del Economists*, **3** (4), July–August

Altbach, P (1994) NAFTA and higher education: the culture and educational dimensions of trade, *Change: The magazine of higher learning*, July–August

Alvarez Garcia, I (1990) Desafios para el desarollo de la educación superior al inicio del siglo XXI, *Revista Latinoamericana de Estudios Educativos*, **XX** (2)

Arredondo Galván, V M (ed) (1992) *La Educación Superior y su Relación con el Sector Productivo: Problemas de formación de recursos humanos para el desarrollo tecnológico y alternativas de solución*, ANUIES-SECOFI, Mexico

Barrow, J, Posner, C and Verma, G (1994) *The Educational Challenge in Newham: The report of the independent inquiry into education in the London borough of Newham*, Newham

Bernstein, B (1992) *Class, Codes and Control, vol iii, Towards a Theory of Educational Transmission*, Routledge and Kegan Paul, London

Bernstein, B (1996) *Pedagogy, Symbolic Control and Identity: Theory and research*, Taylor and Francis, London

Berruecos Villalobos, L (ed) (1998) *La Evaluación en el Sistema Modular*, UAM, Mexico

Brunner, J J (1991) Modernidad y educación superior: notas de discusión, *Educação Brasileira: Revista do Conselho de Reitores das Universidades Brasileiras*, **13** (27), July–December

Carr, W and Kemmis, S (1994) *Becoming Critical: Education, knowledge and action research*, Falmer Press, London

Charmes, J (1995) Una revisión crítica de los conceptos, definiciones y estudios del sector informal, in *El Sector Informal en América Latina: Dos décadas de análisis*, ed V Tokman, pp 33–82, Consejo Nacional para la Cultura y las Artes, Mexico

Dale, R (1990) *The State and Educational Policy*, Open University Press, Milton Keynes

De Leonardo, P (1998) Professions and the growth of private higher education in Mexico, 1810–1980, doctoral thesis, Institute of Education, London

Didriksson Takayanagui, A (1990) *Educación, Universidad y Cambio Tecnológico*, Serie: *Sobre la Universidad*, no. 8, Centro de Investigaciones y Servicios Educativos, UNAM, Mexico

Elliott, J (1989) Knowledge, power and teacher appraisal, in *Quality in Teaching: Arguments for a reflective professional*, ed W Carr, Falmer Press, London

Gázquez, J L (1999) *Iniciativa del Rector General para Reflexionar sobre la Docencia*, Suplemento, Seminario de la UAM, no 1 especial, May

Guevara Niebla, G (1992) *La Educación y la Cultura ante el Tratado de Libre Comercio*, Nexos-Nueva Imagen, Mexico

Guevara Niebla, G (ed) (1992) *La Catástrophe Silenciosa*, Fondo de la Cultura Económica, Mexico

Ianni, O (1997) *Teorías de la Globalización*, Siglo XXI-Centro de Investigaciones terdisciplinarias en Ciencias y Humanidades, Mexico

Latapí, P (1994) Asimetrias educativas ante el TLC, *Comercio Exterior*, **44** (3), May

Martin, C (1994) *Schooling in Mexico*, Ashgate, Hampshire

Martínez Assad, C (1979) *El Laboratorio de la Revolución*, Siglo XXI, Mexico

Melgar Adalid, M (1994) *Educación Superior Propuesta de Modernización: Una visión de la modernización de México*, Centro de Investigaciones y Docencia Económicas, Mexico

Mortimer, P *et al* (1995) *Key Characteristics of Effective Schools*, London University Institute of Education, London

Mungaray, A *et al* (1994) Retos y perspectivas de la educación superior en México hacia finales del siglo, *Comercio Exterior*, **44** (3), March

Muñoz Izquierdo, C (1990) Relaciones entre la educación superior y el sistema productivo, *Revista de Educación Superior*, **xviii** (4), no 76, October–December

Muñoz Izquierdo, C (1992) *Conversación sobre el Cambio en la Educación Superior*, Universidad Iberoamericana, Mexico

Muñoz Izquierdo, C (1995) *La Educación Nacional en el Sexenio 1988–1994*, Universidad Iberoamericana, Mexico

Pieck, E (1996) *Fución Social y Significación de la Educación Comunitaria*, UNICEF, Mexico

Posner, C M (1994) La educación de adultos y el trabajo, in *Necesidades Educativas Básicas de los Adultos*, ed O Zires, Mexico

Posner, C M (1995) Los profesores: agentes de la equidad escolar y social?, in *Educación y Pobreza*, ed E Pieck and E Aguado López, UNICEF, Mexico

Raby, D L (1974) *Educación y Revolución en México*, SEP setentas, Mexico

Reich, R (1991) *The Work of Nations*, Simon and Schuster, New York

Sánchez Sinencio, F (1992) El Centro de Investigación y de Estudios Avanzados del IPN frente al reto de un posible tratado trilateral de libre comercio, *Avance y Perspectiva*, **11**, January–February

Schmelkes, S (1991) Las necesidades educativas de las mayorias ante el Tratado de Libre Comercio, paper presented to the Second Meeting about NAFTA, Tepepan, DF

Schmelkes, S (1999) *Planeación Escolar: Un estudio de intervención*, Departamento de Investigaciones Educativas, CINVESTAV, Mexico

Solana, F et al (1981) *Historia de la Educación Pública en México*, Fondo de Cultura Económica and SEP, Mexico

Stenhouse, L (1985) Action research and the teacher's responsibility for the educational process, in *Research as a Basis for Teaching*, ed J Rudduck and D Hopkins, Heinemann, London

Vielle, J P (1994) La educación de adultos centrada en el trabajo, in *Necesidades Educativas Básicas de los Adultos*, ed O Zires, Mexico

Zapata Marti, R (1994) Globalización modernidad y desarrollo, *Problemas del Desarrollo: Revista Latinoamericana de Economia*, Mexico, IIE-UNAM, **xxv**, January–March

10. Competitive contractualism: a new social settlement in New Zealand education[1]

Susan Robertson and Roger Dale

Introduction

The theme of this volume is educational transitions. In this chapter we will examine the transition in New Zealand education from a system that was part of what was considered a 'world leader' in welfare provision to one now viewed as a 'world leader' in the application of neo-liberal policies to the public sector. Though the New Zealand experiment, as it has widely become known, has attracted the attention of the international community, its rapid and comprehensive restructuring project should be seen as different but not exceptional (Neilsen, 1998). Few restructuring agendas across the Western capitalist economies have been advanced by such a zealous commitment to theory-driven principles of public sector reform (Haworth, 1998). As the century draws to a close, little remains of the old politics paradigm. We argue that in its place a new social settlement is emerging from a transformation in the relations between the state, economy and civil society. This chapter examines the nature of that settlement and its relationship to education in New Zealand.

Education and social settlements: theoretical notes

In this chapter we theorize this transformation as a shift from the post-war social democratic *Keynesian Welfare State* (KWS) settlement to what we call an emerging *Competitive Contractual State* (CCS) settlement in New Zealand. This clearly has major implications for the nature of the education system. We will spend the first part of this chapter outlining briefly what we understand by the notion of 'settlement' and how it relates to the purposes and processes of education systems. We will then give brief examples of what this entails for the reorganization of schools. The major part of the chapter will then be given over to describing and attempting to understand theoretically the new settlement in New Zealand education.

In essence, a social settlement is a temporary period of stability in relationships across what is most simply represented as a triangle of forces in national formations, with state, economy and civil society (each broadly conceived and heterogeneous) as its three points (see Figure 10.1). It is absolutely crucial to recognize that all such national settlements are located in wider global contexts which shape and channel them in qualitatively and quantitatively different ways.

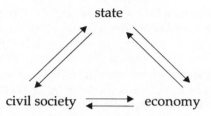

Figure 10.1   State–economy–civil society relation

We may take the Keynesian Welfare State as a paradigm case of what we mean by 'settlement'. In that settlement the *state–economy* relationship was characterized by considerable state intervention in the economy, through ownership, subsidy and regulation. The *economy–civil society* relationship was characterized by full employment and relatively high wages (though for the greater part of the Keynesian Welfare State period the notion of the male breadwinner held sway), while the *state–civil society* relation was characterized by notions of redistribution through both progressive taxation policies and high levels of state provision of public services (the decommodification of public services). This relationship was also characterized by the involvement of public sector trade unions in the provision of such services.

The starting point for the analysis of education in this conceptualization is as part of the state. This is because, as we shall make clear, education is deeply implicated with all points on the triangle and with the relationships between them; it is almost universally a state-regulated if not a state-funded or a state-provided service. It is only the state, for instance, that can require and enforce compulsory school attendance for a specified number of years. And even where apparently 'private' systems of education exist, they – like all other markets – operate in an institutional and regulatory framework determined by the state.[2]

As Figure 10.1 indicates, in framing, however actively, explicitly and broadly, the nature and scope of the regulatory framework for education, the state is subject to two major sources of pressure and influence. The state's relationship to the economy means that it is permanently confronted by three core problems: supporting the capital accumulation process, nationally and internationally (the 'accumulation' problem), guaranteeing a societal context not inimical to the further development of accumulation (the 'order' problem) and contributing to the legitimation of the system (the 'legitimation' problem)

(Dale, 1982). It is in this sense that we can describe the state as an *agent* of regulation (Jessop, 1997). It is important to note that these problems do not exhaust the agenda of education systems; nor do they necessarily always take precedence on that agenda. They do not themselves appear in any necessary order of priority – indeed, it is a central part of our argument that changes in the nature of social settlements are associated with changes in the relative priority of the three core problems, which is increasingly influenced by the national state's location in the world economy (cf Dale, 1998). Possibly most important of all for understanding the relationship between education and the economy is that the 'solutions' to these core problems in the education system are as likely to be mutually contradictory as mutually complementary (Dale, 1989).

It is also crucial to recognize that the form taken by these three core problems in education is not determined by their function. Rather, the way they are presented and what count as acceptable 'solutions' to them also result from the pressures from within civil society. Civil society is the repository of class, gender, ethnic, cultural, regional etc relations and identities. Class structure and gender regimes both contribute to the agenda of education systems and powerfully shape, direct and limit how education systems respond, at the broadest level, to the fundamental problems confronting them. The other major source of influence on the forms in which the problems are presented and the possible solutions to them is the existing structures, processes and traditions, norms and expectations, in short, the institutional structure of the education system. Such structures are never wholly overthrown. However radical the restructuring of a society, educational innovations pass through – albeit modified – taken-for-granted institutional filters. Jessop's (1997) notion of the state as also the *object* of regulation (as well as agent) helps focus attention on the dynamic interplay between the state, economy and civil society.

At its most basic, the agenda for education has to be implemented through the institutional structure of education systems (or, as we shall refer to it below, the education structural settlement). Those structures are made up of a particular pattern of relationships between the education system's *mandate*, what it is considered desirable for it to achieve, its *capacity*, what it is considered feasible for it to achieve and its *governance*, through which combinations of state, market and community institutions it is co-ordinated (see Table 10.1).

Very briefly, we argue that under the Keynesian Welfare State a relatively weak mandate emerged from the politics of education. That mandate was based on legitimation as the first priority for the education system. In such times of prosperity there is a tendency to take for granted the contribution of education to both the control and the accumulation problems. However, in times of relative decline – especially in employment opportunities – a much stronger mandate and one more rooted in the need to address the problems of accumulation and order is laid down by the state and key economic interests at the level of the politics of education. The legitimation problem under the Keynesian Welfare State was addressed by means of the traditional social

Table 10.1 Framework for mapping the changing educational settlement in New Zealand

Sphere	Level	Keynesian welfare state	Competitive contractual state
Global	Global settlement	Internationalization pax Americana/ Bretton Wood	Globalization
National	Social settlement	Priority of core problems: legitimation/ accumulation/order	Priority of core problems: accumulation/ order/legitimation
Institutional	Education structural settlement	Priority of *capacity* over *mandate* and *governance*	Priority of *mandate* and *governance* over *capacity*
		Planning	Devolution
		Regulatory mechanisms – ex-ante – input – professionalism	Regulatory mechanisms – ex-post – outcome – audit
		Universal entitlement	Rights and responsibilities
Organizations	Schools as organizations	– state-determined – procedural bureaucracy – professional discretion – efficiency and equity	– state-co-ordinated – market bureaucracy – community governance – managerialism – audit – efficiency and effectiveness
Self	Identity	Productive citizen	Consuming individual

democratic mechanisms of redistribution and decommodification (Offe and Ronge, 1984), funded from taxation and brought about by the state taking direct responsibility for the funding, control and provision of education. One major consequence of this is that over the Keynesian Welfare State period the mandate for education could be substantially shaped by the professionals within the system. In the case of the New Zealand education system, the mandate for education promoted by the profession embraced a strong sense of social and personal development. Important spheres of the governance of the system were also devolved to the professionals with significant spheres of discretion available to determine pedagogic, curricula and assessment practices. The capacity of the education system was much more important in this period as it was the main means through which the education system was controlled at the level of the politics of education. Education, like other activities in the Keynesian Welfare State settlement, was subject to control through the adjustment of demand in the economy as a whole, what became known in the United Kingdom as 'stop-go' policies.

Crisis and restructuring: Labour's agenda, 1984–90

In New Zealand, the high-water mark of the Keynesian Welfare State period in education is captured in the 1982 OECD *Report on Education in New Zealand*. The examiners noted the emphasis on social and cultural goals, substantial client satisfaction, highly professional administration, high standards, but not extravagant provision. They drew particular attention to the close relationship and the high level of collegiality between the central administration and the teaching profession. The informing myth of the system articulated by the Minister of Education, Peter Fraser, in 1939, is worthy of note here: 'The government's objective, broadly expressed, is that every person, whatever his level of ability, whether he is rich or poor, whether he lives in town or country, has a right, as a citizen, to a free education of the kind to which he is best fitted and to the fullest extent of his powers.' From this we can infer broadly that the New Zealand system did exhibit the features of education systems we suggested would be found in the Keynesian Welfare State regime; considerable professional influence over mandate and governance, with 'not extravagant' provision of resources from the state. Given the changes that were to follow a very short time after the publication of the OECD *Report*, we should note also the references to 'high standards' and 'substantial client satisfaction'. They suggest that the subsequent reforms were not driven by perceived shortcomings within the educational system itself but by wider changes at the level of the national and international economies (Dale and Robertson, 1997).

The impetus for the changes to education was the election of a Labour Government in 1984 at a time of major change. The pressures for change occur at a number of levels: developments within the global economy, in particular the dominance of transnational capital; the ascendancy of finance capital; the rapid expansion of the services sector; and advances in technology (Hobsbawm, 1994). These all combined to create new problems for government. Jane Kelsey observes:

> Governments found it difficult to regulate the flow of money and capital across their boundaries, and to control economic activities through domestic regulation. This in turn restricted their ability to gather taxes and maintain their physical and social infrastructure. Threats by capital to disinvest often backed by warnings of credit rating downgrades, imposed additional constraints on national governments. (1995, p 17)

In its first term of office, the new government set about what is widely recognized as the most rapid and thorough-going programme of neo-liberal economic reform of the last 50 years. Tariffs were abolished or minimized, government subsidies to industry and agriculture were removed, publicly-run enterprises were either sold/privatized or turned into state-owned enterprises with a priority on making a profit rather than serving the public good, the economy was opened up to the forces of international competition, and key regulative Acts were passed, especially the Reserve Bank Act[3] (Rudd, 1993; Kelsey, 1995; Neilsen, 1998). The relationship of the state and the economy became one where the state adopted a hands-off policy and concentrated on maximizing the nation's competitive possibilities both nationally and internationally.

> These developments put into place central rationalities of neo-liberalism, while they dismantled key elements of the rationality and norms associated with the Fordist modes of economic and political regulation. The internationalization of the New Zealand economy was especially important in breaking down the rationality of 'domestic defence'; of the Keynesian 'fortress economy'. It was also fundamental to putting into place the imperatives of international competition which increasingly put direct economic pressure on the core labour and welfare institutions of Keynesian social democracy. (Neilsen, 1998, p 60)

During this first term, Labour paid little attention to the non-commercial sectors of government activity such as education. Indeed, in 1987 a most liberal, professionally influenced document *The Curriculum Review: A Report to the Committee to Review the Curriculum for Schools* was published by the Department of Education. However, in its second term, 1987–90, the Labour government brought the social policy sector and education into view with Prime Minster David Lange himself taking on the position of Minister of Education. He appointed a taskforce, headed by a well-known businessman, Brian Picot, to review the administration of the education system. The report of the Picot Committee published in 1988 was entitled *Administering for Excellence: Effective Administration in Education*. This report became the basis of the subsequent legislation, *Tomorrow's Schools* (1988) which came into force on 1 October 1989. If we have to identify the key date in the process of educational change in New Zealand since World War II, it would be 1 October 1989. This date also indicates the speed with which these reforms were brought about. The Picot Review was announced on 17 July 1987. It reported on 10 May 1998. The *Tomorrow's Schools* White Paper, which was based on extensive consultation on the Picot report (the responses were summarized in a document entitled '20,000 voices'), was released on 10 August 1998 and passed into legislation in the Education Act of 1 October 1989. These changes took place, however, amidst growing tensions within the senior ranks of Labour; there were increasing divisions between Prime Minister Lange and Finance Minister Roger

Douglas over the extent to which Labour should pursue a hard-line neo-liberal restructuring agenda.

Picot's terms of reference demonstrate the direction of the reforms; they concentrated on the administration not the process of education. Two concepts were central: devolution and efficiency. Picot's main recommendations were: 1) breaking up of the Department of Education into a smaller, policy-oriented Ministry of Education and the establishment of an array of specialist agencies, including the Education Review Office; and 2) abolishing all levels of educational governance between the Ministry and each individual school. Schools were all to be run by their own Board of Trustees who were directly accountable to the Ministry on the basis of a School Charter (see Robertson, forthcoming). With the exception of teacher salaries – which are still centrally determined and allocated – schools in New Zealand would have a greater degree of control over how their budgets and funding could be spent. At the same time, *Tomorrow's Schools* did maintain a commitment to some principles of equity; for example, the principles of deficit funding for disadvantaged schools was maintained (Olssen and Morris Matthews, 1997, p 18).

Before the proposals were incorporated into legislation, they were made subject to consideration by groups of interested parties, including some representatives of the education community. This process had produced relatively minor changes to the Picot proposals, but they were sufficient in their perceived impact for the State Services Commission, the body that oversees the machinery of government, to initiate – only six months after the legislation – a further review aimed at turning back the 'backsliding' it perceived had occurred between the publication of Picot and the Education Act based on it. This review produced a number of recommendations that had the objectives of 'implementing the reform programme in full and consolidating the policies that had been implemented' (SSC, 1990, p 3). The report, *Today's Schools: A Review of the Education Reform Implementation Process*, imposed a much more managerialist orientation on schools and closed the temporary openings that had been prised open by the taskforces and which, in some instances, looked as if real power might well be devolved to the community and other stakeholder groups.

The central focus of *Today's Schools* was on improving the management of schools. Its recommendations were directed at refining the structures of education administration and improving principals' and Boards of Trustees' ability to work with them. Perhaps the most significant of the report's recommendations was the proposed restructuring of the Education Review Office. Its numbers were halved and those remaining were to develop, as we outline in the final section of this chapter, a clear review methodology concentrated on outputs and outcomes. These proposals, which were rapidly implemented, had the effect of changing the Education Review Office from a body concerned with *professional* accountability to one that would ensure *managerial* accountability, the purpose for which, in the view of the State Services

Commission, it had been intended before the 'relitigation' that occurred in the post-Picot process (Dale and Jesson, 1993).

The changes to the Education Review Office were only the most visible component of the new regime of administrative control over the education system that was introduced through the reform period. It was felt that the devolution of educational administration to the level closest to those directly involved would enable major changes to take place to education of the kind it was alleged had been stifled by bureaucracy, and especially by teachers' ability to influence the system. Within the form taken under the Keynesian Welfare State settlement, professionals had been successfully able to claim a space for their judgement and expertise and the opportunity to shape the educational mandate. However, teachers' ability to influence the system was now widely constructed as 'provider capture' and perceived as the most serious and pressing of the problems bequeathed by the previous system.

On the other hand, it was recognized that such radical devolution carried with it major problems of accountability. The revamped Education Review Office was the most direct means of addressing these problems but it was located in a context of a range of other reforms to both the regulation and provision of education. The regulatory reforms impinged on education as part of the restructured administration of the public sector. The most important of these were the Public Finance Act and the State Sector Act. It is highly significant that these were directed at the public sector in general and were not education-specific. This can be seen as one of the key features of the reforms in New Zealand. They were not only based on the reform of the administration rather than the content or process of education, but they neither recognized the need for, nor afforded, any special treatment to the education system. From being a distinct entity with its own unique needs, education became 'mainstreamed'; it had no claims to be treated differently from any other state body (Dale and Jesson, 1993). Acknowledging such differences would mean indulging the 'portfolio culture' that was a central target of the reforms.

Under the Public Finance Act of 1989 the emphasis moved from inputs, or the amount of money a Crown agency could secure, to identification of and accountability for outputs, or goods and services, including policy advice. In the case of schools, the Minister of Education would purchase outputs from schools codified in the National Curriculum, the National Administration Guidelines and the National Educational Guidelines for a price. Funding was delivered through a contract between the minister as purchaser and the Board of Trustees as provider. This contract would then be audited by a third party, the Education Review Office. Evidence of value-adding, an extension of the outputs logic, was later added (1992) to the requirements for schools to prove their effective use of resources. However, the Public Finance Act had two potentially conflicting goals: 1) to improve the quality of service and responsiveness to changing client need; and 2) to increase efficient and accountable use of resources. As critics pointed out, an efficient management process could still produce a poor quality product. It might also be added that proof of 'value-adding' often ends up as little more than those activities that are amenable to measurement.

Under the provisions of the State Sector Act (1988), which was based on the assumption that the private sector model of management is superior to that traditionally used in the public sector and that it can be imported to the public sector, all Principals – as Chief Executive Officers in the public sector – were placed on individual contracts of employment and the State Services Commission, as the overseer of all public sector pay agreements, effectively became the 'collective employer' of those working in the 2,600 schools across the country. A central theoretical plank is principal–agency theory which pervades much of the public sector reform in New Zealand and it can be seen to produce a series of 'cascading contracts' between parties in successive principal and agent roles. At the heart of the public sector reforms – including education – is the assumption that if the appropriate administrative structure is in place it is possible for the principal – the government – and eventually the electorate, to bring about the kinds of changes they think necessary. It demonstrates the paradoxical nature of a set of reforms that are hailed as freeing schools from bureaucracy and enabling them to be much more responsive to their communities but that actually subject them to much tighter and more managerial accountability regimes than they had previously experienced.

A key element of the restructuring embodied in the State Services Act in 1988 was the view that the teacher unions would no longer be the 'professional mouthpieces of teachers' (Capper and Munro, 1990, p 151). Rather, that professional decisions were the prerogative of management, now defined by *Tomorrow's Schools* as the Boards of Trustees, not teachers. A further element was that educational matters embodied in regulation should not be written into the industrial awards; matters such as discipline, classification, training and working hours. However, though the unions argued for the inclusion of most matters in which they traditionally had an interest, in many instances the State Services Commission was able to remove these and argue that these issues were entirely employer prerogative. It is a model that, as Capper and Munro observe:

> sees most workplace decisions as being a management prerogative in which unions have no legitimate view. Furthermore, the model idealizes industrial relations as being best carried out as a number of independent interactions between individual workers and their employers. Collective action by unions is to be minimized as an unwarrantable interference in this process. (1990)

Throughout this period the two teacher unions – the New Zealand Education Institute and the Post Primary Teachers' Association – were distanced from the policy formulation process. Indeed, a dominant view of Treasury, the State Services Commission and Picot was that 'rigidities' in the education system were the result of powerful education interest groups and needed to be stripped away. One way of doing this was to manage their input through a framework which established a new set of ground-rules for interest group participation.

Embedding neo-liberalism: contours of the new settlement, 1990–98

The election of a National Government in 1990 did little to alter the direction of the restructuring, even in the face of a nervous public increasingly anxious to limit the power of the state exercised through a flat and simple political structure and head off its zealousness. The combination of a single house of Parliament, along with an electoral system of first past the post, had enabled Labour and now the National Government to pursue rapidly a process of liberalization characterized by both depth and speed. However, public dissatisfaction with the political process and a growing awareness of disempowerment gave rise to a dramatic level of support for electoral reform by the early 1990s (Haworth, 1998, p 58). In 1996 the public voted for a Mixed Member Proportional party and electoral system which would force a coalition approach on the political parties. However, these developments did not impact significantly on the neo-liberal project (Neilsen, 1998, p 64); indeed, the National-led government continued to put into place the remaining elements of the project directly confronting the key institutions and movement of Keynesian social democracy. This meant that National, shored up by a powerful and confident lobby for the reform process mounted by groups such as the Business Round Table and the Employers' Association, committed itself to implementing a range of initiatives that gave priority to reorienting the mandate of education.

This gave further shape and substance to the new educational settlement. The most notable of these, for the purposes of this final section of the chapter, were the creation of the Employment Contracts Act (1991) to dismantle the statist institutions and norms of Fordist industrial relations which legitimated and empowered the unions,[4] the establishment of school markets, the refinement of the school audit process through the Education Review Office, and a continued commitment to the devolution of responsibility to the community for school governance. Labour's public sector legislative regime which changed the governance structure of education, in combination with developments to reorient the mandate of education implemented by the National government, gave rise to four regulatory mechanisms through which the educational settlement within competitive contractualism now shapes schools:

1. managerialism;
2. auditing;
3. markets; and
4. community governance.

Though each is dealt with separately in the following sections, there is considerable interplay in the way in which these affect the organizational structures and practices of schools.

From professional to managerial accountability

The thrust of the new managerialism which has recharacterized the organization of schooling is neatly captured in the slogan, 'let the managers manage' which has pervaded the reorganization of the public sector. Its dominance in the schooling sector can be seen in the notion that an effective school is a well-managed school and that effective school leaders are school managers. Schools have been strongly encouraged to develop a management approach to all facets of their activity, for example, discipline, staff appraisal, school review. Managerialism is viewed as a means of both bringing about changes in school organizations and making professionals more accountable to both the government and the electorate. Such regimes, however, with their focus upon programme-driven budgets, outputs and outcomes, ignore the complexity of school life and reduce the very difficult social and political problems of schools to problems of management.

From inspecting inputs to auditing outcomes

Auditing, in contrast to managerialism, can be summed up as 'making the managers manage' (Schick, 1996) and sits in sharp contrast to the entrepreneurialism implied in managerialism and markets. Audit arises from the desire to focus upon accountability through outcomes and to minimize producer capture. There are several distinctive features of the Education Review Office's approach to auditing worth noting. One is a deeply held suspicion of the interests and motivations of teachers and where teachers are viewed as potentially opportunistic. This means limiting the scope for the exercise of teachers' professional judgement and discretion. Instead, managerialism and contractualism replace professionalism. A second feature is that the Education Review Office is required to ensure every child in a New Zealand school is delivered their 'educational entitlement'. An 'entitlement' is a particular type of social contract between the state and its citizens. This entitlement is made visible in records in schools and stands as evidence of 'good practice' which can then be codified and surveyed (see Robertson et al, 1997). Third, successful organizations are the result of management practices. Whatever the social and economic context of the school, managerial practices are assumed to be able to determine school effectiveness not cultural explanations. Teachers, within this frame, are viewed as managers of learning, managers of records and schemes, and managers of outputs (adding value). Finally, the Education Review Office takes the view that not only do the public have a right to know about the performance of schools, but that this is one means by which parents gather important information in order to form their preferences and make choices in the schooling marketplace. This knowledge about schools is seen by the Education Review Office as best disseminated by the media. However, there is considerable doubt as to whether the reviews undertaken by the Education Review Office provide much insight into the actual activities of schools, particularly given the limited scope of the review process. The outcomes of the audit process for teachers and schools are also shaped by the Education Review Office's approach, which is to limit the information available to schools regarding the review protocols, claiming commercial sensitivity. As a result, in many schools neither the school executive nor the teachers are clear about what the Review Office's team are looking for (see Robertson *et al*, 1997), giving rise to considerable anxiety as to the outcome of a review and a sense of unfairness about the process. Given, too, that a school audit can mean, at best, consolidation of the school's market position or worse – loss of market position – there is considerable anxiety by schools as to the outcomes of the audit process.

From procedural to a market bureaucracy

The introduction of the schooling market is a mechanism for ensuring commitment to the state's new mandate – economic competitiveness – and a mode of governance. The abolition of 'home zones', the introduction of per capita funding and the possibility of schools being able to create their own enrolment schemes enabled and encouraged the development of a 'market' in educational provision. Considine (1996) captures this shift well when he describes it as a move away from a procedural to a market bureaucracy. Markets are intended to promote efficiency, competitiveness and responsiveness to consumer demands. Markets are also a means of disembedding those practices through which the mandate, capacity and governance of the Keynesian Welfare State settlement were driven (see Robertson, 1996) and replacing them with a more individualistic, competitive and entrepreneurial approach central to the competitive contractual state settlement. There are a number of ways in which market-mode now works at the level of schools in the new educational settlement. In order to maintain student numbers in the school and minimize exit (Hirschman, 1979), schools have made internal (curriculum, assessment, pedagogy) and external changes (image, media). Few schools are exempt from this, even rural schools where in theory the market does not exist. Further, declining funds to schools in New Zealand (around a 3 per cent shortfall) have resulted in schools, even small rural schools, seeking a range of means to increase incomes sources. These range from attracting full-foreign-fee-paying-students into the school to the development of school-corporate sector relationships which generate funds and services for the school. Teachers must also be sensitive to promoting their school within the marketplace as well as the consequences of any information in the marketplace which might cause the school to lose its market position. In the first instance, teachers are encouraged to promote the achievements of individual students in the media, to add new subject areas that will highlight the diverse nature of the schooling programme (even at the expense of significantly larger classes in some subject areas) and to manage student public and private behaviour in ways that best reflect upon the school. They must police the boundaries of acceptable and unacceptable school image at all times, in and out of school.

From central planning to devolved responsibility

One of the hallmarks of the reforms from Picot onwards is the view that *communities* should actively participate as 'choosers' and providers of the various public services. The Education Act 1992 provides the legislative framework for giving voice to the community through the election of local Boards of Trustees. Though the voice of the community was to be contained in the School Charter, almost all of the content of that Charter was prescribed by the government and was common to all schools. This has limited the potential for community agency to a set of administrative obligations (Dale and Ozga, 1993, p 81) and the management of the political risks associated with the new modes of governance (market failure, contractual obligations). Devolved responsibility, as a form of legitimation and control, offers little scope for either 'voice' or community agency around shared interests, though there are examples of where social movements have exploited this space by linking the drive for economic independence with matters of political legitimacy linked to New Zealand's colonial past. The Maori revivalist schools – Kura Kaupapa Maori – are examples of this. In the main, the devolution of responsibility to local communities within the settlement framework with its regulatory mechanisms of markets, audit and managerialism minimize the opportunities for genuine community governance and instead promote risk management and individualism (Robertson, forthcoming).

Conclusion

The arguments we have made about the nature of the transition in New Zealand education can be summarized at each of the three levels that we have identified; the global, national and organizational levels. Our fundamental argument is that the transition was stimulated and shaped by New Zealand's position in the global economy which created huge problems for the national economy. In terms of the core problems for education, this meant prioritizing the state's accumulation problems over those of order and legitimation, thus reversing the patterning of the prioritizing of the state's core problems under the Keynesian Welfare State settlement.

We have argued elsewhere that within the new competitive contractual state settlement, accumulation is legitimation (Dale and Robertson, 1997, p

212). That is to say, education's greatest contribution to legitimation is through increasing the size of the national economic pie from which is implied all will benefit. There is little evidence that either of these things have happened. In fact, there has been a widening of the divisions between rich and poor over the past decade in New Zealand (cf Chatterjee, 1998). While the post-war welfare state met its legitimation burden by taking responsibility for a range of social outcomes like health, education and unemployment, the contemporary New Zealand state has reduced its legitimation burden by withdrawing from direct responsibility for those services and promoting policies that encourage individuals to take responsibility for their own economic well-being. In this new settlement, legitimation becomes an individual matter with government's role restricted to providing a context (low taxation, national economic well-being, buying services beyond the minimum state provision) where indirect improvements take place.

There have been two main phases in the transition of New Zealand education over the past decade. The first, largely under the Labour government, concentrated almost entirely on restructuring educational administration. In this phase of the developing competitive contractual state settlement, governance took priority over mandate and capacity. The aim was to rein in an education system that had become insufficiently accountable to either parents or the government, though it should be noted that parents were in the main happy to leave the education of their children in the hands of the 'experts'. This phase was concluded early in National's first term in office (1990) with *Today's Schools* and the completion of the framework provided by the legislative troika: the Public Finance Act/Social Services Act/Employment Contracts Act. Increasingly over the 1990s, the push has been in the direction of increasing state emphasis on the following:

1. the mandate of education (National Administrative and Educational Guidelines, the School Charter and the National Curriculum) so that education became more directly oriented toward support of accumulation;
2. tighter and more focused auditing and policing of the educational mandate; and
3. putting education on a more market footing as part of the individualization of legitimation.

However, an implicit tension between competitiveness and contractualism begins to surface here. Schools are made more responsive through marketization to 'parents' and are more accountable to government through enhanced auditing procedures. Not only is there the potential for tension between these two forms of accountability but neither individually nor jointly do they make the education system more responsive to the needs of accumulation. This may signal both external and internal pressures on the competitive contractual state settlement in New Zealand which could bring about its modification or even its demise.

Notes

1. This chapter draws on an ongoing research project *Toward a Theory of Education in Social Settlements: The emergence of competitive contractualism* funded under the Marsden Award by the Royal Society of New Zealand [#98-UA-120] in which the two authors are principal investigators.
2. See Robertson (1996) for an elaboration of the relationship between the state and the market, in particular that markets are always regulated by the state.
3. Neilsen (1998, p 60) notes that the Reserve Bank Act (1990), one of the last relatively unnoticed acts of the Fourth Labour Government, formally reversed the state's Keynesian-derived commitment to the achievement of wealth redistribution, employment security, increasing wages and stable accumulation. 'This Act subordinated all economic goals to the single goal of maintaining low inflation in a free-market economy' (op cit).
4. This then removed the state from any direct involvement in industrial relations and instead presented the labour market as a field of mutual voluntary bargaining between theoretically equal parties but which in fact radically enhances the power of capital over labour.

References

Capper, P and Munro, R (1990) Professionals or workers? Changing teachers' conditions of service in New Zealand, *Policy and Politics*, **24** (3), July

Chatterjee, S (1998) *Sharing the National Cake in Post Reform New Zealand: Income inequality trends in terms of income sources*, Massey University, Palmerston North, New Zealand

Considine, M (1996) Market bureaucracy? Exploring the contending rationalities of contemporary administrative regimes, *Labour and Industry*, **7** (1), June, pp 1–27

Dale, R (1982) Education and the state, in *Cultural and Economic Reproduction in Education: Essays on class, ideology and the state*, ed M Apple, Routledge & Kegan Paul, London

Dale, R (1989) *The State and Education Policy*, Open University Press, Milton Keynes

Dale, R (1998) Globalization: a new world for comparative education?, in *Discourse and Theory in Comparative Education*, ed J Shriewer, Peter Lange, Berlin

Dale, R and Jesson, J (1993) Mainstreaming education: the role of the State Services Commission, in *Annual Review of Education in New Zealand*, no 2, ed H Manson, Victoria University Press, Wellington

Dale, R and Ozga, J (1993) Two hemispheres – both right? 1980s education reform in New Zealand and England and Wales, in *Schooling Reform in Hard Times*, ed B Lingard, J Knight and P Porter, Falmer Press, London

Dale, R and Robertson, S (1997) Resiting the nation, reshaping the state: globalisation effects on education policy in New Zealand, in *Education Policy in*

New Zealand/Aotearoa, ed M Olssen and K Morris Matthews, Dunmore Press, Palmerston North, New Zealand

Haworth, N (1998) Taking its medicine: 14 years of modern rectitude in New Zealand, *Renewal,* 6 (2), pp 51–62

Hirschman, A (1979) *Exit, Voice and Loyalty,* Harvard University Press, Cambridge, MA

Hobsbawm, E (1994) *The Age of Extremes: The short twentieth century,* Abacus, London

Jessop, R (1997) A neo-Gramscian approach to the regulation of urban regimes: accumulation strategies, hegemonic projects and governance, in *Restructuring Urban Regime Theory,* ed M Lauria, Sage, London

Kelsey, J (1995) *The New Zealand Experiment,* Brigit Williams Books, Wellington

Minister of Education (1988) *Tomorrow's Schools,* Department of Education, Wellington

Neilsen, D (1998) State autonomy and the mode of regulation: neo-liberal restructuring in New Zealand, *Studies in Political Economy,* 57, Autumn, pp 45–71

Offe, C and Ronge, V (1984) Thesis on the theory of the state, in *Contradictions of the Welfare State,* ed C Offe, Hutchinson and Company, London

Olssen, M and Morris Matthews, K (eds) (1997) *Education Policy in New Zealand: The 1990s and beyond,* Dunmore Press, Palmerston North

Review of the Education Reform Implementation Process [Chair: N Lough] (1990) *Today's Schools: A review of the education reform implementation process,* Government Printer, Wellington

Robertson, S (1996) Markets and teacher professionalism: a political economy analysis, *Melbourne Studies in Education,* 37 (2), pp 23–40

Robertson, S (forthcoming) 'Risky business': market provision, community governance and the individualisation of 'risk' in New Zealand education, *International Studies in Sociology of Education,* 9 (3)

Robertson, S *et al* (1997) *A Review of the Education Review Office,* PPTA, Wellington

Rudd, C (1993) The New Zealand welfare state: origins, development and crisis, in *State and Economy in New Zealand,* ed B Roper and C Rudd, Oxford University Press, Auckland

Schick, A (1996) *The Spirit of Reform: Managing the New Zealand state sector in a time of change,* a report for the State Services Commission and the Treasury, Wellington

State Services Commission (1990) *Advice to the Incoming Government,* Government Printer, Wellington

Taskforce to Review Education Administration, Report of (Chair: B Picot) (1988) *Administering for Excellence,* Government Printer, Wellington

11. Poland in transition

Janusz J Tomiak

A single chapter on such an important topic as this one makes it imperative that the readers' attention is drawn to the inescapable difficulties facing its author. It is simply not possible to do full justice to the manifold aspects of the process of a far-reaching and fundamental transformation of a country with a turbulent history, persisting political conflicts, rapidly changing social structure and facing perplexing economic problems which is deeply involved in the search for a new social, political and economic order under very difficult circumstances (Lewowicki, 1996, pp 162–70; Szymanski, 1996, pp 206–17). It is thus necessary to concentrate attention upon the most significant and meaningful influences and developments which in the author's opinion can help in understanding the central features of the ongoing transition in an important country occupying the very heart of Europe.

The background

The summer of 1999 marked the 10th anniversary of the beginning of the end in so far as Communist power in Poland was concerned. A decade may be a convenient period of time to examine the process of transition from the old towards the new order, to discover the difficulties accompanying it and analyse the problems associated with it, particularly those that have not been resolved and still preoccupy the Poles and remain of interest to the rest of the world (Tomiak, 1992, pp 1–10).

In doing this one must not overlook the relevance of the history of the country, especially that Poland is a land in which history remains an important element in influencing the national ethos and still is a force one has to reckon with. This was of great consequence for the developments following the end of the Second World War. The deeply nurtured near universal desire to ensure the re-establishment of meaningful and close cultural political and economic links with Western Europe could then not be realized, bearing in mind the political realities of the post-Yalta and post-Potsdam Agreements which had placed Poland firmly within the Soviet sphere of influence. As the events of 1956, 1968 and 1980–81 (the Solidarity Movement's first bid for power) had clearly shown, Poland was the most likely Central Eastern European country to undermine the unity of the Communist bloc, the first one to try to break away from the stifling control by the Big Brother and abandon the ideology which the nation saw as an unwanted imposition from outside. The ground for the June 1989 turning point had, therefore, been well prepared and when the opportunity for a complete political, social and economic transformation of the country arrived, one could expect that the transition from the old order to the new one would be resolute, swift and comprehensive. The developments following the summer of 1989 have proved that that was very much an exaggerated expectation (Turnowiecki, 1995, pp 200–06).

The stages of transition

Looking back at the past decade as a whole, one can distinguish the following stages of transition:

1. Progressive disintegration, rather than a sudden collapse, of the old system.
2. 'The Big Bang': the introduction of 'shock therapy' to the national economy.
3. Increasing opposition to the drastic reform programme due to the quickly growing social and economic polarization.
4. Change in the political scenario: the return to power of the left-wing political forces.
5. The pendulum swings again: the right-wing coalition regains political control.

The swings of the pendulum indicate that the country has in fact been able to embrace successfully the political process characteristic of Western democratic societies, that is, an orderly form of political change at regular intervals prescribed by law and based upon a free choice by the electorate of one of the programmes proposed by a number of political parties with different ideologies. It is, however, necessary to try to reveal the mechanisms operating behind the scenes which have been producing the swings and have been closely connected with the sequence of transition to the new order, as this is of key importance in this particular inquiry. One must, therefore, examine the different stages of the sequence, identify the different visions of the future held by the parties involved and examine whether their character and the contrasts between them can help in the analysis of the process of transition as such.

It may be useful to point out here that the first stage, that of progressive disintegration of the Communist political and economic apparatus had, inevitably, to be gradual, as Poland was the first ex-Communist country that dared to attempt it and greater speed would have entailed political and – at that stage – even military dangers of the highest order. However, as time moved on, it became clear that the threat of direct Soviet intervention would not materialize. Poland could, therefore, move on to introduce political pluralism and bring in democratic elections (Hardt and Kaufman, 1995, pp 2–15).

The hitherto unanticipated political pluralism brought with it considerable difficulties by creating unlimited opportunities for the creation of new political parties led by inexperienced and over-enthusiastic leaders expecting instantaneous successes. As many as 29 political parties entered the first post-Communist parliament and the problems facing any multi-party coalition government soon became only too obvious. More realistic regulations had to be introduced to limit the number of parties entitled to enter parliament in order to create the possibility of a stable government, capable of ensuring continuity of political initiatives of whatever kind. At the same time it became obvious that proper efforts had to be made to define clearly the options available for the alternative programmes of social and economic reforms in the years to come. To gain deeper insights into this process one must now identify the four most important and politically viable visions of the future.

The Solidarity vision

In 1989–90 the Solidarity workers' movement and its leaders found themselves catapulted into positions of political power and responsibility. The most important of them were Lech Walesa, the first President of the new, post-Communist Poland; Tadeusz Mazowiecki, its first Prime Minister; Leszek Balcerowicz his first deputy; Boleslaw Geremek, the later foreign minister and Jacek Kuron, later minister for social affairs. Their common roots did not prevent them moving subsequently in different directions with some, indeed, becoming bitter enemies. However, in the period immediately following the collapse of Communism in the country, they were united by their opposition to the former regime and by their readiness to rely on the advice of foreign experts and advisers (Balcerowicz, 1993, pp 313–39).

At that time, the chief one of these was Professor Jeffrey Sachs from Harvard University, the author of the famous 'shock therapy', otherwise known as Poland's jump to the market economy. This, in a way, was a very clearly defined plan for action, encapsulating the vision of the new future. Its main pillars were macroeconomic stabilization, liberalization (ie the abolition of price controls and of economic planning as well as the introduction of new laws supporting private ownership and property rights), privatization, constructing a 'social safety net' for those who suffered loss of work and income due to the rapid industrial change and, finally, obtaining substantial financial assistance from abroad for the envisaged reforms. The original enthusiasm for the 'shock therapy' shown particularly by Leszek Balcerowicz, its chief Polish advocate, ensured a rigorous pursuit of the first three objectives. But there were growing difficulties in securing the last two, connected directly to the rapidly growing large-scale unemployment in several extracting and heavy industries which had never experienced it in the past (Sachs, 1993, pp 35–193).

Foreign investors and international financial institutions such as the World

Bank and International Monetary Fund began to receive pleas for immediate help from other ex-Communist countries in Central-Eastern Europe which were also starved of capital goods and modern equipment. Thus, Poland had to compete with numerous other states for such aid.

The ideals of Solidarity as a political force with mass support rooted in the working class could, nevertheless, retain quite considerable popularity in the long run, because the movement stood for patriotism, respect for traditional family values and close contacts with the Catholic Church – all very different from the workers' and trade unionists' natural sympathies in the West. The Solidarity vision, rooted in Poland's unique history rather than in the social and political realities of the last decade of the 20th century, was for this reason guaranteed to survive even the subsequent years of disenchantment with market economics and capitalist competition. Its vision was, in the final assessment, a Poland free from foreign domination, though to the unsophisticated masses this amounted to freedom from overt forms of direct political interference and enforced domination of an alien ideology. Little attention was paid to the dangers of highly sophisticated forms of covert influence and to the social costs of free market economics. In concrete political terms it meant its members' full support for joining NATO and the European Union. As a cohesive political force Solidarity was, however, bound to fragment in the end, as in its original formation it included too great a variety of groups representing a whole range of diversity of outlooks, perspectives and interests (Dudek, 1997, pp 30–84).

The nationalist vision

Right-wing nationalism has always been a significant force in Polish history. In the 19th century, in partitioned Poland, it gained widespread support because many Poles living under foreign rule saw in it the only guarantee of national survival and the only road to regaining independence. After the Second World War traditional nationalism could formally play no role in internal politics but it continued to affect the minds of the young through the influence of the home and the teaching of the Catholic Church, consistently opposing Communist and atheistic ideas. After 1989, a number of political parties came into being, filled with strong nationalist sentiments, much more extremist in character than Solidarity, but they were too fragmented to become a dominant influence in the political life of the country.

The nationalist vision, reflected in the pronouncements and publications issued by the leaders of these parties, was that of Poland as a country totally free from overt as well covert domination by foreign influences and machinations. Values associated with family and religion tended to foster an uncompromising attachment to national traditions and a suspicion of alien influences of any kind or form. In political terms this outlook regarded globalizing as well as European federative tendencies not only with great suspicion, but outright hostility (Jaworek, 1998, pp 3–26 and 92–127). However, lacking unity and effective leadership, the nationalist outlook failed to exert a more significant influence in comparison to the political parties promising prosperity and stability through closer international ties and co-operation. The nationalist vision of a strong state able to cope with the mounting social and economic problems has, none the less, not lost its appeal among all those who were convinced that the government's main task was to defend the national interest through tough measures to stem the tide of spreading crime, corruption and violence.

The liberal democratic vision

Those who favoured complete elimination of the former Communist ideas and Marxist–Leninist principles from national life were all originally members of the Solidarity movement. However, as time moved on, the most determined of the advocates of the 'shock therapy' took the decision to establish a new party, the Freedom Union (*Unia Wolnosci*). They had convinced themselves that the rank and file of Solidarity really wanted to slow down the transition towards the market economy in order to defend the industrial workers against unrestricted competition.

The vision of the future promoted by the leaders of the Freedom Union was that of Poland as a democracy and, at the same time, as a capitalist country, open to home as well as to foreign investors, determined to promote free enterprise and sound economic policies and speedy and efficient privatization, even if the cost of this in terms of social peace and harmony was likely to be high. Sound economic measures included efficient administration of resources, industrial modernization, balanced budget, reducing inflation, introducing convertibility of the Polish *zloti*, joining the European Union but also drastically reducing the superfluous labour force in unprofitable state-owned industries, keeping social expenditure to the minimum and reducing taxation (Balcerowicz, 1993, pp 1–19). This appealed very much to young, enterprising individuals, prepared to work hard and willing to take risks in order to reap high profits. It had much less appeal to the older generation, who expected help and assistance from the state and also to those who were threatened by unemployment and low wage rates.

The pursuit of the Balcerowicz line in the early 1990s and then under the post-1997 coalition between the Solidarity Electoral Movement (*Akcja Wyborcza Solidarnosc*) and the Freedom Union produced positive results for all those who wanted to see the growth of private initiative, an increase in employment opportunities in the newly emerging sectors of the national economy and in the rate of economic growth for the country as a whole, as well as falling inflation. There were, on the other hand, at the same time, literally hundreds of thousands of peasants and workers who considered that they had gained nothing from the shift to market economy. They felt that their standard of living had declined and they took direct action such as strikes and mass protests against what they considered blatant capitalist exploitation. They placed their hopes for a better future in the hands of the new leftist force, the Social Democratic Party of the Polish Republic.

The vision of the united democratic Left

The old Polish United Workers' Party (*Polska Zjednoczona Partia Robotnicza*) wound up in an orderly fashion in 1990. Some of its leaders chose to retire and withdraw altogether from political activities while others decided to create a new party, the Social Democratic Party, thereby retaining their right to continue political activities with a leftist bias, but without an explicit reference to Marxism–Leninism and any open declaration of intention to pursue the Communist policies of the former regime. Their hope, well justified as future developments were to show, was to mobilize effectively all the Poles who were increasingly beginning to experience hardship under the 'shock therapy' policy of the Right and who therefore preferred a return to the policies of their predecessors without, naturally, any explicit desire to see a return to Stalinism.

In 1993, the leaders of the Social Democratic Party succeeded in uniting the left wing of the political spectrum and formed the Union of the Democratic Left (*Sojusz Lewicy Demokratycznej*). That formation was victorious in the general elections of that year after an intensive electoral campaign. They were able to do this with the help of a political vision based on a definite desire to ensure the country's entry into NATO and the European Union and the determination to defend the interests of the working class against any further attempts at rapid privatization, allowing market forces to dominate the economic scene. This was a shrewd and calculated move which earned that orientation both respectability and popularity at home and abroad. It confirmed the movement's pragmatic approach to politics, its natural appeal to those whose standard of living was threatened and, at the same time, its intention to cut the links with the isolationist policies of the past and to gain the support of those who saw clear advantages in a closer integration with Western Europe. By joining the European Union, the Union of the Democratic Left was clearly hoping to establish strong links with Western Social Democratic Parties and strengthen its own position even further.

The Solidarity vision and education

Instilling in the young generation genuine respect for and deep attachment to the traditional Polish values has always been an essential part of the Solidarity ethos. The main direction of the educational effort was thus to be the transmission and not the transformation of the traditional national system of values. Right from the early 1980s and through the subsequent years of Solidarity's suppression by General Jaruzelski under martial law, determined attempts were made by the movement's leadership to ensure that patriotism, devotion to the national cause, respect for the Catholic faith and intimate familiarity with Polish history and literature constituted indispensable elements in the education and upbringing of the younger generation (Davies, 1991, pp 266–89).

Quite naturally, therefore, one would have expected particular emphasis on the content and methods of teaching the subjects connected with the promotion of national identity and the national values system when Solidarity emerged victorious from the struggle for power in 1989. But the movement lost its cohesion and consequently its ability to transform the educational system. Many activists left to join the liberal democrats, having little desire to confine their political and educational efforts to promoting ideas which lacked appeal and which seemingly paid little attention to the more down-to-earth pragmatic considerations without which effective political action is always doomed to failure (Karsten and Majoor, 1995, pp 4–12).

Those who continued their affiliation by no means gave up their vision. Reform proposals tended to stress the need for new epistemological principles, reorienting all educational efforts towards the cultivation of distinctive national educational traditions and the promotion of knowledge explicitly serving national priorities and national needs (Mieszalski, 1994, pp 57–69). In terms of the ideal individual the proposals tended to stress the importance of producing men and women who combined the high principles of Christian morality and the national ethos. And yet, despite the efforts of some of the would-be reformers, the ideal of 'integral humanism' advocated by the great contemporary Catholic philosopher of education, Jacques Maritain, did not gain wide support, perhaps because of its universalistic character, transcending national particularism (Slawinski, 1993, pp 7–9).

The nationalist vision and education

In educational terms the nationalist vision was derived from the principal ideas of the nationalist tradition in Poland, a firm commitment to promoting all kinds of knowledge which would strengthen and deepen a distinctive Polish national identity. The sources of pedagogical ideas and inspiration were, accordingly, the writings of Polish educators for whom this objective had always been of paramount importance. This was tantamount to the cultivation of an idealized image of the Pole as an embodiment of all virtues and a categorical rejection of all forms of alien influences, overt and covert, political and economic, as well as cultural and intellectual. Educational ideas coming from abroad were thus assigned low priority, particularly if they appeared to be linked to the processes of globalization and supranational integration. A particular threat was considered to be the penetration of the national system of education by foreign ideas, criticized for their cosmopolitan and materialistic character.

Strengthening the distinctive national identity in face of all alien influences involved, none the less, also an explicit insistence upon high standards of attainment in both the humanities and the natural sciences. The former were absolutely indispensable for creating proper respect for the rich national heritage and the latter for ensuring that the nation's progress and struggle against foreign competition were not hampered by the neglect of science and technology (Jaworek, 1998, pp 83–87, 142–51).

The nationalist vision of education should be seen as an integrated set of educational principles and objectives associated with not one particular political party but rather with a section of the population oriented towards the traditional value system as well as being generally suspicious of modern integrative political and economic tendencies. For that section of the population post-modernism as such presented no attraction as a feature characteristic of a post-totalitarian society. What all those supporting this vision saw as a worthy replacement for the discredited Communist system was the return to what they considered to be a permanent and indestructible system of values based upon the principle of service and individual commitment to the nation which had to be defended against 'the Other' (Mitter, 1996, pp 110–13).

The liberal democratic vision and education

Those who were committed to the liberal democratic vision of the future have repeatedly insisted that educational change constituted a very important element within the envisaged speedy transition to the new order under the 'shock therapy' strategy. Jeffery Sachs insisted that a shift of emphasis and resources towards higher education was an indispensable precondition for accumulating the human capital in order to ensure a much higher rate of economic growth than had been the case under the Communist rule (Sachs, 1993, p 115). Equal significance was attached also to a rapid growth of opportunities commensurate with the proposed economic and commercial progress for the young and talented pupils with the help of the non-state sector of secondary education. This sector was to be created anew with the help of a number of pace-setters who realized that there was a very considerable demand for it in the bigger cities and the more prosperous industrial and commercialized enclaves in the central and western parts of the country.

An important initiative was the formation of the Civic Education Association (*Spoleczne Towarzystwo Oswiatowe*) which opened dozens of schools clearly oriented towards the cultivation of individual talents and special abilities of their pupils, directed by enthusiastic heads, with intellectually demanding programmes of studies, small classes and numerous optional subjects to choose from and offering abundant opportunities for extra-curricular activities. The overt influence of private schools abroad, operating on similar principles, is in such cases quite obvious. Yet, serious doubts remain concerning the wider and deeper impact of such establishments upon educational change in the country extending beyond the training of the elite (Okon, 1996).

The overall reform of the state education system faced two major problems from the point of view of the proponents of the liberal democratic vision. One was that a thorough reform of the system as a whole had been lacking since the beginning of the 1990s, offering a clear set of coherent proposals as to what it should involve and what should be changed first: the structure of the system or the contents and methods of learning. The second difficulty has been that the cost of a major school reform would, without doubt, be enormous. The liberal democrats have, however, been very determined to keep a balanced budget for very valid economic reasons. Thus, the social pressures for an improved health service, for retraining the unemployed and providing adequate help for the ageing population have meant that educational reform has moved down the scale of national priorities. Only in 1999 was the decision taken by the AWS-UW coalition government to introduce a meaningful structural reform. That, however, was criticized by the opposition and the teachers' unions – not without justification – as inadequately prepared and supported.

The liberal democrats have thus been promoting a vision of well-educated individuals, fluent in foreign languages, intimately familiar with the most recent advances in the world of modern science and information technology, capable of taking correct decisions in the light of the available evidence, ambitious and orienting themselves towards concrete achievements, able to take advantage from the relevant foreign experience and to integrate their own efforts with those of other people (Geremek and Michalski, 1994, pp 6–17). In other words, knowledge of greatest worth – in the Spencerian sense, but brought right up to date – was considered most valuable. The cultivation of attitudes and skills indispensable for the successful economic and managerial performance has been accorded a prominent place in all learning experiences. Providing incentives and offering rewards for high attainment and outstanding academic achievement have become an important feature of the highly competitive educational endeavour (Ministry, 1995, pp 199–210).

The left-wing vision and education

The gradual abandonment, initially tempered with caution, of the Communist order in Poland in 1989–90 ensured that numerous former politicians of the Polish United Workers' Party could, by carefully planned action, retain their influence over a wider sector of the Polish population. Their most determined stand concerned the position of the workers in the nationalized industries and the employees in the social services. They were particularly interested also in trying to protect the unemployed, the old and the disadvantaged from the effects of rapid economic change. They were, however, also interested in changing the educational system, but in the long, rather than the short run. Sensibly, from the point of their electoral appeal, they did not directly resist the proliferation of private educational establishments even if their elitist, right-wing character was quite obvious (Purdue, 1995, pp 145–49).

The left-wing's vision of the future state system of education favoured a strong secular–modernizing bias, devoid of one-sided nationalist and religious tendencies. The left wing was not in any way averse to educational influences from abroad, as long as they were rooted in materialist philosophy and free from any dogmatic assertions. The former vision of 'a new Communist man' was thus replaced by the new vision of well-educated modern citizens, able to think for themselves and motivated by self-interest, though not unaware of the need for broader considerations connected with the notions of social justice and civic participation. Educational reform was viewed in a pragmatic way as a challenging kind of undertaking, requiring adequate preparation and financial backing, and not as a series of *ad hoc* measures designed to produce immediate results in the mistaken anticipation of a high rate of return in the short run. The sequential order of the envisaged transition to a new pattern of education appeared, therefore, as a well-drawn process of planned evolutionary change, based upon international co-operation with a particular stress upon explicit rational foundations rooted in egalitarianism and secular morality (Kruszewski and Kruszewski, 1994, pp 89–105; Kicinski, 1993, pp 110–48).

Reforming the state system of education

The swinging political pendulum over the course of the last 10 years made a more fundamental and thoroughgoing educational reform of state schools difficult. The early Solidarity Ministers of National Education, Andrzej Stelmachowski and Henryk Salmonowicz, as well as the subsequent holder of the office, Professor Jerzy Wiatr, of the Social Democratic party and an ex-Communist, were all engaged for years in discussions with their Ministry groups of advisers and consultants on the pressing need to formulate a plan to modernize and restructure the state educational system. It took nearly the whole decade to finally present to parliament a concrete proposal for far-reaching reform. This was proposed by Professor Miroslaw Handke, the Minister of National Education in the government of Jerzy Buzek late in 1998, after it had been given consideration by – among others – representatives of the Episcopate of the Catholic Church and other churches, the Higher Education Council, the OECD experts in a meeting in Warsaw and also the 61st Session of the Educational Committee of the OECD in Paris in 1998.

The most important parts of the proposal concern the organizational re-structuring of the system confining the basic schools to six years; introducing *gimnasia,* followed by three-year *lycées* or two-year vocational schools, all offering opportunities for continuing further studies in a variety of types of educational establishments at the level of higher academic, advanced, professional and vocational courses of study. The proposal also outlines the future reforms in the content and methods of learning, the modes of assessing pupils' performance, improving teacher training and in-service education as well as proposing new principles for financing education. All this provides the basis for a long and vigorous debate in parliament, particularly because opponents argue that the proposal lacks general support from the teachers' union and the wider society. They demand a slower pace of change, a better prepared set of proposals and a proper financial backing for them, as they will determine the quality of education in the country for decades to come. President Kwasniewski is himself very interested in the educational reform and has issued instructions to form a group of advisers of high reputation to critically examine the contents of the proposal (Ministry, 1998, pp 7–72).

Conclusions

Political pluralism based upon different ideological outlooks does, naturally, involve very different visions of the future among the contestants for political power in a country. Where there is a well-established procedure for the conduct of general elections in an orderly fashion at regular intervals of time, the means are thereby provided for a peaceful transformation of the existing order into a new one which may be based upon a very different vision of the future. How different depends upon the character of the prevailing beliefs among the electorate. This inevitably involves different views concerning education, its principal functions and features (Tomiak, 1997, pp 429–35).

If the visions of the future of education in a country proposed by the different political forces are completely incompatible, problems arise. The consequences of a political change are then bound to be quite far-reaching. They are bound to affect the very foundations – spiritual, ideological and social – of the national system of education in terms of the epistemological principles, concepts of society and the individual as well as in terms of the school structure and the role of the teacher. But the different visions may not necessarily be completely incompatible and they may contain a significant degree of compatibility. This is likely to produce transformation which may be evident, indeed, quite pronounced, in some aspects of education but not in others. That form of transition is likely to be associated with an orderly and gradual change towards a new, modified educational system. More than this. Partial compatibility between the different visions of education of the future can eliminate the danger of conflict between the various interested parties. Fortunately, this has been the Polish case (Mieszalski, 1996, pp 200–05).

A limited, but nevertheless observable measure of tacit agreement in respect of certain uncontested aspects of educational transformation among the most important political orientations has permitted Poland to experience change in certain areas of education over the last decade. The most important has been the growth of the private sector. Both its economic importance from the short-term point of view as well as its social significance from the long-term point of view should not be missed. This sector has enabled the country to produce a new elite of very mixed social background, well trained in the skills and techniques indispensable for efficient functioning of a modern economy. This is an obvious advantage for the future integration of Poland into the European Union. Its wider social and political implications will only become clear with the passage of time. However, a meaningful reform of the state system of education as a whole seems to be far from realization at the present time and the difficult preparatory work that conditions its success leaves still much to be desired.

References

Balcerowicz, L (1993) *Eastern Europe: Economic, social and political dynamics*, University of London School of Slavonic and East European Studies, London

Bandau, S *et al* (eds) (1996) *Schule und Erziehungswissenschaft im Umbruch*, Deutsches Institut für Internationale Pädagogische Forschung, Bohlau, Frankfurt am Main

Davies, N (1991) *God's Playground: A history of Poland*, OUP, Oxford

Dudek, A (1997) *Pierwsze lata III Rzeczypospolitei: 1989–1995* (The first years of the Third Republic: 1989–1995), GEO Publications, Cracow

Geremek, B and Michalski, K (eds) (1994) *Europa i spoleczenstwo obywatelskie* (Europe and civil society), Znak, Warsaw

Hardt, J P and Kaufmann, P F (eds) (1995) *East-central European Economies in Transition*, M E Sharpe, London

Jaworek, R (1998) *Jak zasobny krai doprowadzic do ubstwa* (How to reduce a rich country to poverty), Norton, Wroclaw

Karsten, S and Majoor, D (eds) (1995) *Education in Eastern Central Europe: Educational changes after the fall of Communism*, Waxmann, Munster

Kicinski, K (1993) *Wizje szkoly w spoleczenstwie post-totalitarnym* (Visions of the school in a post-totalitarian society), OPEN Publications, Warsaw

Kruszewski, K and Kruszewski, K B (1994) Playing Monopoly Polish style, in *Education and the Values Crisis in Central and Eastern Europe*, ed V D Rust, P Knost and J Wichmann, pp 89–105, Peter Lang, Frankfurt am Main & New York

Lewowicki, T (1996) Wandlungen des polnischen Bildungswesens: Bedingungen, Bereiche und Wesen der Transformation, in *Schule und*

Erziehungswissenschaft im Umbruch, ed S Bandau *et al*, pp 162–70, Deutsches Institut für Internationale Pädagogische Forschung, Bohlau, Frankfurt am Main

Mieszalski, S (1994) Polish education: face to face with challenges and threats, in *Education and the Values Crisis in Central and Eastern Europe*, ed V D Rust, P Knost and J Wichmann, pp 57–69, Peter Lang, Frankfurt am Main & New York

Mieszalski, S (1996) Drei Fragen an die polnische Schule in der Wende, in *Schule und Erziehungswissenschaft im Umbruch*, ed S Bandau *et al*, pp 200–05, Deutsches Institut für Internationale Pädagogische Forschung, Bohlau, Frankfurt am Main

Ministry (Ministry of Education, Republic of Poland) (1998) *Education in a Changing Society*, Tepis, Warsaw

Mitter, W (1996) Probleme kultureller und nationaler Identitäten im Bildungswesen: Kontinuität und Wandlungen, in *Schule und Erziehungswissenschaft im Umbruch*, ed S Bandau *et al*, pp 110–28, Deutsches Institut für Internationale Pädagogische Forschung, Bohlau, Frankfurt am Main

Okon, W (1996) Erziehung in einer Zeit des Umbruchs, in *Schule und Erziehungswissenschaft im Umbruch*, ed S Bandau *et al*, Deutsches Institut für Internationale Pädagogische Forschung, Bohlau, Frankfurt am Main

Purdue, W D (ed) (1995) *Modernization Crisis: The transformation of Poland*, Praeger, Westport, CT

Sachs, J (1993) *Poland's Jump to the Market Economy*, The Lionel Robbins Lectures Series, the MIT Press, Cambridge, MA

Slawinski, S (1993) Czlowiek w systemie szkolnym (Man within the system of education), *Reforma szkolna* (School reform), 4, pp 7–9

Szymanski, M S (1996) Die polnische Gesellschaft und Schule im Umbruch, in *Schule und Erziehungswissenschaft im Umbruch*, ed S Bandau *et al*, pp 206–17, Deutsches Institut für Internationale Pädagogische Forschung, Bohlau, Frankfurt am Main

Tomiak, J (1992) Educational change in Central Eastern Europe: a view from London, *East/West Education*, **13** (1), pp 1–10

Tomiak, J (1997) Looking back, looking forward: education in Central-Eastern Europe on the eve of the XXIst century, in *Vergleichende Erziehungswissenschaft: Herausforderung- Vermittlung-Praxis. Festschrift für Wolfgang Mitter zum 70. Geburtstag*, ed C Kodron *et al*, vol 1, pp 426–35, Bohlau, Cologne

Turnowiecki, W (1995) Edukacja a proces transformacji w Polsce u progu lat dziewidziesitych (Education and the process of transformation in Poland at the beginning of the 1990s), in *Szkola i pedagogika w dobie przelomu* (School and pedagogy at the turning point), ed T Lewowicki *et al*, pp 200–06, Zak, Warsaw

12. The Russian Federation in transition

Janusz J Tomiak

A thoroughgoing transformation involves the displacement of the old order by the new one, based upon very different aims and objectives and, inevitably, the application of new – and often previously untested – means to attain them. Considerable problems are inevitably created by telescoping the process of transition into a relatively short period of time or arise when the endogenous and exogenous forces promoting and delaying transformation remain in balance. If that state of affairs continues for not weeks but years, the resulting stalemate tends to further complicate the process of transition from the old to the new by rendering it more precarious and volatile. Indeed, depending upon the circumstances, the stalemate may, through its own very nature, lead to quite unexpected developments, sudden political turnabouts and even to major social explosions which are very difficult to predict (Brzezinski,1993, pp 167–77; Williams *et al*, 1996, pp 4–20).

The old system: the USSR

The central features of the Soviet order, so very different from those of the democratic societies of the West, had been well defined and plainly discernible. Effective power was concentrated in the hands of the members of the Politbureau, a small number of carefully chosen and trusted individuals, invariably unanimously supported by the Central Committee, representing the elite of the one and only political party, the Communist Party of the Soviet Union. All the important positions in the country were reserved for the *nomenklatura*, ie a carefully selected group of individuals who were unreservedly loyal to the political leadership and the Communist cause. Intensive political indoctrination was rigorously pursued. An uncompromising stand against the bourgeois states was constantly stressed and observed in the conduct of foreign policy. Assistance was given generously – at an enormous cost – to fraternal Communist parties and political allies abroad. The economic development of the country was centrally planned. The means of production remained exclusively in the hands of the state and individual ownership was limited to the generally accessible basic consumer goods. Foreign investment in the country was eliminated and contacts with foreigners controlled. The armed forces were well equipped with modern weapons, including some of the best and most dangerous in the world.

This set-up was explicitly and emphatically very consequential for education, its aims, organization and control as well as the contents and methods of upbringing. Schools were expected to prepare all pupils to become fully committed builders of Communism, wholeheartedly supporting the political leadership. Epistemologically, knowledge of utilitarian character was given the greatest stress. Religious education was forbidden. The organizing curricular principle established close links between learning and productive work. Polytechnical education was of key significance. All teachers had to be politically committed and actively engaged in turning each pupil into 'a Communist man' – or woman. Parental support was guided by the party activists and passed through overtly controlled channels. Youth organizations' networks strengthened political commitment further by an elaborate ritual and inner discipline (Tomiak, 1994, pp 37–51).

Changing the system was thus extremely difficult and partial and sporadic efforts to change it even into a 'façade democracy' or a 'quasi-democracy' in the 1960s and 1970s were bound to, and did, end in failure (Finer, 1987, pp 421–38, 441–537; Gorbachev, 1987, pp 12–25). And yet, the Soviet leadership in the 1980s, much better informed on the outside world than their predecessors, became fully aware of the economic contrasts between the USSR and the West. Far from catching up with the West and overtaking it, as Nikita Khrushchev had announced in the early 1960s, the Soviet economic performance began to falter and the advantages of peaceful coexistence with other socio-economic systems became evident. The next step, however, the policy of *glasnost* and *perestroika*, ie introducing openness and restructuring in a hitherto rigorously regimented society by Mikhail Gorbachev in the mid-1980s, proved to be the breaking point for the existing set-up (Brzezinski, 1989, pp 53–102; Gorbachev, 1987, pp 135–64; Service, 1997, pp 241–58).

The question which way the country would turn now and what kind of social, political and economic order it would want to orient itself toward, could not, however, be easily answered. The range of possible options seemed quite considerable. Each kind of transformation envisaged required, evidently, pursuing a different path, demanded a different mode of transition, as each contained a different vision of the future. The importance of the years of *glasnost* and of *perestroika* – of what can be called the proleptic (ie the anticipatory) stage for all subsequent developments should not, however, be ignored, although it was a pre-transitional phenomenon. It paved the way for everything that was to follow. This was so, even if Mikhail Gorbachev had planned the reconstruction and not the destruction of Communism (Gorbachev, 1987, pp 17–38; Yeltsin, 1990, pp 188–92).

The stages of transition

Bearing in mind the above considerations, one can make a valid distinction between the following stages of transition in so far as the Russian Federation in the period 1991–99 is concerned:

1. Destruction of the old order – political, social and economic.
2. Formulation of the alternative visions of the future.
3. Confrontation of the conflicting forms of the envisaged transformation.
4. Prolonged political impasse resulting in limited piecemeal introduction of some of the reform proposals.
5. Deepening of the crisis caused by the continuing political stalemate and mounting economic difficulties.

Looking further to the immediate future one can expect:

6. The seemingly inescapable imposition of a new order based upon effective control of the key elements of political authority to ensure the indispensable social cohesion and national survival.

Formally, the Union of Soviet Socialist Republics (USSR), basing its existence and its *modus vivendi* upon the principles of Marxism–Leninism ended as such quite suddenly following the anti-Gorbachev coup in August 1991. With it, the old order collapsed in confusion and deep uncertainty concerning the political, social and economic future of Russia. The old control mechanism disappeared, but the visions of the future were at that time very unclear and it was impossible to predict the future course of events with greater accuracy (Dneprov, 1993, pp 25–28; Holmes *et al*, 1995, pp 228–44; Tomiak, 1992b, pp 137–55; Tomiak, 1994, pp 415–27).

As time went on, the alternative visions of the things to come began to crystallize and formulate around a wider range of political options. Yet, the possible overall political and macro-economic scenarios only gradually, though inescapably, revealed the true complexities of the situation. One could detect that the transition from the old system to some kind of a new one would be thronged with difficulties, arising out of a large number of considerations. Among them, the chief ones were: the unexpected and unforeseen character of the upheaval; fundamental differences of opinion regarding the future among the newly emerging political orientations; the multinational and multicultural character of the old Soviet Union; the history of the country, its very extent, its enormous economic potential and its perplexing diversity; but also its almost total lack of exposure to modern forms of democratic organization and social diversification, successful methods of efficient management of resources, economic competition, a generally respected legal framework based upon the rule of law and, above all, clear-cut concepts of civic obligations and responsibilities binding all citizens in an open society (Birzea, 1994, pp 1–16; Kaufman, 1994, pp 149–58; Tomiak, 1992c, pp 19–34).

In the summer of 1991, the gradually emerging alternative visions of the future in the Russian Federation involved not only disagreements concerning the speed of the transformation and the sequential order of the envisaged reforms, but also very much the direction and the real substance of the transformation. This really complicated the Russian scene, in contrast to most of the other ex-Communist countries in Central-Eastern Europe, where, despite the newly emerging political pluralism a degree of consensus did exist and facilitated the transition to a new order.

One could see that in the Russian Federation there were a number of actors on the socio-political scene right from the start, who tried to assert their presence and to fill the vacuum created by the fall of Communist power in Russia. They all had different origins, they all surfaced suddenly – or resurfaced after decades of complete political impotence – and had to prove that they could swim in the troubled waters of political uncertainty, social confusion and continuing economic decline. They all had to face the challenge of constructing a viable programme of political action, keeping their eyes on the heritage of the more distant past, the need to reconsider the impact of the less distant Soviet era upon Russian society and to clarify their own vision of the future. Most important of them were: the President of the Federation; the newly established political parties; the Russian Orthodox Church; the military; the *nouveau riche*; the Mafia and the old *nomenklatura*. Institutionally distinct, they were in the position to form alliances between themselves and, to a degree, to interpenetrate each other with all sorts of consequences which often lacked logic and wisdom, but had the advantage of political expediency. To make matters even more complicated, the alliances frequently proved to be quite unstable and unreliable, short-lived and disappointing both for the partners who had concluded them as well as for the general public and the electorate, thereby only adding to the confusion which already existed. It is, nevertheless, useful for the purpose of further analysis to identify the key visions of the future and to specify the proposed transitological progressions associated with each vision.

The liberal-democratic vision[1]

The first vision was that of the new Russia as a federal state, based upon political pluralism and market economics. The latter was to include the exchange of goods and services free from governmental interference and excessive regulation; the establishment of open labour and capital markets; unrestricted competition operating within an acceptable legal framework which would provide the necessary stability and security for the efficient functioning of the system (Williams *et al*, 1996, pp 2–19). While the general principles of such a system were thus clearly defined, it gradually transpired that there were additional considerations which could not be ignored and had very much to be taken into account if that system was to work properly. Unfortunately, the principal ones were those that were generally lacking: proper respect for the necessary legal basis which would ensure that all transactions were honoured and all contracts adhered to; adequate measures to be taken to prevent unfair practices such as bribery, violence, corruption and the rapid accumulation of wealth by suspect means; rigorous insistence upon observing the rules preventing tax evasion as well as the appearance of large-scale monopolies; a high propensity towards reinvesting profits at home in new ventures rather than transferring them to private accounts abroad; effective and wise use of foreign aid to the advantage of the population as a whole.

The absence of the above mentioned considerations prevented the first vision from winning decisive support among the wider ranks of the population which felt that they had nothing to gain from this orientation. In particular, the Russian lower house, the Duma, including the majority of the former Communists, ensured that the necessary changes failed to materialize. As the standard of living for large sectors of the population began to sink, pro-market sympathies declined further. This despite the fact that President Yeltsin and the prime ministers appointed by him did their utmost to prevent it. In consequence, the pro-market forces including such parties as the Yabloko Party, Our Home is Russia or the liberal democrats and such capable politicians as Yegor Gaidar, Gregory Yavlinsky and Viktor Chernomyrdin were unable to put into operation their strategy of a decisive transition towards a fully developed capitalist economy. As the evidence of a catastrophic fall in industrial production and a marked decline in agricultural output became indisputable and the consequences of it affected practically the whole of the population, the liberal-democratic orientation started to lose its appeal even among its most keen advocates: the young, enterprising individuals who initially very much believed in the superiority of their vision over all the alternative ones. The growing budget deficit, the mounting problems with obtaining further financial assistance from the international organizations and foreign governments contributed further to the worsening of the situation. The spectacular fall in the value of the rouble in August 1998, for which the pro-market policies of the government were blamed, was yet another adverse development in the long chain of calamitous events. President Yeltsin's deteriorating health, the fall of the pro-market prime ministers Viktor Chernomyrdin and, subsequently, Sergei Kirienko finally extinguished the last hopes for a quick victory of the liberal-democratic orientation.

The nationalist vision

The second vision was that of the new Russia as a great power, able to reassert itself as one of the states exercising a major position in world politics and world affairs. This vision derived its strength from the dissatisfaction and, indeed, the bitterness of the millions of Russians who witnessed the Soviet withdrawal from Central-eastern Europe, the disintegration of the USSR, the consequent decline of the prestige of Russia on the international scene and, finally, the increase in poverty and a substantial reduction in the material standard of living of the majority of the population. The vision of a powerful Russian state appealed particularly to the military, but also found great response among the nationalistically inclined sections of the population. Many representatives of the Russian Orthodox Church, very conscious of its great past and the vital role that it had played in Russian history, not infrequently voiced their support for this vision, mindful of the Church's suppression under Communism and weary of the materialistic outlook of the free marketeers, particularly the very rich, whose ostentatious lifestyle had earned them general disapproval (Brzezinski, 1993, pp 178–81; Service, 1997, pp 527–34).

However, those who favoured this orientation were also unable to attain the degree of strength which would permit them to dominate the political scene in the country and enforce a pattern of transition commensurate with the substance of their vision. They were viewed by the liberally inclined section of the Russian nation as the opponents of the unrestricted play of market economics and free competition and by the ex-Communists as the force harking back to the old Tsarist times, resurrecting right-wing chauvinism and reviving the social distinctions of the age gone by. Their demands were also not welcome to the non-Russians, who still constituted nearly 20 per cent of the total population of the Russian Federation and who were trying to secure for themselves a greater measure of autonomy and self-determination in the different and often quite sizeable, parts of the state (Tomiak, 1997, pp 45–55). Obviously Chechnia is particularly significant here.

Not unimportant was the fact that the mass media were in fact controlled by the *nouveau riche*. Their growing influence over the electorate was more and more noticeable and those who owned them had no inclination to support the nationalist vision. As a result, even such a popular military figure, with a distinguished record of service in the armed forces, as General Aleksandr Lebed, could not exercise a dominant influence over the majority of the population and whip up decisive support for his political programme in the mid-1990s and in the presidential elections of 1996. Other prominent leaders favouring the nationalist cause proved too impatient and much too crude in their political agitation to appeal to the majority of the electorate. In consequence, many people, angered by the growing lawlessness, corruption and violence, but particularly by the growing general impoverishment of the people as a whole, and at the same time by the inability of the nationalist orientation to provide firm guidance and determined leadership, came to the conclusion that the only solution was a return to the Communist order, with or without a significant difference in comparison with the Communist set-up prior to 1991.

The neo-Communist vision

The third vision was the return to Communism, reintroduction of a much stricter system of central control and regimentation, but also the return of greater stability and discipline. This vision appealed particularly to the members of the older generation who still remembered the times when the workers regularly received their wages, however meagre they might had been, did as they were told, did not need to look straight into the face of glaring inequalities and could lead a well-ordered existence, even if that was devoid of the illusory blessings of personal freedom of thought and action. This vision was strongly supported by former members of the Communist Party of the Soviet Union (CPSU), including even those who could well remember the Stalinist terror, the purges and the forced labour camps. For them the evils of unbridled capitalism, the fear of permanent unemployment, unpaid work, high inflation, growing foreign indebtedness, continuing poverty and degradation were unacceptable.

And yet, again, despite the mass rallies, protest marches drawing tens of thousands of demonstrators into the streets, fiery speeches by the leaders of the Communist Party of the Russian Federation, this orientation also was unable to become a dominant political force following the collapse of the USSR. One important reason why it was so was the fact that the young generation had failed to respond to the neo-Communist programme with enthusiasm, even when it declared its support for respecting Russian heritage and tradition (Zyuganov, 1996, pp 122–56). In Zyuganov's words 'capitalism was incompatible with the popular mentality of the Russian people and it could never take root on the Russian soil' (ibid, p 13).

Significantly, the Russian sociologist A O Boronoev expressed a very similar point of view, arguing in a scientific report submitted to a sociological congress in Moscow in 1997 that:

> Researches show... that the Russians have their own systems of values and concepts. They differ in many respects from the structure of values and ideas of the market-ruled world. Such values of a market economy as Property, Household (Business), Labour, Wealth, Fame (Reputation) are insufficiently represented in the Russians' mentality... The country's renovation is impossible... without changes in Russian mentality. (The Russian Society of Sociologists, 1997, pp 24–25)

That suggests, however, that the time-scale of social transformation is of crucial importance and that it renders a fundamental reform of the system in the short run impossible.

All in all, the evidence in respect of the course of events over the period 1991–99 confirms that none of the three main visions concerning the political, economic and social future of Russia could gain the upper hand and decisively enforce the form of transformation it desired. The stages of transition

through which the country was passing over this period of time have, therefore, been of a much less determinate kind than elsewhere, exhibiting some
reforming tendencies at one time and a near total stalemate at another. Because both the forces propelling transformation as well as those impeding it
were at work all the time, the result was a piecemeal, sectoral transformation.
It made itself most clearly visible in those aspects and sectors of the
socio-political set-up where at least a measure of agreement existed, albeit on a
limited scale. Education was a field in which the contesting forces could secure
some significant transformation in certain areas and practically none in others. To examine this process it is first necessary to examine the stated aims of
education, the epistemological principles informing all learning, the concept
of the changing role of the teacher and the curricula, that is the contents and
methods of education (Tomiak, 1992a, pp 33–44).

Education and the liberal-democratic vision

The collapse of the Communist system of education offered an obvious opportunity for the liberal-democratic visionaries to formulate a programme of reform of schools in the country. Boris Yeltsin's first Minister of Education,
Eduard Dneprov, spelt out in very clear, but general terms, the new principles
of educational transformation in the Russian Federation. It should be stressed
that they were the result of several years of deliberation of the Temporary Scientific Research Group VNIK which came into existence in the years of *glasnost* and *perestroika* and included outstanding liberally oriented reformist
teachers such as Shalva Amonashvili, Sofia Lysenkova, Simon Soloveichik,
Vladimir Matveyev, Boris Nikitin and several other individuals. The significance of the proleptic period for the subsequent developments is, therefore,
quite clear (Tkachenko, 1994, pp 48–52).

Eduard Dneprov's principles were: democratization, destatization, the creation of alternative parallel educational structures to the existing ones,
depoliticization, acceleration, enhancement of the teaching of humanities,
differentiation, humanization, lifelong education and placing an emphasis
upon the developmental aspects of education. Behind these principles lay the
conviction that the old Soviet system was rigidly conservative, over-
bureaucratic, too strictly centrally controlled, highly politicized, slow in responding to new challenges, lacking greater diversity and proper emphasis
upon openness and freedom of choice (Eklof and Dneprov, 1993, pp 13–16,
114–18; Tomiak, 1992c, pp 19–34).

The above mentioned principles could provide a firm basis for the consecu-
tive stages of a gradual transition towards a new character of education in Russia, the first step being the preparation of a new law on education embodying
the new principles and the second one being its adoption by the legislature.
Much depended upon Eduard Dneprov himself. Had he been able to continue

his work as the Minister of Education, his draft of a new law in July 1991 might indeed have opened the way to a wholesale transformation of the system of education through a series of stages of transition. But this was not to be. As Eduard Dneprov correctly pointed out in a speech in September 1991, the kinds of educational reforms he was proposing could not proceed 'unless changes took place simultaneously in the legal system, property rights and the political process' (Eklof and Dneprov, 1993, p 16). Yet, far from receiving general support, his programme of reform faced widespread criticism and, finally, determined opposition when he issued regulations prohibiting pre-military training, political propaganda as well as religious instruction in schools. It became clear that the roots of the fourfold alienation: of school from society, of the pupil from the school, of the teacher from the pupil and of both teachers and pupils from genuine educational involvement were deeply buried in the prevailing socio-political environment. These could not be quickly overcome and required overwhelming support for the liberal-democratic vision of society as a whole, which was manifestly lacking.

Emphatically, proponents of democratic reforms were never lacking in Tsarist Russia or even in the Soviet Union – those such as Stanislav Shatsky, Viktor Shulgin, Konstanty Ushinsky, Leo Tolstoy or Vasily Sukhomlinsky – the difficulty was always that there was not enough social mobilization to carry the reforms through in the face of the vested interests of their opponents. Eduard Dneprov's resignation in December 1992 was a very clear indication that the liberal-democratic vision of a new system of national education was not going to prevail. That was a devastating blow to all those who favoured an entirely new concept of the school curriculum, much more open to liberal tendencies and clearly oriented towards providing a greater scope to individual preferences and aiming at a meaningful rediscovery of personal and human values characteristic of an open society.

Education and the nationalist vision

The nationalist vision of education serving the cause of Russia as a great power which was to be respected and universally recognized as such, has not found an exponent who could be compared with the principal advocates of the liberal-democratic one. However, from those who chose to support it came a clear indication that they firmly believed in the importance of education, particularly its power in consolidating the value system based upon patriotism and a firm commitment to serve the country at all times.

The epistemological consequences of this conviction were self-evident. Of primary importance was the intimate familiarization with Russian history, literature and art, but also the mastering of science and modern technology. This had inescapable consequences for the curriculum and the contents of the school subjects as well as the textbooks that had to match the substance of this vision. Similarly, the teacher was to be seen as a person of great significance, commanding general obedience and respect as a key link in the chain of authority. It was the teacher whose role was to give the direction to the whole process of upbringing and to synchronize all educational efforts to prepare the young generation to serve the nation and the country.

The contrasts between this orientation and the alternative visions in educational terms should be underlined. The real source of the strength of Russia, according to the nationalist vision, is not to be sought in the fields of commercial and financial advancement in close association with the forces of a global capitalist system, often dominated by the interests inimical to Russia; nor is it to be sought in a wasted effort to promote on a worldwide scale a radical ideology which possesses inherent weaknesses and has failed to demonstrate its economic viability. The task of the national system of education is to persuade the younger generation that the country's strength and the national well-being are intimately connected, with everybody developing pride in the mother country's greatness and fostering in the young the necessary self-confidence to be able to construct for the nation an equally great future through their own hard effort and commitment.

Education and the neo-Communist vision

The Communist Party of the Russian Federation faced the problem of a successful reconciliation between the incongruent principles of continuity and transformation within the traditional Marxist–Leninist outlook. This problem has led in the past to fierce debates among Western Marxists (Kolakowski, 1978, pp 220–445). For the neo-Communists in Russia in the 1990s it represented a real challenge. There were bound to be differences of opinion in this matter, in that some former Communists favoured the old system of education as it was before the collapse of the USSR in 1991. In respect of both theory and practice, some were willing to accept certain modifications without, however, changing its essential characteristics. It was clear that theoretical considerations had to be combined with political calculations to ensure maximum appeal to the electorate, particularly to those who were wavering and undecided despite their definite lack of enthusiasm for either the liberal-democratic or the nationalist vision of the future.

Important representatives of the Communist Party of the Russian Republic who were also members of the Duma in the mid-1990s tended to stress the Party's commitment to the old Soviet slogan 'All the very best to our children'. They also viewed the process of the democratization of schools in Russia as a positive trend which they wanted to continue if the neo-Communists came to power in the country. They expressed their willingness to accept the existence of a parallel system of fee-charging schools alongside the free state schools. At the same time they deplored the declining prestige and social standing of the teachers, poorly paid – if at all – since the collapse of the USSR, blaming the capitalistic orientation of the post-Communist governments for the lack of strict control mechanisms which previously ensured adequate funds guaranteeing regular payment of teachers' salaries everywhere. They accepted that there had been negative developments in the USSR under the CPSU, but they argued that the new Communist Party of the Russian Federation could not be held responsible for them. On the other hand, they very strongly criticized the contents of some of the new textbooks published with the help of foreign sources such as the Soros Foundation or the Tempus/Tacis initiatives which they considered to be 'anti-Soviet' because of their pro-market bias and preference for liberal democracy (Muckle, 1998, pp 30–33).

Educational transformation

In terms of educational developments, the transition from the old to the new order in the Russian Federation has proceeded along the stages defined earlier in the chapter as a sequence for the evolution of the state system as a whole, with some modifications.

The stage of the destruction of the old order was most evident in education in terms of the disappearance of direct political control mechanisms over educational establishments. The collapse of the Soviet Union, the dissolution of the CPSU, the disappearance of the formerly dominant political leadership removed the one-dimensional character of the central control apparatus. Yet, subsequently, little could be done in real terms to radically change the indispensable educational foundations without which no educational system can function. Here one must, obviously, think of the epistemological foundations of the knowledge to be learned, the contents of learning, the teaching methods and the role of the teacher. In this respect, removing the old, without at the same time being able to bring in the new structures and patterns can only mean creating a vacuum and inviting a disaster. This must, naturally, be avoided at all cost (Furyaeva, 1994, pp 133–37).

Yet effective transformation of an educational system requires a clear choice of one preferred option, selected and given a solid backing by a clear popular majority, so that action could be taken to put it into operation. It is precisely here that the solution of the problem faced real difficulties in Russia in the 1990s. There was no lack of proposals, in fact the different *kontseptsii* came in by the dozens from the whole of the political spectrum only to be indefinitely postponed or rejected because of the unending disagreements both within the legislature as well as between the legislature and the executive. The resulting stalemate precluded any more fundamental changes in the state system of education as a whole. It should be noted, however, that this did not prevent individual and worthwhile initiatives to improve the quality of learning by very determined heads of schools and dedicated teachers–innovators

(Karakovsky, 1993, pp 18–24).

It also did not render impossible the appearance and subsequent growth of private, fee-charging educational establishments at all levels outside the state system. This was made possible by the regulations issued in the early 1990s, which allowed private enterprise to enter the field of education. The disappearance of the omnipotent and omnicompetent Soviet state provided the opportunity for the formation of new educational establishments of various kinds as a private sector. They were all new creations, starting afresh, without the need to free themselves from the burdensome regulatory framework of earlier times. This was a clear advantage which gave them a good chance of surging forward in terms of their inner structure and organization, the content and methods of studies, freedom of experimentation and adoption of the most effective ways of teaching skills and techniques appropriate for the post-Communist society. Well equipped and possessing members of staff who were first-class teachers – often university teachers – schools and colleges of this kind quickly attained the level of success comparable with similar establishments in the most advanced countries in the West. For their students they opened up the way to well-paid positions in those sectors which were short of properly qualified experts – such areas as business, information technology, banking and finance, computer science, investment, communication, co-operation with foreign countries and the like (Heynemann *et al*, 1995, pp 11–24; Kaufman, 1994, pp 150–55; Sutherland, 1998, pp 58–85).

Meanwhile, the state system of education remained largely as it had been before, progressively more and more short of funds provided from the centre and, for this reason, tending to move in the direction of decentralization and regionalization. Movement in this direction has, not unnaturally, been considered dangerous by all those for whom the unity of the country has always been the most important political, social, economic as well as cultural objective.

Conclusions

The analysis of the path of transition from the old order towards the new one in the Russian Federation clearly indicates that that path is not necessarily a simple course which invariably consists of closely interrelated stages forming a visible logical sequence of purposeful action directed at the attainment of clearly defined and generally accepted new goals. That kind of smooth sequential transition is possible only if in the society in question at least three key conditions are fulfilled:

1. There is sufficient consensus concerning the basic rules of political behaviour which have a built-in mechanism ensuring orderly political change, reliably reflecting the views of the electorate and providing the apparatus for putting the preferences of the majority into concrete action.

2. There are adequate financial resources available to put the proposed changes into operation.
3. Proper allowance is made for the time such changes require to be effective.

Lack of agreement concerning the proper functioning of the state organs of power, inadequate financial provision and a naïve belief that more fundamental changes in society can be accomplished speedily with little effort easily destroy the chances of adoption, implementation and realization of even the most highly commendable plans of reform. This is particularly consequential for education, as a vicious circle is then created in that under such circumstances the schools and other educational establishments have little chance of meaningfully contributing to the overcoming of the difficulties in the long run. Pretending that this is not necessarily the case only obscures the nature of the problem and further delays positive action which must be taken in order to save the country from further degradation and enable it to occupy once more a prominent place in the family of nations.

Note

1. I should stress that I am using the concept of liberal democracy in the Western sense. Paradoxically, in the topsy-turvy world of Russian politics, the political formation led by the ultra-nationalist politician, Vladimir Zhirinovsky is also called the Liberal-Democratic Party.

References

Birzea, C (1994) *Educational Policies in the Countries in Transition*, Council of Europe Press, Strasbourg

Brzezinski, Z (1989) *The Grand Failure: The birth and death of Communism in the twentieth century*, Charles Scribner and Sons, New York

Brzezinski, Z (1993) *Out of Control: Global turmoil on the eve of the 21st century*, Charles Scribner/Stewart, New York

Dneprov, E (1993) Reform of education in Russia and government policy in the sphere of education, *East/West Education*, **14** (l), pp 13–34

Eklof, B and Dneprov, E (eds) (1993) *Democracy in the Russian School: The reform movement in education since 1984*, Westview Press, Boulder, CO

Finer, S (1987 repr) *Comparative Government*, Penguin, London

Furyaeva, T (1994) Children and youth in the policy, science and practice of a society in transition: Russia, in *Education and the Values Crisis in Central and Eastern Europe*, Comparative Studies Series, ed V D Rust, P Knost and J Wichmann, vol 4, pp 131–57, Peter Lang, Frankfurt, Berlin, Bern & New York

Gorbachev, M (1987) *Perestroika: New thinking for our country and the world*, HarperCollins, London

Heyneman, S P et al (1995) *Russia: Education in transition*, The World Bank, Human Resources Division Washington, DC

Holmes, B, Read, G H and Voskresenskaya, N (1995) *Russian Education: Tradition and Transition*, Garland, New York & London

Karakovsky, V A (1993) Russia's schools today and tomorrow, *The Bulletin of the Study Group on Education in Russia, the Independent States and Eastern Europe*, **11** (1), pp 18–24

Kaufman, C (1994) De-Sovietising educational systems: learning from the past, policy and practice, *International Review of Education*, **40** (2), pp 149–58

Kolakowski, L (1978) *Main Currents of Marxism: Its origin, growth and dissolution*, vol III, Clarendon Press, Oxford

Muckle, J (1998) Report of a meeting with representatives of the Education and Science Committee of the Duma of the Russian Federation, *The Bulletin of the Study Group on Education in Russia, the Independent States and Eastern Europe*, **16** (l), pp 30–33

Russian Society of Sociologists, The (1997) *The Future of Russia and the Latest Sociological Approaches*, abstracts of reports submitted to the conference, Moscow, 10–12 February

Service, R (1997) *A History of Twentieth Century Russia*, The Penguin Press, London

Sutherland, J (1998) *Schooling in the New Russia: Innovation and change 1984–95*, Macmillan, London

Tkachenko, E (1994) Educational reform in Russia, in *Educational Policy in Russia and Its Constitutional Aspects*, ed J de Groof, pp 45–56, Acco Leuven, Amersfoort

Tomiak, J J (1992a) Education in the Baltic states, Ukraine, Belarus and Russia, *Comparative Education*, **28** (l), pp 33–44

Tomiak, J J (1992b) General trends in Eastern Europe in West European perspective, in *Recent Trends in Eastern European Education*, ed W Mitter, M Weiss and U Schaefer, German Institute for International Educational Research, Frankfurt am Main

Tomiak, J J (1992c) Implications of political change in Eastern Europe for educational policy development, *Journal of Educational Finance*, **17** (3), pp 19–34

Tomiak, J J (1994) Culture, national identity and schooling in Eastern Europe, in *International Perspectives On Culture and Schooling*, ed E Thomas, symposium proceedings, University of London Institute of Education, London

Tomiak, J J (1997) The Commonwealth of Independent States, *in World Yearbook of Education 1997: Intercultural Education*, ed D Coulby, J Gundara and C Jones, pp 45–55, Kogan Page, London

Williams, C, Chuprov, V and Staroverov, D (eds) (1996) *Russian Society in Transition*, Dartmouth, Aldershot

Yeltsin, B (1990) *Against the Grain: An autobiography*, Jonathan Cape, London

Zyuganov, G (1996) *Veryu v Rossiyu* (I believe in Russia), Voronezh, Moscow

13. Education in transition: Slovenia

Mirjam M Hladnik

The new society

The moment of transition in Slovenia can easily be identified as a radical and violent moment of change in the history of the nation. It happened between April 1990 and October 1991 and consisted of four elements. First, the transformation of a one party, totalitarian political regime into a political system of representative, pluralistic democracy. In April 1990 the first free elections were held after 45 years of one party rule and many different parties that existed before the Second World War re-emerged. Some were formed anew. Second, the replacement of the specific Yugoslav interpretation of a state-run command economy by a liberal, free market economy. The replacement took place under drastically changed circumstances because the Slovenian economy lost most of the Yugoslav market in 1991 and consequently most of its property outside Slovenia. Third, the secession from the Federal Republic of Yugoslavia. Slovenia was one of the eight federal units and the first one that was not prepared to accept the hegemonic ambitions of the Republic of Serbia, the biggest and most powerful constituency of the federation. In December 1990 the referendum on the independent Slovenian State was held and an overwhelming majority of the population voted for independence.

Finally, it was the establishment of the sovereign state for the first time in the history of the Slovenian nation. The state of Slovenia was proclaimed in June 1991. The Yugoslav army tried to annul the declaration of independence by taking control of the borders with tanks and air attacks. It was stopped in a 10 days' war and after intense diplomatic brokering was forced to leave the Slovenian territory in three months. It left Slovenia quietly in October 1991.

The transition in Slovenia is in many ways a radical thrust. But it is not a way out of a catastrophe and it is not defensive in character. It may be so because Slovenia was the wealthiest, most economically developed, socially evolved and ethnically homogenous republic in the Yugoslav federation. But it may be also because the transition process had started long before the federal structure showed the first signs of collapse. Since the beginning of the 1980s, the civil society in Slovenia had been discussing the issues of freedom of speech and association, human rights and rights of minorities, multiparty representative democracy, and connected issues. The discussion finally focused on crucial questions about the federal power system and future economic development. As the political situation in the federation deteriorated the direction of transition for Slovenia and its 2 million inhabitants slowly became clear: independence, democracy and membership of the European Union. The transition turned out to have dramatic, radical and dangerous elements. But in general, it has not been a traumatic experience for society and individuals. It was so because the moment of transition was just the culmination of a much longer process of the change in society that lasted 10 years. And it was so because Slovenia avoided war and could deal with its transformation in normal political, economic and ideological terms.

The role of central government in the reconstruction of society was crucial. After the democratic elections were held in 1990, the parliament and government reflected the pluralistic political reality and its main trait, immaturity. Nevertheless, the goals they had to achieve were extremely serious. The reconstruction of society meant a new political and economic order. To establish it, a new legislation for every vital part of society was needed first. Besides that, the crucial role of central government in managing Slovenian society is part of tradition and therefore generally accepted. The immediate consequences of the transition for the state departments were numerous; they were changed, enlarged, extended, renamed and reconstructed. Many departments did not even exist before independence, like the Ministry of Defence or the Ministry of Foreign Affairs, and had to be organized from scratch. Political parties, unions and many other institutions evolved to constitute the newly established democracy. The number of employees in the departments increased enormously to cope with the economic, political and ideological tasks of a new independent state. Yet there were no dismissals of people who were employed in the departments before the transition.

The economic and social stratification systems changed due to different transitional measures that were trying to establish the liberal free market type of economy. One is the so-called de-nationalization. This meant reversing the confiscation process that took place after the Second World War. At that time private property such as real estate, factories, buildings, land, shops, woods, apartments was gradually changed to state property, which was defined as social property. The problems with the de-nationalization are many. For example, the law says the confiscated property is to be returned in the state in which it was before the confiscation. How to return the building which was renovated and enlarged, how to return the wood which became a national park or was burned down, how to return the field where a highway was built? Among these complicated problems a special place is reserved for the Slovenian Catholic Church. It is to recover many different buildings, vast land, woods and national parks but it is not clear yet how this can be done.

The second important transitional economic measure is so-called privatization. This was the means of distributing what had been left of the social property after the former owners got their nationalized property back. Distribution of the social property was based on the presumption that everybody old enough had contributed to the wealth of the country by working. It meant that everybody was entitled to a fair share of what had been left after the conversion from social to private ownership. The shares were distributed in the form of certificates that one could then 'invest' in a certain factory or business as a shareholder. The process of distribution ended in November 1998. With the de-nationalization and privatization processes the social stratification system has changed in the sense that some people or institutions became rich. There was an incredible rise in the number of companies, firms, and small businesses along the way to transition. There were about 2,500 companies in Slovenia before the transition and now there are approximately 60,000 companies, though many of them are only registered and do not function at all. On the other hand, parts of the population suddenly became poor, mainly due to unemployment. Unemployment hardly existed in the previous regime where social rights, from housing to health service, were based on the employment of a person. There were 28,218 jobless people in 1989, now there are about 130,000. Unemployment affects not only older workers but also young people seeking jobs for the first time.

The political vision of the future had been clear and simple from the beginning of the transitional process. The Slovenian state wanted to become a member of the democratic community of states. Slovenia envisaged itself as an equal part of the new integrated Europe, detached completely from the Balkan region and their historic problems. The path eagerly taken was that of democracy, human rights and freedom, which was to lead Slovenia undoubtedly to a wonderful future. The rhetoric of the participants in the transitional process can best be described by the slogan of the ex-Communist Union Party which took part in the elections in 1990 exclaiming: 'Europe Now'. It suggested two urgent needs. The first need was to leave behind the past and the socialist (as we called it) regime. So Yugoslavia and its unsuccessful political, ideological and economic projects: federalism, brotherhood and unity, worker self-management, non-alignment, were rejected The second need was to jump into the future, democratic statehood, capitalist economy, European integration process. So we triumphantly embraced (West) Europe and its promise that any democratic state would be welcomed into the group of 'old' democracies. The most used label for the abandoned past was the *ancien régime*. The most used metaphor for the foreseeable future was 'little Switzerland'. Apart from 'Europe Now', the political slogans were incredibly abstract, like '2000', or 'From roots we grow'.

Gradually the rhetoric became more sophisticated and less funny because history started to be reinterpreted and the leading roles in the *ancien régime* were reconsidered. The starting point was the Second World War. The period before that, the politically and socially important decades between the wars did not count. They were not politically of use to certain new political parties and pressure groups. What was of use was the attack on the regime, which came to power after the Second World War in a revolutionary, merciless way. It was not enough that the previous regime had collapsed; it also had to be completely denigrated. Through the denigration of the Communist regime, the new political options and actors were to be legitimized and new political power established. The battle sides were the classical democratic sides, Right and Left, though in a specific Slovenian set-up. What was not so classical were the political points they wanted to win from the sharp division of society half a century ago: the anti-fascists and the collaborators. Those on the Left wanted to gain from the legacy of the Communists, respected fighters in the anti-fascist coalition, who liberated the country and afterwards took power, rebuilt the country and made the good life possible. They had to minimize the fact, however, that approximately 10,000 Slovenian collaborators were murdered immediately after the end of the war.

Those on the Right did exactly the opposite. They had to minimize the atrocities of the collaborators and maximize the fact that the Communists had committed atrocities on their way to power. They labelled the whole half of a century a disaster for the Slovenian nation and society. The sad victim of the dispute became the simple and never before questioned truth about fascism and the fight against it. The arguments did not go as far as changing the truth, but went far enough to distort it. The winning slogan in the dispute was reconciliation. Due to its exclusive political meaning and (ab)use in the power battle, reconciliation has not happened yet and it is difficult to see how it can happen in the future.

At the very beginning of the transition, a new political actor appeared on the scene who was far more powerful and experienced than the new or old political parties – the Slovenian Catholic Church. It appeared with its own unique rhetoric, ideology and agenda. With the past blurred enough in the process of the reinterpretation of history to disguise its collaboration with the Nazis during the Second World War, the Church gained most out of the dispute. It started openly to propagate slogans about the Church as the guardian of Slovenians through the centuries of oppression, the bastion against the barbaric 'Turks', the cradle of the national culture. The Church proclaimed itself the source and the vessel of the basis of Slovenian nationhood. For its leading role in the history of Slovenians, it used the most updated argument of Christianity as the basis of the whole European culture. It was stressed that it is not the anti-fascist resistance which entitles Slovenia to membership of the West, but its deep-rooted vivid Christian culture. After 45 years of an atheistic regime which kept its activities constrained to the liturgy only, the Church fiercely reclaimed its traditional political and economic role in society.

The political–cultural thrust of the educational system had to serve the transitional vision. It had to be adjusted to the system that was believed to be typical of the democratic, powerful West. Not just adjusted, but made alike, so that it would be able to educate the same democratic, efficient, good citizens. The complete change of the educational system by a reform project, preparations for which had already started in 1992, was conducted also for another reason. It was the legitimization of the new state, new power elite and new political vision. So the new political vision of the future expressed in the educational system has two components. First is the complete reform of the educational system of pre-university level because the educational system has to be changed according to European standards and criteria. In short, 'Europe Now' in education. Second, the complete ideologization of the educational system because it has been turned into a battlefield where different parties want to win as much political credibility as possible. In other words, the reinterpretation of history in education. Throughout the transition the two components have been intertwined in an inseparable way. The goals and aims of school reform have been discussed only in connection to the different political agendas. And every serious political battle has been fought on the ground of the school reform.

The education system as a cultural message system has an ambiguous role in the Slovenian transitional process. On the one hand, school reform is based on modern democratic values that are accepted in civil society and incorporated into the political vision. On the other hand, they are strongly opposed and the reform based on them continuously attacked. The critics argue that such values convey bare liberal ideas, promote selfish individuality and feed cold, instrumental knowledge. To see what the right values to be promoted via the educational system are, it is enough to look at where the critique of the reform comes from. It comes from the political side that is a combination of Christian democrats and other more right-wing oriented parties. Behind them we find again the powerful Slovenian Catholic Church. So, the critics argue, the right values that the educational system should be based on are Christian values, corporatism, tradition and Christian morality. Again, the reinterpretation of history provides the facts, which deny the existence of any other political and cultural tradition in Slovenia. It wants to prove that only Christianity represents the original, national values of every Slovenian. And because these values were suppressed in the past and uprooted by the *ancien régime*, they deserve to be proclaimed again for what they are even more vociferously.

Today we find in the educational field two opposing visions: modernity, human rights, individualism and secularism on the one hand; and on the other, traditionalism, corporatism, Christian values and anti-secularism. Their only common ground is that both are claimed to be basically and thoroughly European by their advocates. In fact, the focus of the dispute on the political vision as expressed in the education system resides in one simple question: which political party will run the Ministry of Education and Sport? For six years the liberal democrats have run it and the other political side has been trying to gain control over it. Gaining the power to manage it means gaining the power to establish the structure of the education system, to define the content of the core curriculum, to control the teachers, to prescribe its fundamental set of values. But there is even more than that. The Ministry of Education and

Sport is viewed as the most important state department because it provides the mechanisms ultimately to define the desirable interpretation of history. And this is exactly the way power in democracy is legitimized and hegemony is established. It is believed that to hold the Ministry of Education and Sport means to hold the levers of power to influence the souls of people in order to rule them. The Slovenian Catholic Church still regards this as its natural traditional task. And so does the other side. This is the reason both need the power to define their interpretation of tradition and history in the first place. Democracy finally provides them with the right circumstances for the struggle.

The new school

The reform of the whole pre-university education system was carefully prepared by endless comparative surveys of educational systems in Europe. Though it is obvious that no 'European' educational system exists, the main rationale behind the reform is to make the Slovenian educational system comparable to it. The main aim of the reform is national assessment of pupil achievement after basic and secondary school and a newly defined core curriculum. On this level, crucial changes have been made, like the introduction of nine years of basic education instead of eight; national assessment of pupil achievement run by the newly established National Examination Centre; a new structure of the core curriculum with the main emphasis on science, mathematics and languages; renewed syllabuses for 40 subjects in primary school. The main idea of the educational reform is to educate pupils for the democratic, market-oriented society. On this level, it is the rhetoric that counts more than anything else. There is no special subject on the European integration process, democracy or civic education in the new structure of the core curriculum. There is only some emphasis on earlier introduction of foreign languages in basic education, which should enable more pupils to develop competent communication skills. Before the reform foreign languages, mainly English, were introduced in the fifth grade of the eight years of basic education. Now children start to learn foreign languages in the kindergarten and more seriously in the third grade of the elementary school. The main values of the school reform are modern values like children's and human rights, tolerance, responsibility and equality of opportunity. Though they sound completely in tune with the main transitional goal of Slovenian society – to become European and a democratic state – they are strongly disputed reform issues, as described above.

The techniques for quality control in the educational system have been drastically changed. Before the transition the education system was tightly controlled via prescribed curriculum, textbooks and didactic methods that were compulsory. Teachers were controlled regularly by inspectors who checked if their written preparations and their oral teaching met all the required elements of a school year plan. Today teachers are free to choose their own methods of teaching, to arrange the themes by their own timetable, and to use the didactic materials they like. An inspector is allowed to conduct direct surveillance in the classroom only on request. The National Inspectorate for Education and Sport is now a more transparent and accurately defined institution than it used to be. It supervises the implementation of laws and other regulations setting out the organization, financing and provision of activities. Also principals and school councils have to control and monitor the educational process. But the real and thorough quality control comes today from another two different sources: first, the parents; second, the national assessment of pupil achievement.

The most important are parents who conduct everyday quality control. The transition has changed them into competent, educated, well-informed and demanding people. Teachers are no longer supposed to fulfil only the state-prescribed educational goals and aims but also the everyday expectations of their pupils' parents. There are formal hours per week and month for parents to meet the teachers, but the teachers are available any time if parents want to see them. What is interesting is that this is not the rule but the way the relationship in education has been changed. So far, I would describe it as quality control because it has this function. It cannot yet be regarded as a partnership between parents and teachers that is necessary for the successful learning process of every pupil. The parents' surveillance of education and teachers as a big transitional change may sound awkward. In Slovenia the schooling (including university level) used to be free of tuition and remains free. It means that people do not demand certain things or services because they are paying for them directly, but if they think they are entitled to them. What has changed the attitude of parents is the different perspective as a result of social changes. The school is no longer viewed as a state-run and state-defined institution, which is always right and cannot be challenged. It no longer represents the system that was regarded as best for people and could not stand any criticism. Today parents know that they and their children have certain rights and that teachers and school should fulfil their expectations.

The second technique of quality control in the educational system is the national assessment of pupil achievement. With this externally controlled examination system standards of knowledge were introduced that were unknown until the school reform. It now means that teachers are free to choose their own methods of teaching, to arrange the themes by their own timetable, and to use the didactic materials they like. But at the end, their pupils have to master precisely the knowledge that is evaluated through the national assessment of pupil achievement. This is rather problematic because the curriculum content and the standards of knowledge were defined by the traditional academic point of view. They are so extensive that there is hardly any time left for thorough learning and understanding.

In general, the education system has been made publicly transparent in two ways. One is the effort that the Ministry of Education and Sport has been investing in public relations and in the participation of teachers. There are books and booklets, a home page on the Internet and open telephone lines available for those who are interested. Many roundtable discussions were organized to inform people about the new elements and procedures in education or about the educational reform. Special attention has been given to the principals, for whom conferences have been organized regularly in a tourist resort on Adriatic coast. Teachers are organized into so-called study groups where the new rules, recommendations or procedures of the Ministry of Education and Sport are discussed. The Ministry of Education and Sport invites principals and teachers to be partners in conducting the educational reform but in fact the teachers do not have many opportunities to participate due to heavy teaching and administrative loads.

The other way that the education system is open to public scrutiny is by its political relevance, as already described. It constantly receives media attention, though this does not necessarily make it more transparent to the public. The fact that the educational system is in the focus of the political power struggle between the two main political sides makes many of the important educational issues incomprehensible to the public. Many parts of the educational reform were not publicly discussed as educational but only as political issues. They have been hotly debated and have produced more emotional and partisan public reactions than comprehensive and tolerant opinions of its members.

The 'good, the true and the beautiful' in the Slovenian educational system have been changed according to the crucial aims in the transitional process. The formation of the independent state, the implementation of a multi-party system and a market-oriented economy mean that the European dimension has had to be introduced into the education system. The process of change is therefore based on the common European heritage of political, cultural and moral values reflected in human rights, the rule of law and pluralistic democracy. So, the true has become everything that is regarded as 'European' and everything labelled 'Balkan' or 'Southern' has been rejected. I would like to stress that this is not a very drastic change because the Slovenians have always regarded themselves as Europeans, closer to the West in their geographical position and their mind-set than to anything else. Also the standards of knowledge that were introduced with the national assessment of pupil achievement follow the earlier idea that pupils have to memorize as many facts, data and information as possible. What is new is the conviction that this kind of evaluation of knowledge is the best one. It is good for teachers, pupils and parents because it gives them the exact information about the success of the educational process. It makes it transparent and effective. Everybody knows who gives and gets what, and those who master the required knowledge can proceed in the system without any other exams. The definition of knowledge has been partly transformed in subjects like history, geography and literature. The only radical change was the abolition of two subjects: Moral Education in elementary school and Self-management and the Basics of Marxism in the secondary school. This was the first change in education at the beginning of the transition and was done without any word of objection.

However, there is another debate that started together with the transition and has been going on intensely for six years. The demands are connected to the atheistic character of the *ancien régime* and are as follows: the return of the history of Christianity as a part of different subjects in the curriculum; and the establishment of a new subject on religions with an emphasis on Christianity as the most important religion in society. A compromise was reached and a new subject was introduced, called Religions and Ethics. Its aim is not to instruct pupils about a certain religion but to inform them about the different religions in the world. Nevertheless, the heated debate on the content of this subject and especially on who will be allowed to teach it is still continuing for reasons described above.

The beautiful has undoubtedly become technology. A lot of money has been invested in installing information technology in schools and introducing computer literacy programmes. Technology represents modernity, progress and best intentions and is probably the only non-problematic affair in the transitional process of the Slovenian educational system.

In the midst of all this transitional turmoil the university level of education has not changed much. There are two universities in Slovenia, the younger and not so influential university in Maribor and the old authoritarian university in Ljubljana, the capital of Slovenia. There are no newly established private or newly created state universities though there are no legal obstacles to this. The secret is the monopolistic status and attitude of the existing universities, especially the University of Ljubljana. A great fear of competition and new ideas prevents any attempt to change the existing structure and content of the university education. It has stayed unchanged in the transitional current of the whole society except for the ruling procedures, which have been changed to secure the exclusive and omnipotent power of the oldest professors.

I would define the described 'transition-in-education' as a case of *déjà vu*. School reform has once again been conducted for the sake of the legitimization of power and the establishment of hegemony. It is interesting that we find a school reform at the beginning and at the end of the transitional process in Slovenia. After the turmoil of the 1960s many countries tried to solve the problems that enraged students by reforming their educational systems. In Yugoslavia, there were some additional political conflicts to resolve, like the liberal government in Slovenia that was replaced by a hard-line Stalinist team at the beginning of the 1970s. In 1974 the Yugoslav Communist Alliance Congress confirmed the platform for the educational reform in the whole country. There was a long period of thorough surveys, comparative analysis and conceptualizing done by experts and well-known educators before it was prepared. The main declared aim of the school reform was to make education more effective with respect to the economy of the country and to make it really equal opportunities oriented. The reform, which established so-called streaming education, was introduced in Slovenia in 1981. This was the starting point of the long process of the changing of society, which culminated in the moment of transition 10 years later.

The introduction of the school reform provoked an unprecedented reaction in civil society. Opposition to the reform by teachers, academics, parents, students, journalists was very well organized, articulated and extremely brave. The reform of the educational system was nevertheless completed, Gymnasiums were abolished, curricula were changed, many new schools were built, huge investments in technology were made. But it was clear that people did not want the reform because it was obsolete in concept, pretentious in aims, and arrogant in its starting point. A lot of damage was done by streaming education to schools, teachers and pupils. The most crucial result of the school reform, however, was a very positive one. After the long public dispute on school reform the right to have an opinion on public issues was won at the beginning of the 1980s. The right to have an opinion about public issues and to state it without fear of reprisals was the basis of the empowerment and courage of the civil society, which was so crucial when the moment of transition came 10 years later.

What will be the important result of the latest educational reform in Slovenia? The Ministry of Education and Sport has just established the National Evaluation Board that will follow the implementation and the impact of the school reform. I do not believe that changing the curriculum and assessment procedures, increasing the hours for maths and science, and installing computers in schools will solve the educational problems but I will wait for the report of the National Evaluation Board. One important result of the school reform is already clear, however. This is the maintenance of power by a certain political party and the legitimization of a certain political vision, which is so crucial in a time of the transition of society. So far, the liberal democrats and their political vision of the future are secure. But I do not think that this will be the last school reform in Slovenia in the foreseeable future.

14. The new South Africa: idealism, capacity and the market

Nick Taylor and Penny Vinjevold

For most South Africans the most unforgettable picture of their new society was the sight on 10 May 1994 of Nelson Mandela's inauguration as President, standing before the world's assembled dignitaries, with a formation of helicopters of the once-feared South African Air Force flying overhead, trailing the multicoloured flag symbolizing the launch of the new rainbow nation. But the start of the country's transition from apartheid dates back more than four years earlier, when on 2 February 1990 President F W de Klerk announced in parliament the lifting of the ban on all political parties, the release of political prisoners – including Mandela, at that stage in his 28th year of incarceration – and the commitment of his government to finding a democratic end to apartheid.

At the time of writing, at the commencement of the second five-year term of the new government, it is still easier to say what the rainbow nation is against than what it is becoming. While the ideals of the new society roll glibly off the tongue and into legislative and regulative frameworks, these are sometimes very different indeed from what is happening in South African streets, workplaces, homes and schools. The present chapter is an attempt to describe some of these tensions in the education system. But first we turn to a brief look at the apartheid heritage of schooling, which to a very significant extent constrains what is possible in the immediate future.

Apartheid education

Apartheid was not born with the National Party government instituted in 1948, but 300 years earlier when the first Dutch settlers landed in the Cape, and reinforced by successive Dutch, British and (briefly) French colonial rulers. It is certainly true that the Nationalists took racial discrimination to new heights of cruelty on a grand scale and obsessive pettiness concerning the smallest detail. The principal manifestations of this system in the education sphere were:

1. *Fragmentation.* At the time of its disbandment in 1994 apartheid education was administered by 17 distinct ethnically-based departments: one for each of the 4 'independent homelands', one for each of the 8 'self-

governing territories' (a precursor to 'independence'), one for African students who remained in the 87 per cent of the country constituting 'white' South Africa, which in turn had a further 3 structures for 'whites', 'Coloureds' and 'Indians', respectively, and a Department of National Education responsible for broad policy.

2. *Glaring inequalities across departments.* In 1990, for example, average per capita expenditure on white students was nearly five times that on Africans. These averages marked further disparities within the different subsystems: thus, while some black schools in the townships could be relatively well resourced, in many rural areas schools may consist of no more than mud buildings in which blackboards, books and stationery are almost unheard of.

3. An ethos and management system dominated by *extreme authoritarianism* (a management training programme which all senior, middle and lower level managers were required to attend in the mid-1980s was appropriately named 'Top Down'). The ideological underpinnings of this culture were provided by Fundamental Pedagogics, a so-called science of education, prominently associated with the University of South Africa – a distance institution which provided by far the largest proportion of both pre- and in-service teacher education – and propagated on all universities and teacher colleges, with the exception of the English-speaking 'liberal' campuses.

The school system experienced exceptional growth in the last three decades, partly as a result of pressure from business for a better skilled workforce, and partly too as the result of an effort to increase the legitimacy of the apartheid state, but largely as a result of political pressure from black youth. Table 14.1 shows this growth: while there was a fourfold growth in the number of black pupils between 1970 and 1996, the number of white pupils increased by only 20 per cent.

Table 14.1 Growth in the South African school population, by race, between 1970 and 1996

	Black	White	Coloured	Indian	Total
1970	2,545,755	812,961	515,336	157,891	4,031,943
1976	3,697,441	903,062	655,347	188,008	5,443,858
1996	9,500,000	980,000	910,000	280,000	11,670,000

Source: Taylor *et al* (1999)

Ironically, the expansion of schooling for black youth, particularly at the secondary level, fuelled opposition to apartheid. Schools, of manifestly inferior quality to those in white areas, provided sites of mobilization for large numbers of students and there was an air of inevitability about the Soweto student uprising in 1976. Apartheid education thus provided the seeds of its own downfall. Unfortunately, it also provided the foundation for one of the most intractable problems faced by the new government. Between 1976 and 1994 black schools were sites of political struggle in which frequent and sustained class boycotts, strong opposition by teachers and students to school visits by district staff, high rates of staff and student absenteeism, and endemic vandalization of school property led to what Christie (1998) has called a school culture inimical to learning and teaching. Christie defines this culture as 'breakdown of rhythmical, disciplined learning and teaching, formally structured in time and space' (1998, p 289); it is characterized by four features:

1. poor physical and social facilities;
2. organizational problems;
3. poor school/community relationships; and
4. poor relationships between the education department and the schools.

A major manifestation of the systemic malfunction caused by the above factors is the internal inefficiency of the public schooling system, as shown by learner progression rates. The most striking statistic in this regard is the calculation by Crouch and Mabogoane (1997) that it takes, on average, 18 learner years of effort to produce one Grade 12 enrollee. Another indicator is that, although South Africa spends a significantly higher proportion of its operating budget on education (budgeted at R48.5 billion, or 22.1 per cent in 1999–2000), than countries like Chile, Egypt, Portugal and Turkey, a far smaller proportion of South African school students go on to tertiary education (Collings, 1999).

Expansion of schooling in South Africa is relatively recent and, given the rapid rate of this growth, the fragmented and inequitable nature of the apartheid system, and the destabilizing effects of resistance, consolidation of the sector was never achieved. It remains one of the highest priorities of the new government to effect this consolidation, through the establishment of a functioning bureaucracy at all levels, and the improvement of operational efficiency.

The first five years of democracy

Achievements

During the first five-year term of the new government three areas of activity were prioritized: reorganizing the 17 apartheid departments of education into a single national department and 9 provincial departments; achieving high levels of representation amongst staff at all levels of the system; and establishing a policy framework which embraces a progressive vision for school reform.

Progress to date in addressing the massive task of restructuring the apartheid education system represents a major achievement for the new government. Apart from the establishment of 10 new departments much progress has been made in terms of changing the composition of the public sector so as to better reflect the racial composition of the country, although progress has been uneven across departments (Munslow *et al*, 1997). (The gender situation is considerably less favourable, with few women in senior management positions.)

In the policy arena the new government has embraced a progressive vision for systemic change, and has made much progress in establishing a number of key policy instruments in the following areas:

1. *Constitutional rights.* The new constitution establishes basic education, and equal access to educational institutions as the right of all citizens (*Constitution of the Republic of South Africa*, 1993).
2. *Administration.* Several policy documents reflect a strong commitment towards adopting new, more participative and democratic ways of thinking about the nature and role of government (DOE, 1995; DPSA, 1995; Presidential Review Commission, 1998).
3. *Qualifications.* The South African Qualifications Authority Act (SAQA, 1995) is the first step towards establishing a coherent framework for the recognition of all education qualifications. Structures which will give effect to the framework have begun to be established.
4. *School governance.* The South African Schools Act (DOE, 1996) makes provision for the establishment of school governing bodies through which parents will exercise considerable authority and responsibility in the governance of schools.
5. *School funding.* The National Norms and Standards for School Funding (DOE, 1998a) establishes principles for redressing past imbalances in financing schools.
6. *Curriculum. The Foundation Phase Policy Document* (DOE, 1997a) and numerous other documents establish the basis for a revolutionary approach to teaching and learning.
7. *Teacher management.* Four instruments – *Norms and Standards for Educators* (DOE, 1998b), *Employment of Educators Act* (DOE, 1998c), *Development Appraisal of Teachers* (ELRC, 1998) and *Duties and Responsibilities of Educators* (DOE 1998d) – aim to align regulations governing teacher qualifications, certification and management, and make provision for establishing a system of performance management for teachers.
8. *Assessment. The Assessment Policy in the General Education and Training Band* (DOE, 1998e) seeks to align assessment with the aims of the new curriculum.
9. *Language.* Mother tongue instruction and respect for all 11 official languages are encouraged by the policy of additive bilingualism (DOE, 1997b).

10. *Gender*. The Report of the Gender Equity Task Team (Wolpe *et al*, 1997) makes recommendations for the establishment of gender equity measures throughout the education system.

Taken together, these documents represent an impressively coherent vision for the thoroughgoing reorganization of South African schooling. The language of the new policy framework is liberatory rather than instrumental. Thus, in the areas of governance and management, emphasis is placed on the need for the civil service and other structures to become more participatory and developmental, rather than focusing on building effective, efficient and accountable systems to ensure delivery.

In effect, these and other new policies tend to foreground the transformation of public schooling and push into the background the strengthening of the foundations necessary for the efficient functioning of the system, such as the institution of procedures for sound human resource and financial management, information collection, and textbook distribution. The daunting task of building the human and systemic capacity which form the foundations on which innovation depends, lies ahead. The following section illustrates some of the challenges faced by government, particularly at the provincial level, in fulfilling this task.

Operational capacity

One of the most revealing indicators of both the differences in management capacity across the provinces, and the high levels of mismanagement in the weaker provincial Departments of Education, is given by the extent to which budget figures were achieved for the 1996–97 financial year. Crouch and Mabogoane (1997) estimate total over-expenditure by the nine provinces to have been some R8.4 billion, or 23 per cent of the R36.7 billion budget. These budget overruns were caused by large increases in spending, mainly in the field of personnel, where 90 per cent of provincial budgets are dedicated to salaries. Estimates for 1998–99 indicate that the situation had further deteriorated, with provinces allocating between 88 per cent and 97 per cent on staff salaries (*Business Day*, 1999a). This situation has had disastrous effects on non-salary expenditure, reducing the money available for textbooks, for example, from R895 million in 1995–96 to R80 million in 1997–98 (Vinjevold, 1999a).

There are clear indications that some of the provincial systems fall into the category described by Munslow *et al* (1997) as being reconciled to gross inefficiency, maladministration and chaos. Evidence for this conclusion includes the existence of thousands of 'ghost' teachers (fictitious persons drawing real salaries) in some of the provinces, and very low levels of productivity amongst teachers and other education officials. Government impatience with these features of the education administration is reflected in the extraordinary outburst against the teaching corps in September 1998, led by then Deputy President (now President) Mbeki (*Sunday Times*, 1998) and followed in close order by the Ministers of Education, and Post and Telecommunications, and the General Secretary of the SA Communist Party. In these circumstances, McLennan (1997) notes, the establishment of order must be the first priority on government's reform agenda. Whether the education system is able to institute systems for the control and regulation of routine functions, while simultaneously achieving all aspects of its reform vision must be open to question.

Nevertheless, notable gains have been made on both fronts. Thus, improvements in financial management in all provinces led to a widespread consensus ahead of Minister Manual's budget speech on 17 February 1999 that significant progress has been made in controlling education spending. For example, according to Reserve Bank figures, in December 1998 the provinces' combined bank overdrafts stood at R1.6 billion, compared with R2.8 billion in the previous year (*Business Day*, 1999b). At the same time impressive equity gains have been achieved in the allocation of spending. First, spending on social services has increased significantly as a proportion of total budget (Crouch and Mabogoane, 1997). Second, a significant internal redistribution within the education system is in process, with inequities in budgetary allocations between provinces appreciably reduced between 1990 and 1996 (ibid). Whether these increases in inputs can be translated into quality improvements is one of the greatest challenges facing the second five-year term of democratic South Africa.

Transformational initiatives: two case studies

The policy initiatives listed above give a flavour of the kinds of transformation priorities targeted by the new government. We now turn to a more detailed analysis of the challenges of implementation through an examination of two key areas of reform: the curriculum, and language policy and practice. This discussion will highlight three general difficulties encountered in the transformation of any kind of social endeavour, but particularly of schooling: the attitudes of those on whom successful change depends, the human resource capacity required for implementation, and the incongruence between market forces and transformational ideals.

Curriculum

Three cardinal goals animate the new curriculum for schools launched in 1998 under the title Curriculum 2005 (DOE, 1997a):

1. The devolution of initiative to all actors in the system: to provinces, districts and schools for the formulation of appropriate curriculum frameworks, to students for taking responsibility for their own learning, and,

above all, to teachers as facilitators of all the processes and products of teaching and learning. Thus, national curricula are framed at very high levels of generality so as to provide space for interpretation by teachers.

2. Targeting higher order learning: thus, in addition to the acquisition of simple information, students will be expected to develop problem-solving and other complex skills, such as analysis, synthesis, critique and conjecture.

3. Foregrounding everyday knowledge, in the form of learner experience, as the basis for developing school knowledge structures and applying these to the solution of non-routine problems and the generation of new knowledge.

In short, the new curriculum aims to be radically constructivist in its epistemology and radically democratic in its management of knowledge. The new government is attempting to move from a regime of strict surveillance and control over what counts as knowledge and who may access it, to the empowerment of all citizens.

The problem with this kind of curriculum is that it depends heavily for its success on teachers who are not only willing to take responsibility, but are able to exercise professional judgement of a very high order. Empirical research conducted under the auspices of the President's Education Initiative (PEI) indicates that at present the majority of South African teachers fall far short of both requirements (Taylor and Vinjevold, 1999). The problem is not that teachers are resistant to the ideals of the new curriculum: indeed, there is evidence that the majority of educators embrace these enthusiastically, and even among those formerly privileged by apartheid there is no significant resistance to the level of goals. But two serious and closely related obstacles do exist. First, it would appear that the majority of the country's teachers have a long way to go before they begin to accept personal responsibility for the processes and outcomes of learning; before they move from an external locus of control where they blame others for their problems and expect the solutions to be handed down to them, to a situation where they exercise initiative and begin to shape and direct what happens in their classrooms and schools. While these attitudes are entirely understandable, given the pervasive effects of apartheid, they will not be overturned overnight.

The second problem relates to the knowledge resources of teachers. The firmest conclusion emerging from the PEI research project is that teachers' poor conceptual knowledge of the subjects they are teaching is a fundamental constraint on the quality of teaching and learning activities, and consequently on the quality of learning outcomes. Implementing classroom practices that result in learning that is more effective and intelligent is not a question of ideology or will on the part of teachers. As we have said, teachers by and large support the intentions of the new curriculum, but lack the knowledge resources to give effect to these in the classroom. No amount of exhortation by politicians or pedagogical guidance by curriculum planners, university and college academics or NGOs is likely to change this situation, unless the knowledge base of teachers is simultaneously strengthened. This is a fundamental systemic problem which affects and limits interventions aimed at improving all aspects of teaching and learning.

In the area of curriculum development, teachers observed by the PEI studies do not have the knowledge base to interpret the broad guidelines of Curriculum 2005 nor to ensure that the everyday approach prescribed by the new curriculum will result in learners developing sound conceptual frameworks. These frameworks are the foundations of the knowledge, skills and values envisaged by the new curriculum policies. In these circumstances, the development and distribution of learning programmes that specify the knowledge required by subject and grade, within a systematic framework, would seem to be an urgent priority. Such knowledge frameworks are essential, not only to devise daily teaching and assessment activities, but also to guide the developers of learning materials and of standardized assessment instruments.

On the issue of pedagogy, many teachers model the surface forms of learner-centred activities, apparently without understanding the learning theories underlying them, and certainly without using them as a medium for enabling learners to engage with substantive knowledge and skills. These methods frequently interfere with student learning, by providing distractions from the core conceptual issues. Consequently, little is learnt. The principal pedagogical question is not whether democratic forms of classroom practice – such as group work or discussion between learners – is taking place, but whether all forms of classroom activity are centred on learning, and result in students consolidating their knowledge and developing new understandings.

The picture regarding what the students observed by the PEI researchers know and can do is dismal. At all levels investigated by PEI projects the conceptual knowledge of students is well below that expected at the respective grades. Furthermore, students are infrequently required to engage with tasks at any but the most elementary cognitive level, and consequently the development of higher order skills is stunted. Books are very little in evidence and reading is rare. Writing is also infrequent and, when practised by students, hardly ever progresses beyond single words or short phrases. The single most worrying observation is the evidence suggesting that many teachers are unsure as to whether reading is specified as an outcome of Curriculum 2005, and that, as a result, some are not teaching reading as an explicit activity.

Teaching, learning and assessment are so closely related in the classroom that they are often not separable into distinct activities. It follows that, if teachers do not possess the knowledge frameworks required to construct learning activities appropriate to their students, then they will also not be competent in exercising the kinds of professional judgements on which all assessments rest. Under these conditions, the immediate development of sets of graded assessment items, in all learning areas and at all grade levels, is likely to be the most valuable assistance that can be provided to teachers in the short term. Such item banks will provide exemplars on the levels of conceptual knowledge and cognitive tasks appropriate to the different grades.

One of the most urgent priorities must be the establishment of quality assurance mechanisms at all levels of schooling, but particularly the systemic assessments envisaged by the Department of Education at Grades 3, 6 and 9 (DOE, 1998e). Given the evidence indicating a failure of schools to impart basic skills in the foundation phase, a simple assessment of literacy and numeracy performance at the Grade 3 level is probably the single most important step required to diagnose the extent of this problem, set standards for teachers, and establish a benchmark against which the impact of the new curriculum can be measured. Similarly, research into factors which inhibit or promote the learning of basic literacy and numeracy in the foundation phase must rate as one of the highest research priorities in the schooling sector.

In the longer term, the quality of teaching and learning can only be improved if the knowledge foundations of teachers are systematically built. Pre- and in-service programmes must teach and deepen conceptual knowledge and higher order skills in all learning areas for both primary and high school teachers. It would appear that, without this foundation, teacher development programmes on curriculum development, pedagogy, assessment, and the construction and/or use of learning materials will find little ground for purchase.

Language policy and practices

The positive effects of mother tongue instruction on learning and the self-esteem of learners have become conventional wisdom in education circles. In addition, since the recognition of the 11 major South African languages as official languages is enshrined as a fundamental right in the constitution, it follows that it is incumbent on government to promote all 11 languages in the country's schools. This the Department of Education has attempted to do through its policy of additive bilingualism, where provision is made for all children to obtain instruction in their mother tongues, and to learn one or more of the other official languages as school subjects (DOE, 1997b). The problem with this policy is that, in keeping with the devolution of authority to school governing bodies, language policy is decided at the school level, where the aspirations of parents do not accord with the multicultural intentions of national policy.

Mother tongue instruction has been tried over many years in South Africa and particularly by the apartheid government. The apartheid state made significant efforts to create optimal conditions for mother tongue instruction – ethnically homogeneous homelands, neighbourhood schools, and single language teacher colleges. All these attempts at mother tongue instruction were undermined and resisted in various ways.

The demise of apartheid and the accompanying elimination of the restrictions on mobility, have led to increasingly heterogeneous classes and schools. In these circumstances the ideal of mother tongue instruction is becoming increasingly difficult to achieve. The PEI research (Vinjevold, 1999b) shows that, with few exceptions, teachers and parents are uniformly desirous of English as medium of instruction, chiefly because they regard English as a means to gaining access to the mainstream national and global society. In the field of language, official government policy is guided by the best research knowledge and the best political intentions. However, it is directly at odds with market forces in the form of parental perceptions and aspirations. Under these circumstances, it would seem wise for government to accept the inevitable and prepare schools and teachers to deliver instruction in English.

Competence on the part of both teachers and learners in the language of instruction is crucial for effective teaching and learning. It follows that initial teacher development programmes must have as a central component the development of linguistic competence in the language of teaching. As an overwhelming number of South African classrooms are moving towards English as medium of instruction, the English language component of initial teacher training courses should be a central feature of all pre- and in-service courses. Furthermore, a knowledge by teachers of learners' primary language facilitates learning and improves relationships between teachers and learners. For this reason initial teacher education courses should include a compulsory component of a major language of the region in addition to the language of instruction.

As it seems likely that there will be low levels of English linguistic competence amongst teachers for the foreseeable future, it is important to investigate the factors that will optimize teaching and learning under these conditions. For example:

- ways of mediating knowledge between teachers and learners through teacher assistants who speak the language of pupils;
- bridging classes in the language of instruction; and
- the use of storybooks and other textbooks and learning materials.

Conclusion

During the first five years of South Africa's first democratic government the Department of Education has restructured the administration of schooling at the highest levels and established a coherent progressive policy framework. These are impressive achievements, given the extent to which apartheid education had become entrenched, not only in the spheres of administration and policy, but at all levels of practice as well. The new policy vision strikes a balance between developing excellence for competing in the global society, on the one hand, and expanding real educational opportunity, on the other. The devolution of responsibility to provinces and schools and high-skill curriculum goals are directed towards promoting excellence, while the drive to equity is promoted by compensatory funding formulas, affirmative staffing practices, and multi-cultural language policies and curriculum processes.

Progress towards both kinds of educational goals has to date been severely constrained by institutional malfunction in all parts of the system. Improving systemic efficiency will undoubtedly be a major objective during the second term of the new government. And the extent to which this is achieved is likely to depend in large measure on finding the right balance in four areas: between authoritative and devolutionary management practices, between operating and staff costs, between prescriptive and constructivist curriculum and assessment activities, and between market and multicultural considerations in language usage. Above all, policy inclinations based on the best political intentions must be tempered with the needs of pupils, teachers, schools and parents, as determined by careful research into the conditions into which reform is launched.

References

Business Day (1999a) Provinces are starting to make headway on debt: but rising staff costs are hampering capital expenditure and service provision plans, 21 January

Business Day (1999b) Manuel slays SA's provincial beasts, 15 February

Christie, P (1998) Schools as (Dis)Organisations: the 'breakdown of the culture of learning and teaching' in South African schools, *Cambridge Journal of Education*, **28** (3)

Collings, J (1999) Poor returns from the lion's share of funding, *Financial Mail*, 19 September

Constitution of the Republic of South Africa (1993) *Act 200 of 1993*, Government Printer, Pretoria

Crouch, L and Mabogoane, T (1997) *Key Numerical Indicators 1991–1996*, Centre for Education Policy Development, Evaluation and Management, Johannesburg

Department of Education (DOE) (1995) *White Paper on Education and Training*, *Government Gazette*, **357** (16312), Government Printer, Pretoria

DOE (1996) *The South African Schools Act, Act 84 of 1996*, Government Printer, Pretoria

DOE (1997a) *Foundation Phase (Grades R to 3): Policy Document*, Department of Education, Pretoria

DOE (1997b) *Language in Education Policy, Government Gazette*, **383** (17997), Government Printer, Pretoria

DOE (1998a) *National Norms and Standards for School Funding*, Department of Education, Pretoria

DOE (1998b) *Norms and Standards for Educators*, Department of Education, Pretoria

DOE (1998c) *Employment of Educators, Act 1245 of 1998*, Government Printers, Pretoria

DOE (1998d) *Duties and Responsibilities of Educators*, Department of Education, Pretoria

DOE (1998e) *Assessment Policy in the General Education and Training Band. Grades R to 9 and ABET, Government Gazette*, **402** (19640), Government Printer, Pretoria

DPSA (Department of Public Service and Administration) (1995) *White Paper on the Transformation of the Public Service, Government Gazette*, **365** (16838), Government Printer, Pretoria

ELRC (Education Labour Relations Council) (1998) *Development Appraisal of Teachers*, Department of Education, Pretoria

McLennan, A (1997) Into the future: restructuring the public service, in *Managing Sustainable Development in South Africa*, ed P FitzGerald, A McLennan and B Munslow, Oxford University Press, Cape Town

Munslow, B, FitzGerald, P and McLennan, A (1997) Sustainable development: visions and realities, in *Managing Sustainable Development in South Africa*, ed P FitzGerald, A McLennan and B Munslow, Oxford University Press, Cape Town

Presidential Review Commission (1998) *Developing a Culture of Good Governance*, Report of the Presidential Review Commission on the Reform and Transformation of the Public Service in South Africa, Government Printer, Pretoria

SAQA (South African Qualifications Authority) (1995) *Act No. 58 of 1995*, Government Printer, Pretoria

Sunday Times (1998) Teachers who live by the rules of criminals, 13 September

Taylor, N and Vinjevold, P (1999) Teaching and learning in South African schools, in *Getting Learning Right: Report of the President's Education Initiative research project*, ed N Taylor and P Vinjevold, Joint Education Trust, Johannesburg

Taylor, N *et al* (1999) Systemic and institutional contexts of schooling, in *Getting Learning Right: Report of the President's Education Initiative research project*, ed N Taylor and P Vinjevold, Joint Education Trust, Johannesburg

Vinjevold, P (1999a) Learning materials, in *Getting Learning Right: Report of the President's Education Initiative research project*, ed N Taylor and P Vinjevold, Joint Education Trust, Johannesburg

Vinjevold, P (1999b) Language issues in South African classrooms, in *Getting Learning Right: Report of the President's Education Initiative research project*, ed N Taylor and P Vinjevold, Joint Education Trust, Johannesburg

Wolpe, A, Quinlan, O and Martinez, L (1997) *Gender Equity in Education: Report of the Gender Equity Task Team*, Department of Education, Pretoria

15. South Korea

Terri Kim

This chapter outlines the story, from 1992, of the South Korean state's new visions of the future, the current economic and cultural changes, the shifts in the cultural valuation of knowledge and the new educational reforms.

It is suggested that 1992 is the latest moment of transition in South Korea. This was when a civilian government took power and signalled the end of 30 years of military regimes. Those military regimes have often been given credit for the country's economic growth and have been simultaneously condemned for political repression. In assuming the presidency of the new civilian government, Kim Young Sam promised to make a break with the authoritarian practices of the past, eliminate bribery in government, and make government more open and accessible to the people. The long-term strategy was to weaken the political power of the military itself.

In his immediate campaign for 'clean government' Kim concentrated on disclosing government corruption and punishing high-ranking civil servants and hundreds of public officials. Also, business leaders, former military leaders, and several MPs were brought to trial (McCann, 1997, pp 10–14). The most dramatic event in this process was the trials which began in 1996 of the two former Presidents, Chun Doo Hwan and Roh Tae Woo, on charges of mutiny, sedition, corruption and bribery.

The overall popularity of the new civilian government was, however, low. Leading opinion makers in South Korea were cynical about the arrest of the former Presidents and the punishments. The civilian government's new motto, 'Correct and rebuild South Korean history' (*Yerksa Baro Sewooki*) was seen as an attempt to gain popularity and distract public attention from Kim Young Sam's own involvement in political corruption.

There were also problems with overall economic performance from the early 1990s. Growth in GNP fell from 8.4 per cent in 1991 to 4.8 per cent in 1992, the lowest in 12 years, followed by a 17.4 per cent increase in wages (National Statistical Office, ROK, 1993). South Korea seemed to be losing its international competitiveness. There was a widespread sense that the South Korean 'miracle' had reached an end. A series of disasters occurred in 1993: for example, gas explosions in Seoul and Taegu, the collapse of the 15-year-old Songsu Bridge over the Han River in Seoul, and the collapse of the Sampoong Department Store resulting in over 650 deaths. Charges were made that the disasters were caused by poor engineering and ethical weaknesses in Korean industry. Public demands were made for greater economic justice, social welfare and environmentally sound and sustainable growth.

New visions of the future and changes in the state's political and economic apparatus

Against this background, the civilian government affirmed the vision of 'Correcting and rebuilding South Korean history'. The vision was threefold: 1) the reunification of the two Koreas; 2) the internationalization and globalization of the South Korean economy and culture; and 3) the development of a free market economy balanced with liberal democracy. Accordingly, President Kim Young Sam proposed a first summit meeting between the leaders of the two Koreas as an initial step towards reunification. However, the sudden death of the North Korean leader, Kim Il Sung, in July 1994 frustrated this idea.

North Korea successfully maintained its regime (by a father–son succession) and its ideological position against South Korea and the United States. After the sudden collapse of Soviet influence in 1991, and the subsequent and rapid absorption of the former Communist economies into global markets, North Korea made no substantial adjustment to the end of the cold war; its troops entered the demilitarized zone in 1996 and it fired a missile into Japanese airspace in 1998 (*The Korea Herald*, 9 January 1999). However, while maintaining its political and military hardline, North Korea had to increase contact with the outside world to prevent economic collapse. North Korean foreign trade has involved South Korea as well as Japan, Germany and other countries (McCann, 1997, p19). Economic co-operation between South and North Korea has shown notable signs of increase – except for a short drop in 1998 due to the South Korean economic crisis (*Joong Ang Ilbo*, 22 April 1999). The North Korean economy was already on the verge of collapse from the mid-1990s, and recently famine occurred. There has been an increase in the number of North Korean defectors – among whom were high-ranking political figures and their relatives (*Far Eastern Economic Review*, 26 October 1995). This increased further the sense of political crisis and insecurity in South Korea.

Under the same slogan, 'Correcting and rebuilding Korean history', the South Korean civilian government (1992–97) led by Kim Young Sam was determined to achieve *Segyehwa* (globalization). His vision of globalization, however, was based on popular views of globalization at that time such as the rise of a borderless transnational economy, the new revolution in information communications and technology, and lifelong learning (Kim, Young Sam, 1996, pp 7–16). The civilian government asserted that the principles of national development in the era of globalization must be fundamentally different from those of the past era of modernization and industrialization. According to this view, internationalization was a concept for the 19th and 20th centuries, whereas globalization is the concept of the knowledge-intensive era of the new century (Chang, Hyun, 1998, pp 6–7). National opinion supported the political rhetoric about globalization, even though there seemed to be lack of awareness about how to achieve it. Nevertheless, President Kim Young Sam declared 1994 to be a milestone in the pursuit of economic globalization (Presidential television address on New Year's Day). Since then, proposals for globalization have come from various government ministries, scholars and members of the Federation of Korean Industries. The government has developed both international and domestic policies to attain globalization.

At the international level, globalization policy has focused on making South Korea a more visible and influential member of international society. In the name of globalization, the government sought ways to improve the international image of South Korea and its level of international communication. One measure was to strengthen the work of the Korea Foundation overseas. Another measure was to join, as the second Asian nation (after Japan), the OECD in 1996.

The civilian government's domestic response to the external pressure of globalization and free market economies was expressed in its project of liberalization and internationalization of the domestic economy. The civilian government tried to reform the economic system before South Korea was forced to open its domestic market to foreign commodities and services. To cope with the new regional trading blocs – such as the European Union (EU), North American Free Trade Agreement (NAFTA) and Asia Pacific Economic Cooperation (APEC), as well as transnational corporations (TNCs) – the civilian government in South Korea intended to reform the earlier model of a state-guided and protected economy and to promote a free market economy.

Since 1994 there has been rapid reconstruction of political and economic institutions in South Korea. For example, as a first step towards economic liberalization, the civilian government dissolved its Economic Planning Board, which had been the main body for economic policy-making in South Korea from the 1960s. The Kim Young Sam government attacked the current banking system. The reform disclosed corrupt connections between banks and business borrowers. A lack of transparency and accountability had permitted corruption in capital accumulation by the *chaebols* – the large conglomerates – through privileged loans or taxes, labour control, and protection from outside competition; in turn, business leaders had provided the political funds to prolong military governments (Cotton, 1995, pp 83–94). These close links between the *chaebols*, the banks and military governments in South Korea used to be thought necessary for rapid economic development. With hindsight, this kind of alliance between the *chaebols* and the government is now blamed for the current economic crisis in South Korea. However, the new monetary policies meant the bankruptcy of small and medium-sized businesses and simultaneously undesirable expansion of the *chaebols*. With the increase in their economic power, the *chaebols* became more politically independent of the state than before.

The urgent need for genuine economic restructuring was already visible, before the major economic crisis of November 1997. Subsequently, as a condition of the International Monetary Fund's (IMF) rescue package of a record $58 billion on 3 December 1997, South Korea was expected to go through a restructuring process. The new vision of the future by the Kim Young Sam government had to fit within the Structural Adjustment Programme imposed by the IMF and the World Bank.

Amid the economic crisis, the civilian government led by Kim Young Sam ended in charges of corruption and in public humiliation. The successor of Kim Young Sam was another civilian, Kim Dae Jung, the leader of the opposition party and the most visible dissident in the country, who earlier had been imprisoned and exiled.

Assuming the presidency in the economic crisis in 1998, Kim Dae Jung proclaimed a new state vision of the future: 'A Second Nation-Building' (*Je Yi-ey Kuen Kook*). Unlike the former civilian government led by Kim Young Sam, which concentrated on condemning the faults of the past, this new civilian government claimed political legitimacy and credibility from its ideas about the future. Despite the difficult economic situation of individuals, the new slogan has seemed to be effective enough in convincing the public of the necessity of socio-economic restructuring process for the survival of the nation.

Besides its vision of the future, the government's slogan was also a means to legitimize the new governing elite who are from the Cholla province, which has been oppressed politically for more than 1,000 years in the history of Korea. To reduce this chronic regional friction in Korean politics, Kim Dae Jung mandated a bureaucratic re-organization, immediately after his election. Overall, this reflects a sudden shift of power in the state apparatus in a moment of transition.

Within its own political rhetoric of 'the second nation-building', the new civilian government has officially advocated 'The Third Way' – borrowing the phrase of the Blair government in the United Kingdom – to combine free market ideology with new social democracy. President Kim asserts: 'We will convert from authoritarianism to democracy and change from a government-controlled system to a free market system. We will shift from nationalism to globalism and move away from confrontation between North Korea and South Korea and seek national security and reconciliation simultaneously' (*Time Magazine*, 17 August 1998, p 21). Subsequently, President Kim Dae Jung has devised a new term, '*Djnomics*', which has become the central theme of the present economic agenda in South Korea: to construct transparent corporate governance, prudent financial management, co-operative labour relations and efficient government administration (The Ministry of Finance and Economy, 1999, pp 51–66). In the current process of making the South Korean economy a free-market system, the previous role of the government and its political and economic apparatus are changing with the shift from a highly nationalistic command economy. In the 'sweeping structural reforms', the Kim Dae Jung government has decided to sell the first Korean bank to a foreign enterprise. The government's restructuring programmes also include the *chaebols*.

By 1999, a year after it verged on default, South Korea seems to have survived successfully the most difficult moment of the economic crisis. The country has already reduced indebtedness, upgraded its international credit rating, stabilized its currency, reduced interest rates and begun the steps deemed necessary by the IMF to restore economic vitality.

Changes in the social and economic stratification systems and their cultural impact

Thus, the political and economic transition in South Korea which started in 1992 has been speeded up by the current restructuring process after the major economic crisis of 1997. On 5 December 1997, the IMF and the South Korean government made an agreement on the Structural Adjustment Programmes, mentioned earlier, that required austere monetary measures, restructuring of the financial and banking sector, the opening of the stock market, a market-oriented macro-economic policy, deregulation, trade liberalization, flexibility of the labour market, and the reduction or elimination of government intervention (IFWEA, 1999). Accordingly, the government is compelling the privatization of Korea Telecom, Korea Electronic Power, POSCO (which is the largest steel maker in Korea), Korea Heavy Industry (which is a shipbuilding company), and state-owned universities. Privatization is now accompanied by foreign investment. Private sector institutions of various kinds are now open to foreign investors. For example, Volvo took over Samsung Heavy Equipment in early 1998. In the stock market, the number of shares owned by foreign investors has been increasing rapidly.

In this restructuring, forced retirement, and occupational retrenchment were common. It became usual for employers to insist that workers accept so-called 'voluntary retirement'. The unemployment rate has risen quickly. In November 1997 right after the economic crisis the unemployment rate was 2.9 per cent, equivalent to 574,000 people. The figure jumped within a year, to 7.8 per cent or 1.6 million people at the end of 1998 (*The Korea Herald*, 4 January 1999, p 3; IFWEA, 1999). The pattern of lifelong employment provided by the *chaebols* has ended abruptly.

In 1998 South Korea experienced economic recession, of which the main economic indices were an 8 per cent unemployment rate (compared with 2 per cent in 1997), a negative 5 per cent economic growth rate (compared with a growth rate of 5.5 per cent in 1997), and a 28 per cent drop in investment (IFWEA, 1999). Employed workers as well as unemployed irregular workers are suffering from wage decreases and unstable conditions of employment. In terms of income reduction, the highest income group lost 0.3 per cent of income, the second group 9.9 per cent, the third 9.9 per cent, the fourth group

11.8 per cent, and the lowest income group 17.2 per cent (IFWEA, 1999). This indicates a widening gap between the poor and the rich, marking a change in the social and economic stratification system of South Korea.

Subsequently, the state has implemented social security measures. For example, the government expanded the range of unemployment benefits to all kinds of workplaces and started the National Pension System in April 1999. Also the government has offered thousands of unemployed people public work, such as cleaning streets or taking care of public forests and has improved the unemployment insurance system (IFWEA, 1999).

Despite the real-life difficulties in the moment of transition, the South Korean people appeared through strong patriotism to be united culturally once more. As reported in newspapers, a nation-wide campaign, called 'Save the nation' was strongly supported by the public. During the campaign, people in South Korea were selling or donating their rings and jewellery or anything else that contained gold. This was presented in the media as a consensus by South Koreans to survive hard times – together.

Cultural changes

Unlike other Asian countries, where the economic crisis undermined the political legitimacy of autocratic governments (eg those of Mahathir Mohamad in Malaysia and Suharto in Indonesia), the Korean economic crisis did not bring about a political challenge to the fundamental legitimacy of the new government. The second civilian government led by the former dissident Kim Dae Jung provided a democratic forum to re-balance the political power of different interest groups. To the extent that Koreans have begun to use democratic political mechanisms to advance their interests in the moment of transition, Korean cultural values seem to have worked out differently from 'Asian values', as these have been popularized by leaders of the Southeast Asian countries and embraced by intellectuals there.

The South Korean way of political development amid the economic crisis may be a challenge to the conventional 'Asian model' of development, which was thought to be underpinned by Confucian cultural values. Fukuyama (1999) notes that Korean cultural values entwined with the Confucian principles may have diverged from the conventional Asian model to accommodate European democratic themes, not least because Koreans have been actively engaged in social and political struggles in the strong movements of students and labour unions against autocratic governments for the last four decades.

Fukuyama may, however, be wrong. It is possible to connect this form of Korean political democracy with traditional Confucian principles rather than European ideas. Confucian axioms embody the concept of the mandate of heaven which gives legitimacy to rulers and the duty to govern well; otherwise, rulers can be overthrown (Hsu, 1932).

In the Confucian state, knowledge and political power were united, as scholars and rulers together defined the nature of governing authority and explored its limits (Guy, 1987, pp 1–7). The process of recruitment for government offices was linked with the education system. Thus, institutions of Confucian scholarship not only reflected ideas of government, but they also affected the government of ideas. To sustain good government on these Confucian principles, South Korea developed Confucian civil-service examinations, as early as the fourth century AD, to select, on meritocratic principles, a well-cultivated elite (Lee, Ki-baik, 1985). The present moment, however, has had an impact on this traditional cultural valuation of knowledge and the long Confucian education tradition in Korean history.

Changes in cultural valuation of knowledge and educational reforms

Since 1992, education has been prioritized in the state's reform projects (Ministry of Education, ROK, March 1999). However, what was once valued as pedagogically good is now being considered as bad. As noted earlier, the legitimacy of military governance was devalued immediately by the first civilian government led by Kim Young Sam (1992–97). Accordingly, the prestige as well as popularity of military schools diminished in South Korea. This sudden shift in cultural values resulted from the deliberate political action of the civilian government to denounce the earlier military culture in South Korea. This emphasis in the reforms of the first civilian government is continuing with the second civilian government of Kim Dae Jung.

Nevertheless, it is suggested here that educational changes overall have been relatively insignificant. Educational policies have tended to be immediate and piece-meal solutions to urgent problems. For instance, since the inauguration of his presidency in February 1998, Kim Dae Jung – like Kim Young Sam – has urged educational policy-makers to reduce educational burdens and costs on students and parents, caused by the examination-oriented school curriculum and the severe competition for university entrance examinations.

These pressures – immediate and urgent – on parents and pupils have been important in South Korea, when success in life has been much dependent upon entering a few top universities. Despite the severe competition in university entrance examinations, South Korea has fast developed a mass higher education system, boasting the second highest rate of enrolment (per 10,000 of the population) in colleges and universities in the world, after the United States (UNESCO, 1994). One report from the Ministry of Education estimates Korean parents spent more than 9.6 trillion won on legal and illegal private tutoring for their children in 1998 (and at that time one US dollar bought about 1,200 won). This sum was a 70 per cent increase compared with 1994.

However, this highly competitive educational culture has produced corruption in formal education and selection procedures in South Korea. Private tuition outside the schooling system became illegal in South Korea, and this has intensified secretive methods, in which rich families pay very large amounts to hire professional tutors for their children. The problems erupted in a series of scandals in 1998, reinforcing the urgent need for drastic reforms by the government. Under the current law, all private lessons are banned except for regular courses offered at authorized private education institutions and tutoring by college or university students. Eventually, as a rapid solution to relieve current burdens on both educational consumers and providers, the Kim Dae Jung government suggested abolishing examinations in schooling by 2001 (MOE, 1999). Examinations are now seen as pedagogically harmful in South Korea. Thus, unlike in the other sectors of public life, there has not been a major reconstruction of the education system in South Korea. South Korean educational reforms have mainly focused on immediate problems, solved on short-term views.

Only *parts* of the state's educational vision of the future have been clear. For example, new learner-centred 'open education' has been stressed against the broad context of 'internationalization and globalization' (The Presidential Commission on Education Reform, ROK, 1997; MOE, March 1999). However, the new open education system has not been explored beyond formal education, which is very much under the control of the Ministry of Education. The practical measures have been routine: the government has provided IT education programmes and installed English proficiency classes in primary schools. The Ministry of Education also founded the Korea Multimedia Education Centre in 1997, which operates EDUNET – a free total educational information system (MOE, 1998, pp 134–35). According to official arguments, this open education system and the new learner-centred schooling will provide a creative educational environment fit for the 21st century (MOE, 1998, p 130).

For example, the civilian government's educational vision of internationalization and globalization has focused on how to make South Korea visible in international educational arenas. Korea joined the APEC Education Forum, which was formed in 1992 as part of the Asia Pacific Economic Cooperation (APEC) (MOE, 1998, pp 121–22). Also, after joining the OECD at the end of 1996, South Korea has formally become an observer on the OECD Educational Committee, and has actively engaged in international seminars on the issues of Human Resource Development (MOE, 1998, p 123).

It is only recently that the government has started to stress the significance of 'culture' in the educational vision of the future. For instance, the South Korean government declared 1998 the year of the Korean Culture, and hosted the World Cultural Exposition (which was held in Kyongju in September 1998). The Korean National Commission for UNESCO has also proposed a plan to establish an international centre for intercultural understanding in the Asian region by 2003 (Ministry of Education, ROK, March 1999).

At least, the new educational vision of the future includes some educational provision for the future reunification of the two Koreas, as stated in the civilian government's five-year educational development project (1999–2003). In fact, Korea is now the only country that is still divided as a consequence of the cold war, although the two Koreas have been a single nation ethnically, linguistically and culturally for the last 5,000 years.

Nevertheless, there is still lack of a substantial educational provision at a practical level to achieve an effective reconciliation and the subsequent reunification of the two Koreas. While the state formulates various policy measures to improve international and intercultural education, paradoxically, teaching and research on North Korea are strictly under the surveillance of the South Korean government. On North Korea, South Koreans still lack sufficient freedom of expression. For instance, during the presidential election campaign in 1997, a professor had to face criminal charges, after publishing a children's book titled *I am Reunification Generation One* (translation), which was allegedly considered pro-North Korea. Ironically, North Korea is still considered the most dangerous enemy within and 'the Other' in South Korea. In this context, the recent increase of refugees from North Korea has significant educational implications.

The South Korean government has maintained the principle of political separation in dealing with North Korea. Nevertheless, inter-Korean trade and economic co-operation grew markedly in the 1990s, even when the nuclear problem in North Korea was at its peak in 1994. Subsequently, South Korea by 1995 had become the third largest trading partner of North Korea, following Japan and China, and the second largest exporting country next to Japan (Lee, Hyun-Hoon, 1998, p 85). President Kim Dae Jung's new 'sunshine policy' also reflects this principle by focusing mainly on the economic dimension.

Overall, it is clear that the South Korean government has tried rapidly to accommodate to a new global economic challenge. However, the government's education reforms have not been at the centre of the recent transition. There have been no *fundamental* changes in the education system in South Korea, despite the other changes in political, socio-economic and cultural arenas. The educational system, apart from stressing 'internationalization', remains centralized under the Ministry of Education. By keeping the infrastructure of education the same, under the control of government bureaucrats, the system of higher education in South Korea has remained relatively rigid and remarkably uniform.

The reforms have much of the right rhetoric – creating internationalization and learner-centredness. However, what South Korea is changing towards remains unclear and will remain so, until the unification of the two Koreas has become clear as a cautious and practical political and economic possibility.

Conclusion

At the start of this chapter, it was argued that Korea had entered a stage of transition in 1992 and has gone through a sudden collapse and reconstruction of the state apparatus, socio-economic stratification systems and the state's visions of the future.

In fact, Korean history has been constantly turbulent. It is often said that during the last two thousand years Korea has suffered more than 960 foreign invasions. Against this turbulent history, it can be argued that Korea has undergone multiple transitions. More precisely, it is argued here that since Korea was forced to become a part of the world economic system at the turn of the last century, there had been at least three transitions before this latest one in 1992.

For example, Korea entered a moment of transition in 1894 through the *Kabo* reform, during which the traditional Confucian State system was drastically transformed into a modern nation state system by adopting the Japanese model of modernization. One aftermath of this transition was Japanese colonization.

The second transition occurred in 1945, when the end of the Second World War brought independence suddenly to Korea. One consequence was an abrupt national partition. People in the South had to accept US military governance for the next three years. After the three years of trusteeship, the first Republic of Korea was established in the South as an independent modern nation–state in the Korean peninsula, within the US vision of liberal democracy and capitalist market economy.

The third transition came with the military *coup d'état* on 16 May 1961. The subsequent military regimes in South Korea transformed the state apparatus and created a strong 'developmental state'. Under the bureaucratic-authoritarian military regime led by General Park Jung Hee, a new South Korean socio-economic stratification system emerged, and the state's vision of becoming a newly industrializing economy was realized.

These illustrations of several moments of transition in South Korea support the view that 'transition' is not new but has been a constant historical challenge to South Koreans. What is stressed in this chapter is the fact that South Korea is going through another, possibly the last moment of transition in the 20th century. The consequences are not yet clear.

In the period of Kim Young Sam's government (1992–97), the state's new vision of the future consistently focused on 'globalization' (*seghyehwa*), with neo-liberal policies such as flexibility of labour market, privatization, and the 'lean' state. The current government led by Kim Dae Jung continues to promote this globalization project, under the new conditions externally imposed by the IMF loans.

The next four to five years, a period more or less equivalent to President Kim Dae Jung's remaining time in office, are likely to show the after-effects of this moment of transition – how strongly the South Korean economy will have survived; how North and South Korean relations will have evolved towards a re-unification or war; and consequently how South Korean education will have been 'globalized' and transformed in the context of old and new power relations.

References

Chang, Hyun (1998) Management implications of the ideological discourse of globalization and re-engineering in South Korea, in *Perspectives on Korea*, ed Sang-Oak Lee and Duk-Soo Park, pp 1–15,University of Hawaii Press, Honolulu, Hawaii

Cotton, J (ed) (1995) *Politics and Policy in the New Korean State: From Roh Tae-Woo to Kim Young Sam*, St Martin's Press, Longman, New York

Fukuyama, F (1999) Asian values in the wake of the Asian crisis, paper presented at the International Conference on Democracy, Market Economy and Development, held in Seoul, February

Guy, K R (1987) *The Emperor's Four Treasuries: Scholars and the state in the late Ch'ien-Lung era*, Harvard University Press, Cambridge, MA

Hsu, L S (1932) *The Political Philosophy of Confucianism, an Interpretation of the Social and Political Ideas of Confucius, His Forerunners, and His Early Disciples*, George Routledge & Sons, London

International Federation of Workers' Education Association (IFWEA) (1999) Instruments of globalization, in the Asia International Study Circles Project (http://www.ifwea.org/)

Kim, Young Sam (1996) *Korea's Reform and Globalization*, Korean Overseas Information Service, The Government Press, Seoul

Lee, Hyun-Hoon (1998) Northeast Asian economic co-operation and its relation with inter-Korean economic integration, in *Perspectives on Korea*, ed Sang-Oak Lee and Duk-Soo Park, pp 77–90, University of Hawaii Press, Hawaii

Lee, Ki-baik (1985) *A New History of Korea*, tr Edward W Wagner and Edward J Shultz, Harvard University Press, Cambridge, MA

Lee, Sang-Oak and Duk-Soo Park (eds) (1998) *Perspective on Korea*, University of Hawaii Press, Hawaii

McCann, D R (ed) (1997) *Korea Briefing: Toward reunification*, M E Sharpe, Armonk, New York

Ministry of Education, The Republic of Korea (1998) *Education in Korea 1997–1998*, The Government Press, Seoul

Ministry of Education, The Republic of Korea (1999) *Educational Development: The outline of five-year planning*, Ministry of Education, Seoul

Ministry of Finance and Economy (1999) *Djnomics: A new foundation for the Korean economy*, The Government Press, Seoul

National Statistical Office, Republic of Korea (1993) *Major Statistics of Korean Economy, 1993*, The Government Press, Seoul

The Presidential Commission on Education Reform, The Republic of Korea (1997) *Education Reform for the 21st Century – To Ensure Leadership in the Information and Globalization Era*, PCER Report, November, The Government Press, Seoul

UNESCO (1994) *Statistical Yearbook*, UNESCO, Paris

16. Change as normality: education in Ukraine with special reference to the Crimea

Crispin Jones

And where is she, Ukraine, mother Ukraine?
Yevgeny Yevtushenko, *Zima Junction*

Introduction

Ukraine is a fascinating example of an educational transitology, its 20th-century history being a set of more or less violent changes rather than revolutionary eras, culminating in its emergence as a 'new' state towards the end of the century. And like other new states in Europe, as elsewhere in the world, codifying or even inventing their own unitary past is a serious business and remains a principal purpose of state education. In addition, international trends such as globalization and local variation and circumstances make this aspect of education an uneven and even politically dangerous process. During transitologies, as in revolutionary periods, organizing the education system is a central and challenging task. To modify it in terms of such key issues as visions of the future and of the past is nigh on impossible. Indeed, the case can be made that transitologies are more difficult for education than revolutions, as the changes are less clear-cut, the directions more difficult to delineate and respond to.

To demonstrate this process, this chapter looks at the two recent transitologies (1914–24 and 1986–97) and the violent intermission between them in Ukraine, formerly the Soviet Socialist Republic of Ukraine. Within this broader context, the issues posed by the Crimea, an autonomous region within the state, are looked at in more detail as they reveal more clearly still some of the educational issues that have arisen.

Ukraine: the context

Like many other parts of the old USSR, Ukraine is less well known as an independent state, although it has a long (and contested) history. It is second only to Russia in size as a European state and has a population of some 52 million people, again large by European standards. Its neighbours are Belarus, Hungary, Moldova, Poland, Romania, Russia and Slovakia, all of which have a place in the new state's history. Its capital, Kyiv (formerly Kiev), founded by Norsemen, was the centre, from the 10th to 13th centuries, of the first great Slav culture and state, Kievan Rus. Argument continues to wage between Russia and Ukraine as to which is its true descendant. Under Stalin, the desire for parthenogenetic explanations more generally led to the suppression of all alternative theories and the liquidation of their proponents – some 85 per cent of Soviet archaeologists being 'purged' in four years in the 1930s (Ascherson, 1995, p 44). The solution to the argument is probably neither, as Kievan Rus was effectively destroyed by the Mongols in 1237 and the territory squabbled and fought over just about ever since. With so many powerful neighbours and being at the eastern margin of Europe, Ukraine has always been a frontier land, a border, boundary and march land, which more powerful states have invaded or ruled for much of its history – Scandinavians, Lithuanians, Mongols, Cossacks, Poles, Russians, Turks, Swedes, Austrians and Germans. Making sense of this history and creating what is, to many intents and purposes, a new nation–state is a major test for Ukrainian education as well as the other institutions of the fledgeling state.

A final contextualizing point is that the ethnic diversity in the country is complex. The great majority (nearly three-quarters) of the population are Ukrainians but the Ukrainian language was in decline until independence in 1991 with Russian being widely spoken, although Russians are less than a quarter of the population. There are many other small minorities, particularly along Ukraine's borders, befitting its complex history. One of significance for this chapter is the Tatar minority who live mainly in the Crimean Autonomous Republic, as their status poses significant questions for the state education system and indeed, for the state itself.

Transitologies in Ukraine

Ukraine's history is fascinating but cannot be gone into in great detail here (but see Ascherson, 1995 and Reid, 1998 for popular accounts). It is important, however, in that because it has been so turbulent, it has led to a far more stable state than was ever expected on independence in 1991. This paradox is one that the two transitologies and the violent intermission may help to explain. As in many other post-Soviet states, this century has seen two transitologies in Ukraine, one around the First World War and the 1917 Revolution and the other following the collapse of Communism. However, the intermission between the two in Ukraine has had the net consequence of a common feeling throughout much of the population that wherever possible, extremes and conflict should be avoided. Such a sweeping assertion needs amplification.

The first transitology occurred around the First World War and its after-math. It was followed by a long and mostly violent period, an era of volcanic upheaval which dramatically changed people's lives but which left the education system of the Ukraine similar at the end of the period to the education system at the start. It is, however, crucial to an understanding of the transitology that came after. This long period of turmoil is really in two interrelated parts, the result of Stalin's and Hitler's depredations, the one from about 1929 until 1939 and the other from 1939 until about 1953. Although a case could be made for a division, it is perhaps more helpful to bring the two together. The final transitology could be seen as starting in 1991 with Ukraine's independence, although 1986, when the Chernobyl nuclear power plant exploded, is seen here as its starting point. This transitology is now ended as the Ukrainian state settles down in its new guise and its educational system seems to have equally arrived at a pattern that is likely to continue.

The first transitology 1914–24

The first transitology starts in 1914 when many Ukrainians, some in the Austro-Hungarian Empire and others in the Russian Empire, were conscripted into opposing armies to spend years fighting one another. Ukrainian nationalism, which had never died under the years of imperial rule despite attempts to destroy it, continued to excite the minds of many of the intellectual class, especially teachers. The Tsar's 1876 Edict of Ems, which forbade Ukrainian in schools, removed all Ukrainian language books from the schools and exiled many Ukrainian nationalist teachers into Great Russia, had failed to kill the language, in schools as well as in the wider society. It had, however, set a pattern. Ukrainian as a language has remained a point of contention even up to the present with some Russians still asserting it is only a dialect of Russian.

The wave of nationalism and political change that started to sweep through the losing empires in 1917 did not pass by Ukraine. In March 1917, a *Rada* or parliament was established in Kyiv. Following the October Revolution in Russia later in the year, Red Army troops moved into Ukraine and, ignoring independence claims by the *Rada*, re-established Moscow rule. In 1918, the German Army moved in as part of the Brest-Litovsk settlement, while at the same time, in the west of the country a short-lived Ukrainian Republic was declared in the Polish-speaking Austro-Hungarian ruled part of the country in the dying days of that empire. This double history continued in the aftermath of the First World War.

The Wilsonian principle of self-determination left Ukraine still divided (Boemeke *et al*, 1999). In the west, Polish nationalism took drastic expression. In the chaos of the war and its aftermath, what today might be called 'ethnic cleansing' led to 1.5 million Ukrainians being killed in the period 1914–21 and a 'plantation' of 200,000 Polish settlers being established. In education the

Ukrainian language and the study of Ukrainian history were yet again banned; this was the more poignant as the first chair in Ukrainian History had been established in 1894 at the Polish-controlled university of Lviv in western Ukraine.

In Russian-dominated Ukraine, the story was even worse. The 1917 collapse in Russia led to the long civil war, mostly fought in Ukraine territory, itself at that time divided between Poland, Russia, Czechoslovakia and Romania. For three years, five armies fought in Ukraine – Red, White, Polish, Ukrainian and Allied (60,000 French troops) plus Cossack bands. All, save the Allies, attacked Jews and there were massacres, with anything between 50–200,000 being killed (Reid, 1998).

When peace was restored, Ukraine entered into a modest golden age. *Korenizatsiya*, the educational policy that encouraged the development of indigenous cultures and traditions in education and elsewhere, was implemented across the new Soviet Union. It was part of Lenin's policy towards the national minorities, although more cynical people might suggest that such policies were essential if the old Russian Empire was to be kept. What it meant was that by the end of this particular transitology, started by the assassination of Archduke Ferdinand in another province of the Austria–Hungarian Empire, a clear new vision of the future, 'Communism', was in place in Ukrainian education. In theory, children were being taught that the old, oppressive empires were dead and that a new era of proletarian solidarity, of which they were to be the vanguard, was just beginning under the benign leadership of Lenin and the Union of Soviet Socialist Republics. 'Bliss was it in that dawn to be alive…'. Yet, despite the rhetoric, anti-Russian sentiment continued, as did anti-Semitism. Four years into a new Soviet education system, Lenin died and Stalin came to power. The transitology had ended, although this was not perceived at first.

Stalin and Hitler

To have had the attention of Stalin was bad enough. To have had Hitler as well was a disaster for the Ukraine. Their malign influence is in two parts, the first starting with the accession to power of Stalin and ending with Hitler's death and the second ending with the death of Stalin. It was a period of almost unprecedented horror. Comparisons in this case are often without value but suffice to say that probably no European country suffered more during that period. It reduced a country and its education system recovering from the First World War and the civil war backwards to where it had been during the most disadvantaged periods in the past. Only towards the end of the period, in the 1950s, was the education system and the society restored to levels it had known in the early 1920s.

The first part starts shortly after Stalin came to power in 1928. By 1929, 'dekulakization' – the 'abolition of the kulaks as a class' – commenced in

Ukraine. Ukraine, the breadbasket of the Soviet Union, was a prime target for its associated collectivization. In three years, 12 million Ukrainians were deported, most never to return. In 1930, the great political purges began, causing yet more suffering and deaths. In education, *korenizatsiya* was abolished as it was alleged that such national education accentuated national differences as against class solidarity and as such incited national enmities. In some contexts the argument may have merit but in this one it had none. Again, Russification was the main political and educational agenda, apart from the purges. And, to cap it all, the Great Hunger. Between 1932 and 1933, some 5 million more Ukrainians died from hunger or 'exhaustion' as official documents of the time euphemistically described it (Conquest, 1970). The purges of 1937 to 1939 are a ghoulish postscript. No numbers for Ukraine have been made available, but given the total Soviet estimate of 1 million killed and 12 million sent to the gulags, the numbers for Ukraine must have been considerable. (The scale was staggering: in the 1980s, a mass grave for 200,000 people dating from this period was found at Bykivnya near Kyiv (Reid, 1998, p 122). The first part of the violence had ended with Ukraine devastated, its education system a shadow of the official picture. For many other Soviet citizens, the outbreak of the Second World War in 1939 made little difference to their lives. Needless to say it was different for Ukraine.

The second part of this period started in 1939 with the Molotov–Ribbentrop pact and the subsequent division of Poland. The Soviet Union gained that part of Galicia always considered part of the Ukraine by them and many Ukrainians living in Galicia. A young and ambitious Russian politician from western Ukraine, Nikita Kruschchev, organized by 'popular demand' the incorporation into the Ukrainian Socialist Republic of this new acquisition. (It was Kruschchev who gave Russian Crimea to the Ukraine in 1954: a 'father to the nation'?) Less well known is that he organized the deportation of anything between 800,000 and 1.6 million people, 10–20 per cent of the total population of this newly acquired territory in the two years before the German Army arrived in 1941.

Many Jews had remained behind in Ukraine after the arrival of the German Army. Indeed, they had nowhere to flee to at that time. Behind the army was the SS. When they left in 1943–44 most of the Jews, some 2,250,000 people, had been murdered. These included the famous Jewish communities of cities like Odessa (180,000 murdered) and Kyiv (175,000 murdered). Perhaps the most famous atrocity was that written about by Yevgeny Yevtushenko in his poem on the massacre at Babii Yar (Yevtushenko, 1966). In the poem he notes continuing Russian anti-Semitism, for the Nazis were helped by their Romanian allies and by a small numbers of anti-Semitic Ukrainians. Reid tells the harrowing story of how 'Shooting the Jews' became a popular children's game in some areas, such was the scale and ferocity of the extermination (Reid, 1998, p 157). A further 1,750,00 Ukrainians were also killed in the carnage of those years. Hitler is said to have ordered that the only education Ukrainian children needed should be reduced 'to one sentence: the capital of the Reich is Berlin' (ibid, p 158).

In 1944, the Red Army returned. In March, the Crimean Tatar population, accused by Stalin of collaborating with the Germans, was deported, an atrocity further discussed later in this chapter. Many of the men had just returned from service in the Red Army. Stalin, mindful of his minorities, also incorporated Czech Ruthenia into the Ukraine SSR, where he could keep a closer eye on another group of potentially dissident Ukrainians (Weinberg, 1994, p 778).

Post-war re-construction was slow but was eased by the massive investment in the Crimea, the home of the Soviet Black Sea Fleet. The education system was rebuilt along the lines established in the 1930s and 1940s, forming the pattern that remained in place, with minor alterations, until the collapse of Communism. It is a familiar system, well described by Nigel Grant and others (Lane, 1978; Grant, 1979). The long disastrous space between the two transitologies could be said to end at this point, although people had to wait for the death of Stalin until 1953.

The impact of this long period on the Ukraine of today and the transitology that subsequently took place is clear. Stalin's accession to power is a turning point in Ukrainian history and a lot more besides. A twisted vision, or version of a vision, was imposed on a people. The vision of the future of Communist rhetoric and the actuality of his monstrous reign left Ukraine in a state of almost quietude. Nothing could be that bad again or should be allowed to be. Add the German invasion on top and Ukraine could have gone in one of two directions – outright nationalism or its rejection. In many ways it has moved in the latter direction. The rhetoric of Communism remained, in education as elsewhere, but real belief in it had gone for most Ukrainians. The education system of the early Soviet pioneers was elaborated and improved but the history that it taught and the values and visions of the future that it espoused were less firmly established. Marxist–Leninism had less power than Christianity in secular schools across the rest of Europe and the history of Ukraine as told by parents, grandparents and other friends and relatives bore little relation to that which was taught in school. An education system of denial had been carefully erected throughout Ukraine. The stage was set for the second transitology. Nowhere was this clearer than in the Autonomous Region of Crimea.

Crimea: the context

Ascherson's book (1995) makes it clear that the Crimea, although now part of the Ukrainian state, has a long and fascinating history and one central to Europe's vision of itself. As part of Lenin's strategy to hold the old Russian Empire together in the new USSR, Tatar Crimea was made an autonomous republic within the Russian SSR in 1921, recognizing the Tatars' long history in and control over that particular place. The Tatar language was recognized but Stalin, against the wishes of its users, forced the change from a Roman to a

Cyrillic script, a change which still causes resentment amongst the language's users, despite changing back in 1997 (Nissman and Hill, 1997).

In 1941 the German army arrived in the Crimea. As described earlier in this chapter, large and prosperous minority populations like the Jews were wiped out by the Germans. 61,000 other people, mainly ethnic Germans, were also removed from the Crimea by them. (Most of the large German community had been internally exiled by Stalin in the face of the German attack.) In 1944, the Russians retook the Crimea. Stalin, wrongfully claiming widespread support for the Germans by the Tatars, 'abolished' the Tatar nation, removed its autonomous status and deported them off to Central Asia in a horrific deportation programme. Starting on 18 May 1944, 200,000–250,000 Crimean Tatars were sent into exile. The Tatars estimate this expulsion killed some 110,000, half the expelled: official Russian estimates admit to 45,000 between 1944–48 (Wilson, 1994). Wherever the truth lies, the expulsion was near-genocidal in its impact on the Tatars and was the last in a long line of Russian attacks on their nation (Kozlov, 1988), as Table 16.1 illustrates.

Table 16.1   The decline of the Crimean Tatar population, 1783–1993

Year	% of Tatars in Crimear
1783	83
1897	34
1937	21
1945	0
1989	1.5
1990	5
1993	10

Source: Derived from Open Society Institute (1996)

With the removal of the Tatars, Russians were encouraged to immigrate and take their place in the new industries and services supporting the expanding Soviet Black Sea Fleet based at Sevastopol. In 1954, Nikita Krushchev made the Crimea a region of the Ukrainian SSR, which made geographic sense but which was based on the apparently reasonable assumption of the continuation of the USSR. It was not a reasonable assumption.

Transitology in Ukraine and the Crimea, 1986–97

The collapse of belief in the Soviet Union by Ukrainians was not a sudden affair but had a long pre-history, some of which being described earlier in this chapter. A series of post-war events are also significant, the invasions of Czechoslovakia, Poland and Afghanistan, the unmasking of Stalin, particularly in his

Ukrainian atrocities like the mass grave of Bykivnya. But perhaps most of all in the Ukrainian case it was Chernobyl. On Friday 26 April 1986, a nuclear power plant at Chernobyl, just north of Kyiv, blew up. The Gorbachev-led USSR tried to cover up the disaster as did the local Ukrainian Communist Party; to this day, the full consequences of the explosion are still unclear. In Ukraine as in the rest of Europe, many thousands have died, and many more will continue to die into the millennium from its consequences. Indeed, 150,000 people are still displaced in Ukraine as a result of the catastrophe (United Nations High Commissioner for Refugees in Ukraine, 1997). The nationalists in Ukraine, as the news came slowly out of the government information machine, found that this was the last straw. Western Ukraine had always remained nationalist but this disaster spread the disillusion with Moscow rule across the whole of Ukraine. However, it must be said that Ukrainian nationalism really grew in response to the collapse of the Soviet Union rather than being a cause of the collapse. As in Eastern Europe, the protests against the Soviet system started early but the collapse, when it came in 1990–91, was relatively sudden and, thankfully, peaceful.

Pictures of the French Revolution's Tennis Court Oath and other images of critical moments in national self-determination are heroic myths for the main part. The critical juncture in Ukraine was more prosaic. The aborted coup against Gorbachev by hard-liners in August 1991 was decisive. The Ukrainian Communist Party leadership was in a quandary. Soviet power had collapsed and the nationalists were gaining strength to fill the vacuum. The issue was fast becoming who was going to lead an independent Ukraine rather than whether or not it was to become independent. Leonid Kravchuc, a former Party ideologue, put it clearly, albeit crudely, before the decisive vote in the *Rada*, speaking in Russian: 'Today we will vote for Ukrainian independence, because if we don't we're in the shit' (quoted in Reid, 1998, p 215).

The collapse of the Soviet Union meant that the new state of Ukraine had two large areas that still saw themselves as rightfully belonging to the new Russian Federation, a peninsula, the Crimea, which was Russian speaking and Russia oriented as well as the eastern part which was similar (the Donbass). The new government in Kyiv had to tread a delicate path between the various factions, nowhere more carefully than in the Crimea (Wilson, 1993). The changes following the collapse of the Soviet Union were made more complex in the Crimea by the return of many of the Crimean Tatars who had been expelled by Stalin. The Tatar population rapidly increased, from 38,000 in 1989 to some 260,000 in 1993 (Open Society Institute, 1996, p 27). Now mainly speaking Russian – only half speak Tatar well (ibid) – they returned to the Russian-speaking Crimea, wanting to re-assert their national identity and cultural 'ownership' of the peninsula. However, Ukrainian nationality law, based on international convention (Abdureshitov, 1996), initially excluded many Crimean Tatars from citizenship, as they were not resident in Ukraine on its gaining independence, as they were still in exile and they cannot speak Ukrainian, an alternative criteria for citizenship (Fraction of Kurultaj of Crimean Tatar People, 1996). Thus the majority were still without Ukrainian citizenship and because of that, without work. Work in state-controlled enterprises is restricted to Ukrainian citizens and with privatization of the economy of Crimea remaining underdeveloped, rates of unemployment remain extremely high (over 40 per cent), despite the Tatars having high rates of educational qualification, acquired in their exile (Zubarev, 1996).

The population in the Crimea in 1997 consisted of between 60 per cent and 65 per cent Russian, 20 per cent to 23 per cent Ukrainian, 10 per cent Tatar and 1 per cent others, mainly Germans and groups from other parts of the former Soviet Union, especially the Caucasus states (Piskun, 1996). Nearly all are Russian speaking, even the Ukrainian minority. However, the new Ukrainian state insisted that the state language, and the language of instruction in Ukrainian schools, should be Ukrainian (*Kiev Post*, 1997). Yet the state had been mainly Russian speaking when it was part of the USSR and the language of instruction in the schools had been Russian. The scene was set for a dangerous confrontation over educational and other social provision which could easily lead to conflict and violence (Bremmer, 1994).

So how is the education system in the Crimea attempting to deal with these issues? The language of instruction in the schools is supposed to be Ukrainian, with Russian as the first foreign language. The Tatars want Tatar to be the medium of instruction for their children and the first foreign language for all other children attending Crimean schools. The Russians want Russian as the language of instruction and English, Ukrainian or German as the first foreign language. The Ukrainian state wants Ukrainian to be the language of instruction but is prepared to be flexible in areas where there are other large language groups. This is because only about 50 per cent of 'Ukrainian' Ukrainians are really fluent in the language. However, for example, now 90 per cent of first graders in Kyiv are in Ukrainian medium schools – while 76 per cent of the adult population speak Russian – with clear evidence of the gradual Ukrainianization of everyday speech in Kyiv, despite its earlier low status. Russian/Ukrainian bilingual conversations are common and not seen as threatening (as is also the case in Catalonia but not in Quebec (Arel, 1996)). President Leonid Kravchuk in 1993 said, 'When we talk about bilingualism, it is always about the defence of one language – Russian: but I would like it to be about the defence of two languages, Ukrainian as well' (Solchanyk, 1993 p 3). Data for the Crimea are not available but it is likely similar patterns of multilingual language use are increasing. The reasons, according to David Laitin, are threefold: first, economic return for changing to the state language; second, an appreciation of the loss of status of a previously high status group (the Russians); and third the converse, namely the increase in status of a formerly low status group, viz the Ukrainians (Laitin, 1996).

There are other issues. What history, what literature and what social education should be taught are also vexed questions. What influence should religion have in relation to education is another. The various groups within the

Crimea, and across Ukraine more generally, have different aspirations and understandings. Coupled to that is the fact that the education system is near to collapse due to chronic underfunding. Teachers are seldom paid, the buildings are crumbling and new schemes to improve things have to cost nothing or be funded by external sources.

Other signs of ending are also apparent. In 1997, a new NGO programme 'Integration into Ukrainian Society of Crimean Tatars, Armenians, Bulgarians, Greeks and Germans formerly Deported from Ukraine' started, funded by the Soros Foundation. It indicates a willingness to co-operate between the various parties previously feuding over their place in the new Ukrainian sun. Furthermore, in April 1997, national elections left President Leonid Kuchma and his party just short of absolute majority in parliamentary elections as left-wing parties gained 42 per cent of the vote. The Ukrainian nationalist parties were heavily defeated. Given that Ukraine now has a relatively stable economy and hyperinflation has gone, these are all signs that Crimea and Ukraine in general have passed through their current transitology.

Chernobyl still casts a cloud over the Ukraine but it is a very different state now. The vision of the future in 1991 was a confused one, agreeing on one thing only, that the old Soviet Union was finished. Differing visions in the Crimea were more sharpened versions of those found elsewhere in the new state. But as the changes in language use indicate, the people of Ukraine are rightly reluctant to return to the imposed excesses of the past. Communism and all its works have been ostensibly rejected but its emotional legacy is a powerful one, albeit a quickly fading one. Russia has been rejected but Ukraine not completely accepted. The fears of internecine violence of the early 1990s have faded if not quite disappeared. But given that Ukraine was compared to Yugoslavia in terms of its explosive ethnic mixture, with the Crimea being the detonator, the Ukrainian state has to some extent defied expectations. For this, the period under Stalin and Hitler must claim some credit. The horrors that extended over much of this century influenced most Ukrainian families. With increasing economic stability, the wish to plunge into ethnic conflict has diminished.

Other elements in the transitology also have helped in the stability of the new state. Communism has been rejected and the free market adopted with more or less enthusiasm according to market position. Political parties on democratic lines are evolving and maturing. It is, for example, unlikely that a party would repeat the famous slogan of the ultra-nationalist party in an early election: 'vote for us and it is the last time you will have to vote'. Truthful, but it was rewarded with few votes. The old party elite has realigned itself to new values without losing too many of its former privileges. Modern Ukraine looks Westward rather than to the North. Membership of NATO and the EU is sought, not unrealistically, in the medium term.

Finally, the education system has evolved in line with the new state's uncertain steps into the free market economy. In 1993, the Association of Non-state Owned Educational Institutions of Ukraine was formed. Over 100 private educational institutions, from nursery schools to private universities are members, most accredited by the Ukrainian Ministry of Education (ANIEU, 1999). Higher education, with over 1,000,000 students in some 280 universities and other degree-awarding institutions, is moving away from the priorities of the Soviet era with its emphasis on military technology and centralized control to a new emphasis on the humanities, economics and management education and some degree of institutional autonomy (EdNU, 1999). As Petro Mykolaiovich Talanchuk, the Minister of Education said in 1993: 'Now that we are not geared to the Soviet Union we have less need to manufacture products such as aircraft carriers' (MacGregor, 1993, p 12).

Initial fights over language and cultural issues, at their most extreme in the Crimea, have gone underground if not faded away. The curriculum has been completely changed, rejecting the former Marxist–Leninist curriculum, although difficulties remain over the content of history and literature curricula. Ukraine's recent past and the position and role of the existing groups within the state remain a delicate subject. Ethnic Russian wishes to remain Russian and the Tatar dream of a homeland remain difficult educational as well as broader political issues. The education system seems similar to the one that it has replaced but the Ukrainian emphasis on gradualism and consent seems to be successful, although familiar issues remain. As Cerych noted in the broader post-Soviet context, educational systems like that of Ukraine face difficulties over resource levels, the balance between decentralization of education and the need to maintain state unity, the continuing need to find more appropriate curricula content and related initial and in-service education for teachers and, perhaps most importantly, to maintain the drive to develop and maintain effective quality control systems (Cerych, 1997). All this within the broad context of supporting national unity and nation-building through the educational system (Kotasek, 1996). It is one of the good things that has emerged from a frightening history that Ukraine's education system has emerged from its transitology looking far more effective in meeting the educational needs of its citizenry than it was before.

Note

I am grateful to Bob Cowen and David Coulby for their helpful comments on earlier drafts of this chapter.

References

Abdureshitov, N (1996) Principles of restoration of citizenship in the former Soviet States, in *Citizen: Information Bulletin # 1–2*, ed E Chubarov, 'Assistance' – Foundation on Naturalisation and Human Rights Simferopol, Crimea, Ukraine

ANEIU (Association of Non-state Owned Educational Institutions of Ukraine) (1999) *Association of Non-state Owned Educational Institutions of Ukraine,* http://www.ednu.kiev.ua/ aeiunfp/index_e.htm, accessed 18 May 1999

Arel, D (1996) A lurking cascade of assimilation in Kiev?, *Post-Soviet Affairs,* 12 (1), pp 73–90

Ascherson, N (1995) *Black Sea: The birthplace of civilisation and barbarism,* Vintage, London

Boemeke, M *et al* (ed) (1999) *The Treaty of Versailles: A reassessment after 75 years,* Cambridge University Press, Cambridge

Bremmer, I (1994) The politics of ethnicity: Russians in the new Ukraine, *Europe-Asia Studies,* 2, pp 261–83

Cerych, L (1997) Educational reforms in Central and Eastern Europe, *European Journal of Education,* 32 (1)

Conquest, R (1970) *The Nation Killers: The Soviet deportation of nationalities,* Macmillan, New York

EdNU (1999) *Ukraine's National Higher Education System,* http://www.ednu.kiev.ua/ edu_h_e.htm, accessed 18 May 1999

Fraction of Kurultaj of Crimean Tatar People (1996) Principles of restoration of citizenship in the former Soviet States, in *Citizen: Information Bulletin # 1–2,* ed E Chubarov, 'Assistance' – Foundation on Naturalisation and Human Rights, Simferopol, Crimea, Ukraine

Grant, N (1979) *Soviet Education,* Penguin, Harmondsworth

Kotasek, J (1996) Structure and organisation of secondary education in Central and Eastern Europe, *European Journal of Education,* 31 (1)

Kozlov, V (1988) *The Peoples of the Soviet Union,* Hutchinson, London

Laitin, D (1996) Language and nationalism in the post-Soviet Republics, *Post-Soviet Studies,* 12 (1), pp 4–24

Lane, D (1978) *Politics and Society in the USSR,* Martin Robertson, Oxford

MacGregor, K (1993) Three goals of Mr Ten Percent, *Times Higher Educational Supplement,* 5 March, p 12

Nissman, D and Hill, D (1997) Ukraine: Crimean Turks return late to Latin script, *Crimean Home Page:* www.current.nl/users/sota/alfabet.htm, accessed 4 June 1997

Open Society Institute (1996) *Crimean Tatars: Repatriation and conflict prevention,* Open Society Institute, New York

Piskun, O (1996) Institution of citizenship in Ukraine, *Migration Issues,* 1 (1), pp 16–18

Reid, A (1998) *Borderland: A journey through the history of Ukraine,* Phoenix, London

Solchanyk, R (1993) The politics of language in Ukraine, *RFE/RL Research Report,* 2 (10), pp 1–4

United Nations High Commissioner for Refugees in Ukraine (1997) *Migration Studies: Ukrainian Analytical-Informative Journal,* 2 (3), pp 32–36

Weinberg, G (1994) *A World at Arms: A global history of World War II,* Cambridge

University Press, Cambridge

Wilson, A (1993) Crimea's political cauldron, *RFE/RL Research Report* (no 45)

Wilson, A (1994) The elections in Crimea, *RFE/RL Research Report* (no 25)

Yevtushenko, Y (1962) *Yevtushenko: Selected Poems*, tr R Milner-Gullard and P Levi, Penguin, Harmondsworth

Yevtushenko, Y (1966) *The Poetry of Yevgeny Yevtushenko: 1953–1963*, tr G Reavey, Calder and Boyars, London

Zubarev, V (1996) The role of NGOs in rendering assistance to former deported peoples, which come back, in *Citizen: Information Bulletin # 1–2*, ed E Chubarov, 'Assistance' – Foundation on Naturalisation and Human Rights, Simferopol, Crimea, Ukraine

17. Education in the United Kingdom

Nigel Grant

The United Kingdom of Great Britain and Northern Ireland is often used as synonymous with Britain and England as if they were all the same thing, which of course they are not. The countries are very different in size, which is one of the reasons why this confusion of definitions arises. England has about 50 million population (a little smaller than the Ukraine), Scotland 5 million (about the same as Denmark or Finland), Wales 3.5 million (about the same as Albania) and Northern Ireland a million and a half (the same as Estonia). Scotland has its own legal system, national church and administration, and Northern Ireland has its own administration (and is religiously split), whereas Wales and England are in effect parts of the same country. England created the English language, which gave rise to the language of the United States, Canada, Australia, New Zealand, and which is much used in South Africa, India, Pakistan, Bangladesh, ex-colonial Africa and as a second language in many other countries, probably about half the world's population. It is also now spoken as a first language in Scotland, Wales and Ireland, whatever other languages are used. At the moment of writing (1998), all power rests with the Parliament at Westminster, where all the countries are represented, the Scots and Welsh having slightly more members than their populations would justify, though they are obviously still a small minority. In education, the Scots and Northern Irish systems are distinct from the Anglo-Welsh, which comes from their former status.

The countries came together in different ways. England, the largest and richest, has always dominated, and first of all united (under Norse pressure), then expanded and conquered Wales, assimilating it into its legal system in 1536, abolishing Welsh traditional law and applying the English legal code, and replacing the Welsh language officially. England also conquered Ireland, starting in the 12th century, and joined with it politically in 1801. Edward I (Longshanks) of England invaded Scotland in 1296, but met resistance under William Wallace and Andrew Moray and then under Robert Bruce. Longshanks' son, Edward II, reinvaded Scotland, but was defeated at Bannockburn in 1314, and peace was finally signed in 1328, after a declaration of sovereignty in 1320 (the Declaration of Arbroath), stating that although they all protested their loyalty to the crown, Scotland was not the king's to give away. Scotland was henceforth recognized as an independent kingdom (but not always treated as one). Scotland and England were frequently at war, but were dynastically united in 1603 (the Union of the Crowns), when Elizabeth Tudor died childless and her nearest relative, James VI of Scots, came to the throne of England as James I of Great Britain and of England (hence United Kingdom of Great Britain) and departed for his richer kingdom. The 'Great' of Great Britain was never a grandiloquent term, but simply to distinguish it from Little Britain or Brittany.

The common dynasty was not effective in ensuring peace – the two countries could be still occasionally at war, although they shared the same sovereign – but a Union of the Parliaments was entered into in 1707. Technically, the two Parliaments were abolished and a new one, the British Parliament, was created, but it still met in Westminster and followed its conventions. Most of the members still thought it was the same one with a few additional Scots; many of them still do (like John Major, the former Prime Minister, much given to talking of 'a thousand years of British Parliamentary history', which suggests an ignorance of history or of arithmetic or both).

The single kingdom was not entirely incorporating. The law and the churches were exempted from union (the English politicians did not want to tangle with the Scots lawyers or the divines of the Church of Scotland), and a separate educational system grew up from this, and it still is separate and differently structured. It was also there a long time before the English one, which when it did take shape included Wales as well. This did not require any new legislation, for England and Scotland were kingdoms (officially united as equals) whereas Wales was a principality of the English crown. But in taxation, economic policy, war and peace and foreign policy they became in effect the one country of Great Britain, and joined in building the British Empire and all that came from that.

The next addition came when the Irish rose again in 1798, which gave the British a bad fright, for both Catholics and Protestants rose and had French support, but it was badly organized and the rebellion was crushed, and steps were taken to unify the two countries by creating a United Kingdom of Great Britain and Ireland by abolishing the Irish Parliament (since it was limited to the Protestant Ascendancy and most of the Irish population was Catholic there was little protest at this), and since the British Parliament was officially abolished too, a new one was set up, the United Kingdom of Great Britain and Ireland. But since this too continued to meet at Westminster and followed the same conventions, most members there too still thought of this as an annexation.

This was the United Kingdom that fought in the First World War, but in 1916 came another rising in Ireland, with terrorism being used by both sides and eventually Britain conceded independence to the Irish Free State (later the Republic), except for Northern Ireland. This area had been 'planted' by James I and VI with Scottish and English Protestants. These now make up about 60 per cent of the population in the six counties of Ulster, who were determined not to come into an independent Ireland, which they regarded as priest-ridden, as most of it is Catholic. Eventually civil war broke out between the 'Hard Liners' and the 'Free Staters', those who demanded freedom for all of Ireland, complete and indivisible, and those who were prepared to accept the British terms for the partition of Ireland. The Free Staters won, and most of Ireland became independent but Northern Ireland remained within the United Kingdom, containing a population with a Protestant majority in six counties of Ulster. The three others – Cavan, Moneghan and Donegal, including the most northerly part of Ireland – are in the Republic. This is the situation that still exists today.

There is a great deal of confusion over names. England is the largest country. Wales was incorporated into England, and shares the same legal code but is no longer annexed to that country. Scotland never was part of England, despite attempts to make it so. Britain is therefore England, Wales and Scotland. No part of Ireland is therefore British. The United Kingdom of Great Britain and Northern Ireland (as it is called on all UK passports) consists of Britain and Northern Ireland, not Britain and Ulster, just six of Ulster's nine counties, bordered by a wiggly line which many organizations and all churches ignore, in the north-east of Ireland. The United Kingdom is messy to an extent of which few are aware.

The use of the term 'Anglo-Irish' is quite common as a term, and is admittedly rather neater than 'between the United Kingdom and the Republic of Ireland', but is quite wrong and deeply offensive; the Scots and Welsh are not 'Anglo' anything. There are similar confusions with Ireland. As mentioned already, no part of Ireland is British, including Northern Ireland. Actually, it is North-Eastern Ireland; it is not Ulster, but only a part of it. Nor will the name of 'Eire' for the Republic do either, for Eire is simply the Irish for Ireland. There is much confusion over names and flags, partly because little history is learned now, at least not the kind dealing with the past of our own countries.

England, of course, speaks English, which has spread to many other countries, including Scotland, Wales and Ireland, and has become tantamount to a world language. Scotland has two native languages of its own, Gaelic and Scots. Gaelic is a Q-Celtic language, closely related to Irish (Gaeilge), but is now spoken by very few, 65,000 according to the last Census. Scots is a Germanic language, related to English but not a dialect of English, although it is still often classified as such. It developed separately from the Anglian dialects and interchanged vocabulary with it. Most Scots can probably understand it to some extent at least and some speak it normally, but there are no figures as Scots lost all official recognition since the Union with England. It is used for conversation and literature, but never (so far) officially. Wales has Welsh, spoken by about 20 per cent of the population and used in the schools and for literature. It is a P-Celtic language, and is much used in the media and in culture. Nearly all Welsh also speak English, to which like the Scots they have given their own pronunciation, as have the Irish. In Ireland, the official language in the Republic is Irish along with English, taught in all schools and understood by perhaps 20 per cent of the population. It is a Q-Celtic language, very close to Gaelic (which originally came from it, as did the name of the country) but English can be understood by virtually the entire population.

In 1979, attempts to devolve power to Scotland and Wales were frustrated by an amendment which required 40 per cent on the electoral register to vote for it in a referendum, including the double-entered, the removed, the ill and the dead. This was not met in Scotland, though a majority voted for it very narrowly, and the Labour government fell in the row that followed. In Wales, the majority voted against by four to one, as Wales had no experience of having its own legal system, and the Welsh devolution act was repealed quite easily, as was the Scottish, in spite of protests. In the election that followed, the Conservatives under Margaret Thatcher came to power, though Scotland and Wales continued to vote Labour. They both took a great dislike to Thatcher, who had come to power over the entire United Kingdom on English votes, not Scottish or Welsh (who were obviously a small minority). The attitudes and policies of the Thatcher administration were determinedly English and based on the free market. The period from 1979 to 1997 has often been called the period of Thatcher, but to most Scots and Welsh (and increasingly to the English), it is looked back on as a time of nightmare.

Thatcher fell from power eventually, and John Major took over until 1997. She did a great deal of damage, destroying nearly all the manufacturing industry and asserting the supremacy of Middle England. She was essentially an English nationalist, and aggravated the discontents of the Scots and the Welsh, but also of the English, as the supremacy of the market began to make less and less appeal there too. Meanwhile, the Conservatives became very unpopular and some even corrupt, and the party was swept from office in 1997. A Labour government was elected with a huge majority, the largest in UK history. The Conservatives lost all their seats in Scotland and in Wales, and they had none in Northern Ireland in any case, so that they were now reduced to being an English shires party.

Meanwhile, the differences among the nations that constitute the UK were making themselves clearer, even in England. Scotland had actually had a Conservative majority in 1956 but since then it has had its legal system, its administration and its distinctive educational system governed by the party that has *lost* the elections in Scotland. Support for the SNP (the Scottish National Party, now more left-wing than Labour) rose significantly. The new Labour government brought forward a referendum on Scottish devolution as they had promised in their manifesto, and this was passed, this time with a huge majority, on 11 September 1997.

A Welsh referendum was held a week later, and was narrowly passed by the last vote in Cardiganshire. The support for the PC (Plaid Cymru, the Welsh National Party), was stronger than before, but Labour was still dominant and the main voice for Welsh devolution, as it had been for Scottish. The Welsh had further to go than the Scots, of course. They had voted No in 1979, had no tradition of having their own laws, and in any case the Welsh Assembly was to have much less power than the Scottish Parliament. In Northern Ireland there was a lengthy and complicated process of making peace between the Unionists and the Republicans, the IRA called off its policy of violence (though it has not yet decommissioned any arms). This agreement was reached on Easter Day 1998 and approved by a referendum in Northern Ireland and the Republic, and an Assembly was set up there too.

Approaching the turn of the millennium, the United Kingdom was showing a clear change from being an Anglicized and centralized state to being a genuinely federalized group of nations as the new parliaments and assemblies prepare to take over the whole of education, health, internal economic affairs, the police, law and order, leaving foreign policy and defence to the United Kingdom government. The odd thing is that there is to be a Northern Irish Assembly, a Welsh Assembly, a Scottish Parliament, but not as yet any Parliament for England or any part thereof, apart from a London Assembly whose powers are far from clear. There are some moves towards having elected mayors in certain of the larger cities, and some suggestions of regional governments like Northumbria, Cumbria, Yorkshire, East Anglia, the South-West (Cornwall and Devon), Kent, Mercia and so forth, but so far there has been little enthusiasm for reviving the historical nationalities, as it is a long time since any of them had a nation to belong to. But England is another matter.

The trouble with England is that it is so big, and accustomed to act as if it were the whole of the United Kingdom with a few extra bits tacked on, whatever the constitutional position was. England had been one country since the Middle Ages, and conquered or tried to conquer the others. It must be remembered that although England was dominant in the Empire the Scots, Welsh and Irish were important accessories in its creation; as a glance at the nominal roles shows, there were more Scots and Irish in the British Army or the Indian and Colonial Civil Services than the numbers of their populations would warrant. Poverty at home, plus the lack of any political self-government, plus a tradition of wandering or adventurism (and the chance of wealth and power over subject peoples) did much to explain this.

But the Empire is gone, and so is the wealth that it helped to create. The United Kingdom was left impoverished and much less powerful after the Second World War, and eventually had to go in with the European Union as its world role changed. The United Kingdom is now a member of the EU, in which *everyone* is in a minority. The Scots, the Welsh and the Irish are quite happy with this, but England has not yet got used to the loss of wealth and Empire, to not being dominant any more as the small nations become self-governing and England has to come more and more into contact with foreigners, possibly being governed by them in some things in the EU (though its powers too are still being discussed).

Britain has also become more multicultural since the 19th century (as have many other European countries), as first Irish, then Italians, then Indians and

Chinese came in and settled. In the 20th century more Indians and Chinese, then Pakistanis, West Indians, Bangladeshis, East European Jews and many others arrived, until the ethnic minority population now amounts to about 5 per cent of the population. There are 'ethnic minority' groups all over the United Kingdom, in London, Birmingham, Bradford, Glasgow, Edinburgh, Swansea and Belfast, although London has the highest number (it is still much richer than the rest), and most of the immigrants or their descendants seem determined to keep their religions, diets, dress and even their languages. They are quite prepared to learn English and the English ways, but few of them have any intention of discarding their own cultures as well; they do not wish to *become* English. Similarly, most of the Scots, Welsh and Irish get on quite well with the English and would disclaim being anti-English, but they are not English and have no intention of *being* English. This is still hard for many English to accept, having been used to dominance not just in these islands but in the world and seeing it all fade away as even the smaller nationalities are asserting their own identities and giving this a political expression. The United Kingdom, willingly or otherwise, is becoming much more multicultural and more pluralist.

In education there has been a messy situation, for the systems developed in different ways, and never really came together. The Scots were early to develop an educational system, though it did not come under the state until 1872, by which time the United Kingdom was in charge and Scottish independent development was constrained. The English system was slow to start, as most schooling was then carried on privately. There was an Education Act in 1870 to 'fill the gaps'. The English Act was intended to ensure basic education for 'the instruction in reading, writing and arithmetic to the children of those classes which support themselves by manual labour', the rest being done privately. The Scottish Act was to ensure basic 'education for the people of Scotland'. That is why 'public schools' (ie expensive private schools, 'independent schools') are much stronger in England, where they take in nearly 10 per cent of the children, than in Scotland, where they take in just over 1 per cent.

Consider the powers to have schools 'opt out' from local authority control, a reform introduced by Thatcher. In England, something like 3,000 schools opted out, but in Wales the figure was three schools and in Scotland one. It will be up to the new Parliament to decide what to do about that, for it will be in charge of the entire educational system. This obsession with market forces, pushed hard by the government of the time, clearly exerted little appeal on the Scots and the Welsh.

The Welsh educational system developed as an adjunct to the English, and is still structurally similar. They still have the same examination system, and the Welsh like the English still have this strange usage whereby most pupils over the age of 16 study three subjects (usually cognate) *and nothing else* for A levels, and most universities specialize in one subject for three years. Admittedly, the course is finished in a shorter time but at the cost of being extraordinarily narrow. But the Welsh educational system, though structurally the same as the English, is quite different in ethos. Influenced by Methodism and the Welsh language (which all children now study), it is more egalitarian than the English. The secondary schools are nearly all comprehensive (as is the case in Scotland too), but the so-called 'National Curriculum' applies here too, as in England and nowhere else in the United Kingdom (in spite of the title). The same legislation holds for England and Wales as yet, with some amendments to respond to Welsh needs.

The Irish system used to be unified, but the Republic and the North of Ireland have moved apart since the independence of the Republic. The Republic's system falls outside our remit, but the North has followed a policy of being as different as possible. They still hold on to an 11+ system of selection for secondary schools, adopted under English influence, just in time to see it discredited in the country of origin. This was known as the policy of 'keeping step in step with England', but more generally was known as 'keeping one step behind England'.

In England, where of course the great majority live, education has been erected to being one of the government's priorities. This transition is probably since 1997, as the Blair government tries to create a more civilized society from the wreckage left by Thatcherism. It is a very class-ridden country, much more so than Scotland, Wales or Ireland where they are more meritocratic than socially elitist, though social class still has a role there too. Now England, like the rest of the United Kingdom, has a Labour government, and finds itself wondering where it is going. The Labour government's power is considerable, with a huge majority and little effective opposition and strong popular support, but a sense of direction is not as clear as it might be. They know where power eventually rests, with the middle classes (or people who aspire to join them) of Middle England, and know that they achieved power so dramatically by not frightening them with more taxes and public spending and are determined to hang on to that for as long as they can.

For that reason, they have clung on to some Conservative policies and spending plans, and are no longer as working-class as they once seemed to be, and seem more concerned with presentation ('spin-doctoring') than with the content of policies. They seem determined to abolish the hereditary House of Lords (though that is taking a long time) and to increase democracy in the United Kingdom. This is going to be a slow process, and some are showing increasing impatience, and many are still suspicious of greater European involvement, particularly over the single currency. Some think this is inevitable, but others fear that this will be a step towards a federal Europe (although some would welcome this).

There seems to be a great deal of caution, and in education there are no plans at the moment for major reforms, save for Education Action Zones, where attempts are being made to have areas of deprivation given priority in raising standards by a national plan with more money, private as well as public (a kind of 'partnership deal' that the government is so keen on just now). The long-term aim is to raise educational standards for the whole of England, but less on the structural patterns of the school system, which is no longer a great issue of comprehensive versus selective schooling; that is now more pragmatic and rather less ideological than once it was. England is now trying to raise educational standards for the whole people, not just for one group or class, but that is bound to take a very long time indeed before the long-standing favouritism of the middle classes is laid to rest without bringing their standards down. Private schools in England are still quite strong, and there are no plans to close them; the government policy is to level standards up without putting more taxation on the middle classes. This obviously will be a difficult task, and in the future will have to use higher taxes, for none of this can come all that cheap.

We have seen this with higher education, which has expanded enormously in the United Kingdom in the last few years with the conversion of polytechnics into universities, some of them on several sites. In England, the two oldest universities of Oxford and Cambridge still dominate the field but some of the others are coming up. In Wales, most go to Welsh universities but some go to English ones. Of course, the Welsh have the same examination system but in Scotland, where the school examinations are different, very few go down this route, having distinguished ancient universities of their own.

Higher education is very expensive, and with the huge increase in numbers something had to be done to recover some of the costs. The government not only increased the student loan system (which they had inherited from the Conservatives) but also introduced a charge for student fees (a loan again, but one which will leave a debt for students to repay over a period as soon as they are in well-paid jobs). This applies to the whole of the United Kingdom for the time being, but when the Scottish Parliament and the Welsh and Northern Irish Assemblies take over the entirety of education in their own countries, that will be up to them. They may keep, moderate or abolish student fees and the loan system, and will not have to regard what England does as a model; it will be entirely up to them and to nobody else. So far, the numbers coming forward for university entrance do not seem to have declined, but we will have to see what the Scots, Welsh and Northern Irish do. But it cannot stop there; at present, the Irish universities in the Republic keep 20 per cent of their places for students from the North, and this could expand elsewhere in the EU, where policies on university finance and student loans and student fees vary enormously. There will be the need for some harmonization here too as student numbers going to study across European boundaries increase.

Transition in the United Kingdom continues as a hesitant process, much slower and more cautious than most expected as we see the European agenda exerting some pressure and wonder what is actually going to happen. There is an enormous mess to clear up, of course, in the United Kingdom as a whole, in the other countries and in Europe. At the moment, the United Kingdom has one of the lowest standards in education of the European countries, strongly outdistanced by Germany, Denmark, France, Spain, Sweden, Finland, Austria, the Netherlands and Belgium – almost every country in the EU except Greece and Portugal by any measure of educational attainment. That could be one reason for the current emphasis on raising standards in the schools. Some schools in England are excellent and distinguished (and in Scotland, and in Wales and in Northern Ireland), but the worst in all the countries are beyond comprehension. There is a task for all parts of the United Kingdom to take up here, or it will be left as a low-skilled and uneducated nation to face the next millennium, and it depends on all the countries, not just on one.

The government is well aware of the size of the tasks facing it, and also knows that it cannot do it alone. The smaller countries are becoming autonomous, and some may even go independent. In any case what happens will be up to them, together or alone. The United Kingdom over a long period tried to operate as a single country, which it seemed to do quite well, but was impoverished by two world wars and had to join (hesitantly) with Europe. It tried the Anglocentric free market model under Thatcher, but that did not work either, and since 1997 is now trying a new direction, in education as in other things. It will not be one country, in education at least, but a pluralist group of countries, autonomous at least, within the European Union. There is not even any guarantee that the United Kingdom will be a kingdom for all time, for some voices have been raised in favour of an eventual republic. It is not part of the political agenda, but once we have disposed of hereditary peers, it is not inevitable that we should stop there. Once we have raised standards in schools, made the country more democratic and devolved authority to its parts and become more European, what is now the United Kingdom could well become a federalized group within the EU and be genuinely educated up to EU standards; we can no longer rely on the slogan 'British is best', if we ever could. This transition is now in process; I may even see the results in my own lifetime.

Further reading

Bell, R E and Grant, N D C (1977) *Patterns of Education in the British Isles*, Allan and Unwin, London

Kay, B (1988) *Scots: The mither tongue*, Mainstream, Edinburgh

McClure, J D (1986) *Why Scots Matters*, Saltire, Edinburgh

18. Crisis and reform in US education: *A Nation at Risk*, 1983 and all that

Andreas M Kazamias

Prologue

The contemporary comparative historian surveying the world educational landscape in the second half of the 20th century, would be struck by the 'crisis and reform' scenarios that have been salient in the dramaturgy on the state and on the future course of US schooling and more broadly of US *paideia*. Personally, I have been a professor of comparative education, teaching in US universities, on a regular basis since 1958, a course called 'School and Society'. Surveying my course notes and outlines in preparation for this writing assignment, I was struck by the fact that, on every occasion, I would introduce the subject with 'the crisis in education', what I would call 'educational *crisology*', and I would end the course with the problematics of educational reform, namely, the proposals as well as the actual innovations or reform policies that were being initiated for the purpose of overcoming the crisis. It would appear, therefore, that in the United States, the period since the Second World War has been one of recurring 'crisis and reform', dramatic episodes performed on the schools' theatrical stage.

In probing further into my course descriptions and lecture notes, and reflecting on the more recent work of distinguished US educational historians, I was able to identify distinct epochs at different historical conjunctures, in terms of both the discursive construction of the crisis (the crisology) and the concomitant meliorist reform cures. In this connection, at least three transitional historical phases or epochs can be identified, each with its own conceptual and reformist physiognomy, and each reflecting its own constellation of values. However, to a degree more or less, all are characterized by:

1. millennial thinking about schooling;
2. a utopian belief in the school as a panacea, including the notion that 'social hell' could be salvaged through the common school (Tyack and Cuban, 1995, pp 1–3); and
3. a 'scholiocetric' and social instrumentalist or social efficiency reformist ideology.

The three epochs/phases could be described as:

1. the 'schools without scholars' phase, located roughly in the decades of the 1940s and 1950s;
2. the 'schools without "minds", subjects or souls' epoch, located roughly in the 1960s and 1970s; and
3. the 'schools without scholars, minds, subjects or souls' era, situated roughly in the 1980s and the 1990s.

None of these phases can be said to represent a radical transition in the US saga of 'crisis and reform' in education. But of the three, the most recent – that of the 1980s and 1990s – can at this historical juncture be assessed to be perhaps the most worthy of the appellation transitology. This chapter focuses on the last one, which we call 'A Nation at Risk, 1983 and all that'.

Historical reflections on the revolt against the schools (1955–83)

Two well-known US educational historians have recently used the metaphor of the 'swinging pendulum' as a constructed image to conceptualize and interpret the post-war educational 'crisis and reform' waves or what I have called 'episodes'. Diane Ravitch has viewed the problem of educational reform in the United States since the 1940s in terms of an 'educational pendulum' that has swung back and forth from progressivism to traditionalism in school knowledge, that is, the curriculum, and pedagogy. In the historical conjuncture of the 1950s – the period of the East–West competitiveness, the cold war and the *Sputnik* scare – the 'educational pendulum' was swinging from the progressive paradigm of 'life adjustment education' to the traditional paradigm of 'academic excellence'. In the mid-1960s, 'the calls for academic excellence had faded away, drowned out by the rising tide of social conflict in the cities and the disorders on college campuses' (ibid). During the ensuing decade, the educational pendulum was swinging back towards progressive reforms centring in what we would call the 'pedagogical atmosphere' or climate of schooling and focusing, among others things, on the reconstitution of the social and pedagogical power relationships. By the mid-1970s, in Ravitch's historical construction, the educational pendulum was beginning to swing back towards the traditional paradigm. Parents were calling for a 'back to basics' curriculum demanding the restoration of academic standards and discipline. And with one eye looking back to the first 'crisis and reform' era and the other looking forward to the third era, Diane Ravitch had this to say in 1983, taken to be the year of our transitology, with the appearance of the epoch-making Report of the National Commission on Excellence in Education, *A Nation at Risk*:

> The latest swing of the educational pendulum has now taken us back, at
> least rhetorically, to the post-Sputnik era, when educators, policymakers,

and parents feared that America's schools were producing (as one book was titled) 'second-rate brains.' *The fear expressed in the most recent batch of commission reports is that the United States, through the failings of its schools, is losing the international competition for jobs and markets. When Sputnik was first launched by the Soviets, critics worried that the United States was falling behind in the race for space, technological prowess, and military superiority. Today, they worry less about falling behind in the space race, but just as much about the lags in our technological innovation and our place in the world economy... The continuing spread of interdependence in the global economy will make it difficult for American schools to neglect the basic subjects.* (Ravitch, 1983; italics mine)

With some modifications, the metaphor of the swinging pendulum as a constructed image to view the cyclical 'crisis and reform' waves in US education has also been used by Carl Kaestle. Kaestle cast a historical glance further back than Ravitch into the 19th century, the period of Horace Mann and the formation of the common school, and he highlighted certain 'broad swings of the pendulum' at different epochs since that time. In a similar vein as Ravitch, he recognized 'opposing constellation of values' at the 'opposite ends of the pendulum's arc', during the recent post-war period (Kaestle, 1985).

From a heuristic point of view, there is much to be said about the pendulum metaphor. Without using it, back in the early 1970s, I had made pretty much the same observations as those of Ravitch about the reform waves in the previous couple of decades But having lived through the post-war reform period, particularly the period of the 1950s and after, I was able to make some additional pertinent observations and historical assessments. Specifically:

1. The 'crisis and reform' dramaturgy and the attack on the public schools continued unabated in the 1970s. An influential report entitled *The Reform of Secondary Education: A Report to the Public and the Profession* by The National Commission on the Reform of Secondary Education in 1973 averred that the large city school systems were 'on the verge of complete collapse'. The Commission went on to say: 'these schools are at the bottom in academic accomplishment' (The National Commission on the Reform of Secondary Education, 1973, p 8).

2. I also referred to two other characteristics of the reform discourse of the 1970s. One was the critique of US schooling by 'radical' critics like Samuel Bowles and Herbert Gintis whose afflatus was a then fashionable neo-Marxist school of thought. In their widely read book (1976), Bowles and Gintis had called for a 'socialist' transformation of the capitalist order, as being the 'key to [educational] reform'. They argued that schooling in capitalist America contributed neither to economic efficiency nor to social equity, an indictment that led other radical critics of that time, such as Ivan Illich, to advocate the abolition of schools altogether and the 'deschooling' of society.

3. Another feature of the 'crisis and reform' discourse of the 1970s was the notion that schools should pay more attention to their traditional economic function. This entailed, among other things, the development of vocational skills as well as the 'vocational socialization' of the future worker who would participate both as worker and citizen in a capitalist industrial society.
4. Finally, I had argued that most of the reforms that were attempted during the period prior to the 1980s were reformist rather than radical in that they were internally 'scholiocentric' and pedagogical; they sought to reform the schools within the existing political-structural framework and the existing system of values. Consequently they were not as successful as expected.

Constructing the 'crisis and reform' discourse: *A Nation at Risk* (1983)

Writing at the very beginning of the decade (1980), David Tyack, another eminent US historian, and his co-authors Michael W Kirst and Elisabeth Hansot hypothesized that 'educational reform in the 1980s may be quite different from most educational reforms thus far'. The reason for this prognosis was sought in the 'unprecedented' socio-economic and educational conditions at that historical juncture, particularly the apparent 'declining loyalty' to public education (Tyack *et al*, 1980, pp 253–54).

In retrospect, it was not only that reform in the 1980s appeared to be 'quite different'. As indicated below, the constructed combined 'crisis and reform' discourse appeared to be different as well. This transitology is clearly presaged in the apocalyptic educational reform manifesto *A Nation at Risk: The Imperative for Educational Reform* issued by the National Commission on Excellence in Education (NCEE) in 1983. The oft-quoted prologue of this reform manifesto set the stage and the tone of the unfolding new dramatic episode and the ensuing 'great school debate':

> Our nation is at Risk. We report to the American people that… the educational foundations of our society are presently being eroded by a rising tide of mediocrity that threatens our very future as a Nation and a people. What was unimaginable a generation ago has begun to occur – others are matching and surpassing our educational attainments… Our society and its educational institutions seem to have lost sight of the basic purposes of schooling and the high expectations and disciplined effort needed to attain them. This report… seeks to generate reform of our educational system in fundamental ways and to renew the Nation's commitment to schools and colleges of high quality throughout the length and breadth of our land… The world is indeed one global village. We live among determined, well-educated, and strongly motivated competitors… Knowledge, learning, information, and skilled intelligence are the new raw materials of inter-

national commerce and are today spreading throughout the world… If only
to keep and improve on the slim competitive edge we still retain in world
markets, we must dedicate ourselves to the reform of our educational system for the benefit of all – old and young alike, affluent and poor, majority
and minority. Learning is the indispensable investment required for success
in the 'information age' we are entering. (NCEE, 1983)

In this epoch-making text, US public schooling was indicted for being at best
mediocre; academic standards and indicators of student performance in key
subjects such as science and mathematics were, according to the report, deplor-
ably and dangerously low compared to those of the United States' chief international competitors, eg Japan and Germany; schools were blamed for 'a steady
decline in industrial productivity'; school curricula were found to be 'homoge-
nized, diluted, and diffused to the point that they no longer have a central purpose'; compared to other nations, American students had low expectations,
spent much less time on school work and on homework; and teachers were
poorly prepared in subjects to be taught and poorly paid (NCEE, 1983).

Obviously, this prestigious National Commission and the White House
that endorsed its report felt strongly that US public education was in a deep
crisis, a state of affairs that placed America and the nation 'at risk'. The American public should become aware of the seriousness and the plausible dire consequences of this social malaise. To avert a national catastrophe, a strong
public commitment must be made to educational reform and the pursuit of excellence in education along the lines recommended by the Commission. However, public commitment to *excellence* and educational reform, according to
this national commission's clarion call for change, must not be made at the expense of an equally 'strong commitment to the *equitable treatment* of our diverse population'. In the words of the Commission:

> The twin goals of equity and high-quality schooling have profound and
> practical meaning for our economy and society, and we cannot permit one
> to yield to the other either in principle or in practice. To do so would deny
> young people their chance to learn and live according to their aspirations
> and abilities. It also would lead to a generalized accommodation to medioc-
> rity in our society on the one hand or the creation of an undemocratic elitism
> on the other. (NCEE, 1983)

Excellence and equity/equality in education, therefore, must be the activating
ideals of the necessary movement or the imperative for educational reform.
Towards these ends the National Commission on Excellence in Education
made certain recommendations that, in its judgement, would help overcome
what it diagnosed to be the crisis in US education in the early 1980s. 'Our recommendations, are based on the beliefs that… a solid high school education is
within the reach of virtually all, and that life-long learning equips people with
the skills required for new careers and for citizenship.' In abbreviated form, its
recommendations included the following:

1. '[That] State and high school graduation requirements be strengthened and that, at a minimum, all students seeking a diploma be required to lay the foundations in the Five New Basics by taking the following curriculum during their 4 years of high school: (a) 4 years of English; (b) 3 years of mathematics; (c) 3 years of science; (d) 3 years of social studies; and (e) one-half year of computer science. For the college-bound, 2 years of foreign language in high school are strongly recommended in addition to those taken earlier.'
2. '[That] schools, colleges, and universities adopt more rigorous and measurable standards, and higher expectations, for academic performance and student conduct.'
3. '[That] significantly more time be devoted to learning the New Basics.'
4. That teacher preparation be improved and teaching be made 'a more rewarding and respected profession'. To accomplish these goals: (a) 'persons preparing to teach should be required to meet high educational standards, to demonstrate an aptitude for teaching, and to demonstrate competence in an academic discipline... (b) salaries for the teaching profession should be increased and should be professionally competitive, market-sensitive, and performance-based... (c) school boards should adopt an 11-month contract for teachers... (d) school boards, administrators, and teachers should cooperate to develop career ladders for teachers... (e) substantial non-school personnel resources should be employed to help solve the immediate problem of the shortage of mathematics and science teachers'.
5. '[That] citizens across the Nation hold educators and elected officials responsible for providing the leadership necessary to achieve these goals' (NCEE, 1983).

Annus mirabilis (1983), and after

Attacks on the public schools for their shortcomings and failures, as noted earlier, pre-dated 1983 and the appearance of *A Nation at Risk*. But such apocalyptic language, 'trenchant rhetoric' and 'bashing of public education', as those found in this text that emanated from the highest echelons of government – the Commission was appointed by Terrell Bell, the then Secretary of Education, and the report was endorsed by President Ronald Reagan – were quite unprecedented. (See also Berliner and Biddle, 1997.) Furthermore, the rhetoric and the content of this report were echoed, very often in similar apocalyptic language, in a host of other 'crisis and reform' texts that appeared around the same time or in the immediate years that followed. Some of these texts were the work of individuals, others of committees or academic study groups. Many joined the chorus in lamenting the plight of public schooling. But, in traditional US fashion, they also optimistically reassured the US citizens that there was indeed a road to salvation and, as the framers of *A Nation at Risk* put it: 'America can do it'.

The literature – both primary texts and secondary sources – on the great school debate in 1983 and the immediate years after is legion. Given the constraints on space and scope that a study of this nature imposes on the writer, we shall of necessity limit ourselves to brief analyses of selected, representative and widely publicized 'policy' reports by high-profile national groups or organizations. Further, it should be noted here that our thesis is that the distinguishing element of the 'crisis and reform' transitology, as reflected in *A Nation at Risk* and kindred texts, is the emphasis that was placed on the 'political economy' of schooling and on the related 'neo-liberal' market oriented economistic conception of education, as well as the relationship(s) between schooling and American economic robustness in a competitive and interdependent global *kosmos*. Consequently, we shall: 1) focus on that distinctive element in the 'crisis and reform' literature; and 2) seek to illuminate it by contextualizing it, that is by placing it in the contemporary historical context.

A report to the President of the United States from the Business–Higher Education Forum (1983) linked America's industrial competitiveness, so 'crucial to our social and economic well-being', to the upgrading of skills for those who teach mathematics and science (Gross and Gross, 1985, p 64). So did *Educating Americans for the 21st Century*, 'a plan of action for improving mathematics, science and technology education for all American elementary and secondary students so that their achievement is the best in the world by 1995', a voluminous report by the National Science Board Commission on Pre-college Education in Mathematics, Science and Technology (1983). Interestingly, this text was issued in September 1983, just five months after the reform manifesto *A Nation at Risk*. Like its predecessor, this text bemoans the sorry state of US public education, especially the inadequate grounding of school-leavers in basic areas such as mathematics, science and technology; it emphasizes the foreign challenges to US industrial and economic supremacy; and it proposes what it perceives to be 'sweeping and drastic changes' in the content and pedagogy of the aforementioned basic subject areas. *Educating Americans for the 21st Century* in 1983 set the following ambitious, but according to it, attainable goal for 1995:

> The improvement and support of elementary and secondary school systems throughout America so that, by the year 1995, they will provide all the nation's youth with a level of education in mathematics, science and technology, as measured by achievement scores and participation levels (as well as other non-subjective criteria), that is not only the highest quality attained anywhere in the world but also reflects the particular and peculiar needs of our nation. (National Science Board Commission, 1983)

The linking of public schooling with economic growth, social well-being and national survival, and the underlying 'human capital theory' were clearly expressed or implied in other widely publicized and influential reports. In the same year again (1983) as that of the *A Nation at Risk* manifesto, the Task Force on Education for Economic Growth of the Education Commission of the States (ECS) produced 'a comprehensive plan to improve our nation's schools' called *Action for Excellence*. According to this plan: 'Improving education in America can legitimately be called crucial to our national survival' (*Action for Excellence*, 1983, pp 3, 46). Two years later, another report, called 'A Statement', and characteristically titled *Investing in Our Children: Business and the Public Schools* (1985), echoed the same ideas and concerns as those in *A Nation at Risk* on the educational crisis, on the imperatives for reform (setting high standards, monitoring achievement, curriculum reform), on improving teacher education and 'enhancing and strengthening the professional roles of teachers', and on 'educational excellence'.

'The business of America is business!'

Aside from obvious similarities in the 'crisis and reform' sagas among the aforementioned reports, *Investing in Our Children* (1985) is especially significant for our purposes for yet another reason. It illustrates the predominant emphasis being placed on the 'economic' aspects and purposes of schooling and the concomitant involvement of business in the reform of US public education.

It is of crucial importance to point out here that US education, as Cohen and Lazerson have documented, has, at least since the beginning of the 20th century, been 'intimately related to the American corporate order', and 'closely tied to production'. Schooling, as human capital theory tells us, 'has been justified as a way of increasing wealth, of improving industrial output, and of making management more effective' (Cohen and Lazerson, 1977, in Karabel and Halsey, 1977, pp 373ff.). US public schools have always been expected to provide the skills and types of knowledge that would contribute to economic growth, national wealth and a free enterprise capitalist economy. Additionally, they have also been expected to 'socialize' the future worker into the US capitalist work ethic, which, in many respects was coextensive with being a good US citizen. Furthermore, and related to the above, the business community has always been involved in education (Timpane, 1984, p 389). As the highly popular US President Calvin Coolidge is said to have stated in the 1920s: 'The business of America is business' (Spring, 1982, pp 16ff. Also see: NEA, 1918; Goodlad, 1983; Kliebard, 1986).

In his important historical study (1986), Herbert Kliebard documents the centrality of the social efficiency idea in the ever recurring US politico-educational controversy around the curriculum question 'What Knowledge is of Most Worth?' posed by Herbert Spencer in the 19th century. (On the recurring controversy over Spencer's question, see Cremin, 1988, p 377.) In

Kliebard's historical construction and interpretation, the social efficiency version of 'what knowledge is of most worth' (in contrast to the other three that
constituted the arena of curriculum politics in the 20th century, viz, the hu-
manist, the developmentalist and the social meliorist) emphasized a technocratic utilitarian conception of education, vocationalism, and a managerial,
business style in running education. The social efficiency reformers emphasized the 'cult of efficiency' school ethos (Callahan, 1962), and a Taylorist style
of scientific management (Kliebard, 1986; Konstantellou, 1992). From this conceptual lens the quality and worth of school knowledge, curriculum subjects
and, more broadly, school learning do not give priority to and they are not assessed in terms of their intrinsic human worth, nor, as Aristotle would say, the
degree to which they contribute to civic virtue, the cultivation of the 'soul', or,
more broadly, to *paideia* (culture). Instead, they give high priority to 'instrumental rationality', to 'marketable' knowledge and skills, to 'observable reality' that is measurable on tests designed by experts, and to the smooth
transition of the students from school to the world of work. Kliebard under-
lines this historic US educational–cultural idiosyncrasy as follows:

> Humanistic subjects, to take one example, were not exactly delegitimized;
> but their standing *vis à vis* the frankly occupationally oriented subjects in the
> curriculum waned significantly. Even subjects commonly associated with
> the academic curriculum, such as mathematics and science, became sanc-
> tioned not as important ways of knowing or as invaluable repositories of
> knowledge but as indispensable vehicles to achieving certain high-status oc-
> cupations. (Kliebard, 1990, p 25)

And in summarizing the characteristics of the social efficiency 'technocratic
ideology' of US schooling, Arthur Wirth in 1983, the transitology *annus
mirabilis*, wrote:

> It [the technocratic ideology] tends to assume that only observable behavior
> is real, that everything real must be measurable, that learning consists of
> mastery of discrete components, and that the good person is operationally
> defined by scoring well on expert-designed tests. It is the competitive
> achievement model designed to help winners get ahead vocationally and to
> reinforce the attitude that in this world it is each person for her/himself.
> (Wirth, 1983, as quoted by Konstantellou, 1992, pp 153–54)

From the above reflections, it is patently clear that 'social efficiency' and all
that this term connoted and denoted in the educational sector, particularly
types of school knowledge, an educational culture and a school ethos for purposes of economic efficiency in an advanced capitalist 'enterprise culture' *par
excellence*, have historically been quite dominant as an educational *cum* pedagogical ideology, or as 'policy talk' and 'policy action', to use Tyack's and Cuban's apt terminology (1995, pp 40–41). But the pre-eminence and paramount
importance given to public schooling for economic efficiency and for the accu-

mulation of national wealth, nay for national survival and the economic hegemony of the country in a global and interdependent *kosmos* have no historical
parallel.

'Chorused' reverberations

Glancing at what followed the *annus mirabilis* (1983), one cannot but be im-
pressed by the reaction and the impact which the seminal texts of this salient
date, especially *A Nation at Risk*, had on both 'policy talk' and 'policy action', as
applied to the recurrent episodes in the history of American 'public school reform'. The 'crisis and reform' dramaturgy, as constructed in 1983, mainly by
the National Commission on Excellence in Education, reverberated at the
state and local levels across the nation and was repeated in almost identical
scripts/scenarios by several new actors – individuals, political groups, professional organizations, business groups, think tanks and the like. To take but a
few examples. In a widely disseminated and frequently referred to report entitled *A Nation Prepared: Teachers for the 21st Century* (1986) by the Carnegie Forum on Education and the Economy, one hears the same mantras, such as
'that America's ability to compete in world markets is eroding'; that 'American
children are in limbo – ignorant of the past and unprepared for the future';
that in periods of economic crises 'Americans turn to education'; that 'they
rightly demand an improved supply of young people with the knowledge,
the spirit, the stamina and the skills to make the nation once again fully competitive'; and that in the new pursuit of excellence, Americans must recognize
the essential truth that 'success depends on achieving far more demanding
standards' (Carnegie Forum on Education and the Economy, 1986). Referring
to what occurred in 1983–84 as a 'turnaround', John F Jennings, a counsel for
the Committee on Education and Labor of the US House of Representatives,
in an article titled 'The Sputnik of the Eighties' (1987), bemoaned the dire consequences of the economic misfortunes that allegedly '[were] seeping into the
American consciousness'. 'The Sputnik of the 1980s', he averred, 'is economic
competition, and the United States is beginning to recognize that the educational attainment of its people is an intrinsic element of national economic
well-being.' In this pronouncement, it was further noted that following the
1983 reform manifesto, 'most state and local reform was focused on increasing
academic standards for all children and on raising the professional competence of teachers'. Also noted was the increased involvement of 'corporate
leaders' in the 'crisis and reform' dramaturgy (Jennings, 1987, pp 104–06).
Most vociferous indeed, among the actors that joined the chorus, were the
corporate leaders and the business community. Writing in 1984, Michael
Timpane, the Dean of Teachers College, Columbia University, noted, as mentioned above, that 'the involvement of business in education is not new'. Indeed, 'for the first half of this century, that interest was pervasive'. Then, in the

1950s and 1960s, it waned. But in 1983, the process of re-establishing connections between business leaders and public education 'has accelerated greatly'. According to Timpane, 'the most notable change in the past year [1983–84] has been the increased involvement of businesses in education policy-making' (Timpane, 1984, pp 390–91). Among the corporate leaders who were asked to testify before Congress in favour of expanding federal aid to education in 1987, Charles Marshall of the American Telephone and Telegraph Company was quoted as stating the business world's interest in education in, what else, but 'business' language!

> We are not interested in education simply for altruistic reasons; we need knowledgeable, well-educated highly skilled employees if our business is to succeed. The educational system prepares the young people from whom we will enlist our future employees. If their preparation falls short, we wind up with less able employees and it is more difficult for us to reach our goals. (quoted in Jennings, 1987, p 106)

Reflections and reflexivities on *A Nation at Risk,* 1983 and all that

In their recent seminal historical study on the trajectory and *problematique* of educational reform in the United States, Tyack and Cuban have, correctly in our judgement, pointed out that the recurrent reform episodes, as 'policy talk' and 'policy action', have been 'intrinsically political in origin', and that 'the ideologies of progress or regress in schooling are political constructs'. They explain:

> Groups organize and contest with other groups in the politics of education to express their values and to secure their interests in the public school... Leaders have used them [ideologies] to mobilize and direct reform, persuading followers that they were joining a triumphal upward march to a utopian future or arresting a devastating backward slide. In both cases, people have held that their beliefs were supported by facts, but 'progress' or 'regress' in education lay much in the eye of the beholder. (Tyack and Cuban, 1995, pp 8, 38)

'On matters of grave importance, style, not sincerity, is the vital thing!' (Oscar Wilde)

There is much to support this view about the 'crisis and reform' episode surrounding '*A Nation at Risk,* 1983, and all that'. At that historical juncture, certain elite groups in the American society, such as business leaders, high-ranking academics (eg presidents of universities and distinguished professors of mathematics and sciences), members of school boards, and, of course, high echelon political leaders, were able to construct and publicize a 'crisis and reform' discourse that appeared to be quite effective. A breakdown of the membership of the NCEE and other committees, commissions and similar bodies speaks quite eloquently to their status. For example, of the 18-member NCEE: six were academics (four university presidents and two professors); three were members of school boards; five were school people (two principals, two teachers and one superintendent; two were corporate leaders; one was a former Commissioner of Education, and one a former State Governor (NCEE, 1983). Tellingly, there were no representatives from labour, the humanities, the social and educational sciences or ethnic studies.

Paul Peterson of the Brookings Institution, who had served as *rapporteur* for the Twentieth Century Fund's Task Force on Federal Elementary and Secondary Education Policy, has argued that most of the influential educational commission reports of the times (early 1980s) were indeed political statements. They all produced policy analyses 'of dubious value'. As political documents they tended to 'exaggerate' the problems they addressed and 'dramatize' their subject matter. Perhaps because of their 'style' rather than their content and 'sincerity', to refer to Oscar Wilde's famous dictum, they seem to have had 'a major impact'. According to Peterson: 'Not only have the reports been given widespread publicity and not only have they spawned new activity in many state legislatures, but it would not be surprising to find that in the next few years test scores improve, public confidence returns, and fiscal support for public education increases' (1985, pp 113, 116). In retrospect, while there is considerable evidence to support the first part of this statement, namely, that the reports had considerable impact, the prediction of progress in the second part was not borne out. Writing in 1989, Chester E Finn, Jr, a well-known 'centrist conservative', who served as President Reagan's Assistant Secretary of Education (1985–88), and a strong supporter of the 'policy action' advocated by the National Commission on Excellence in Education and other similar commissions, commented that the nation was 'still at risk'. Finn quoted William J Bennett, President Reagan's Education Secretary, as having reported:

> American education has made some undeniable progress in the last few years... But we are certainly not doing well enough fast enough. We are still at risk. The absolute level at which our improvements are taking place is unacceptably low. Too many students do not graduate from our high schools, and too many of those who graduate have been poorly educated. Our students know too little, and their command of essential skills is too slight... And the entire project of American education – at every level – remains insufficiently accountable for the result that matters most: student learning. (Finn, 1989, p 17)

The 'crisis and reform' episode in context

The script of the educational 'crisis and reform' dramatic episode of the 1980s, dubbed 'A *Nation at Risk*, 1983 and all that', was written at a critical transitional period in recent US history. Contemporary historians and other knowledge-able students have testified that during the decade of the 1970s and early years of the 1980s US society and its version of the 'welfare state' were in a state of crisis. According to a contemporary writer:

> The powers of the American state are now deployed in a massive business offensive. Its basic elements are painfully clear. Drastic cutbacks in social spending. Rampant environmental destruction. Regressive revisions of the tax system. [Looming trade wars.] Loosened constraints on corporate power. Ubiquitous assaults on organized labor. Sharply increased weapons spending. Escalating threats of intervention abroad. (Cohen and Rogers, 1983, quoted in Apple, 1990, p 156)

Others have seen the social and economic crisis of the period as: 'the increase in poverty, the defunding of the educational and social programs that took many years to win and that are still crucially necessary, the attempts by right-ist groups to impose their beliefs on others, the widespread deskilling of jobs, the lowering of wages and benefits for many others, and the loss of whole sec-tors of jobs' (Apple, 1990, p 156).

Eric Hobsbawm, the eminent social historian, and others have seen, during the early part of this period (the 1970s), a crisis of the 'states', like the welfare states of the United Kingdom and the United States, that still believed in the Keynesian remedies or prescriptions of economic policies. In the 1970s, ac-cording to Hobsbawm, a small group of radical economic liberals, who advo-cated an 'unlimited and unrestricted free market', emerged into prominence. These 'neo-liberals' were against Keynsianism, a mixed economy and full em-ployment, and they zealously championed the old liberal doctrines of atomistic individualism and *laissez-faire*. It was no accident, Hobsbawm has added, that the Nobel Prize in Economics, established in 1969, was awarded to Friedrich von Hayek in 1974, and two years later (1976), to Milton Friedman, both quite well-known and still influential 'neo-liberal' political economists. The political–ideological conflict between the Keynesians and the emerging neo-liberals is clearly stated as follows:

> The battle between the Keynesians and the neo-liberals was neither a purely 'technical' dispute among professional economists, nor a search for ways to deal with novel and complex economic problems. It was a conflict of oppo-site and irreconcilable ideologies...The neo-liberals believed that the 'invisi-ble hand' of Adam Smith's free market would unavoidably produce the maximum increase of the 'wealth of nations' and the best possible distribu-tion of wealth and income, a position which the Keynesians rejected. (Hobsbawm, 1995, Greek translation, p 523)

Similar analyses of the neo-liberal political–ideological offensive against Keynesianism, the welfare state and the so-called 'liberal consensus' of the 1950s and 1960s, and the enthronement of neo-liberal tenets such as individualism, the market, and 'get the state off people's backs' had been made earlier by other writers (Armstrong *et al*, 1984; Mishra, 1984). What is particularly relevant for our purposes here is the historical verdict/interpretation that the neo-liberal politico-economic ideology was able, in Hobsbawm's words, 'to influence decisively government policy in the 1980s'. Such influence was evident both in Britain and the United States, during the political ascendancy of different forces, namely, the so-called New Right or New Conservatism/Neo-conservatism, associated with Margaret Thatcher and the Conservatives in the United Kingdom and Ronald Reagan and the Republicans in the United States. The most important policies credited to Thatcherism and Reaganomics, according to Armstrong *et al*, were 'restrictive monetary policy; cutbacks in welfare provisions; tax cuts; privatization and deregulation; and union bashing' (1984, pp 406–21).

Unpacking the recrudescent US 'liberalism' and 'conservatism' in the 'crisis and reform' transitology, *A Nation at Risk*, 1983 and all that'

Neo-liberalism and a recrudescent neo-conservatism as social philosophies unavoidably influenced 'policy talk' and 'policy action' in the arena of education, pedagogy and schooling. This was reflected to a degree more or less, explicitly and openly or tacitly, in the dramaturgical 'crisis and reform' sagas and policy scenarios analysed above. A dominant thread in the neo-liberal educational conceptual tapestry and policy template, as woven in the texts and other discursive statements and/or practices, was 'instrumental rationality' and a technocratic and functionally utilitarian type of education: that is, reforming public schooling for the purpose of providing a type of instruction and knowledge that would be useful and instrumental in promoting economic growth and serving 'national' economic – read mainly business – interests. For in unpacking *A Nation at Risk*, the nagging question that crops up for reflection is: '*whose nation was at risk?*' The US public high school, in short, was to be 're-invented' by hitching it onto the wagon of a free market economy and an 'enterprise culture'. The traditional, always pervasive, but in a sense, rather *polysemic* socio-educational doctrine/ideology of 'social efficiency' was reconstructed, and rewritten, into a monophonic mantra: education/schooling for economic efficiency in an individualistic money culture. There were other strands or themes in the constructed educational 'crisis and reform' space, under consideration here, that are ancillary to the aforementioned central one and can be said to be within the neo-liberal/neo-conservative Reaganomics of the 1980s. One was the emphasis being placed on excellence, more than on equity; on higher more rigorous and measurable standards, particularly in core curriculum areas and 'the New Basics', such as science, mathematics, English, social studies, and computer science; and on quality education measured in terms of achievement and tests. Another, was the call for more discipline in the schools and more 'disciplined effort' in order to attain the high expectations of schooling.

The 'policy talk' and 'policy action' in this 'crisis and reform' transitology was further characterized by other notions whose afflatus must have been the recrudescent US liberalism and conservatism of the late 1970s and early 1980s. One had to do with the strong emphasis being placed on the role of the states and local school districts to implement reforms and deliver educational services. In the words of the NCEE: 'State and local officials, including, school board members, governors, and legislators, have the primary responsibility for financing and governing the schools, and should incorporate the reforms we propose in their educational policies and fiscal planning' (NCEE, 1983). Then there was the emphasis on 'competitiveness' in the international markets and the global economy, and the need to be at the top in the Student Achievement Olympics such as those staged by the International Association for the Evaluation of Educational Achievement (IEA). Finally, and equally prominent and relevant here, was the nationalistic, and the 'we are and must be the greatest' tone or 'noise' that pervaded much of this genre of 'politico-educational' literature.

Epilogue: looking backwards toward the future

With 'A Nation at Risk, 1983 and all that' the recurrent debate on US public education had taken a new turn. The script of the 'crisis and reform' dramaturgy was in many respects revised. The effort was made to 'restructure' and reorient US public education, particularly the US common high school. The envisaged trajectory, as shown in this essay, was 'a neo-liberal turn to the right', in concert with the neo-liberal and neo-conservative social philosophy promulgated and quite dominant at the time. Such a 'swing to the right', to refer to Kaestle's conceptualization of the 'pendulum metaphor' mentioned earlier, reflected different and 'opposing constellation of values for the public schools'. In 1985, Kaestle wrote:

> At the opposite ends of the pendulum's giant arc are located opposing constellations of values for the public schools. At one end we find freedom, equality, child-centeredness, education for social harmony, education for the whole child, and so on. At the other end we find rigorous intellectual training, education for developing the workforce, accelerated and enriched education for the gifted, and education for international competition.

To the latter part of which statement, one could add the other neo-liberal and 'rightist' values we identified earlier, viz, discipline, order, excellence, standards, 'back to basics', and 'less but stronger state'.

The restructuring and reorienting of US public schooling along such lines, that is those adumbrated in this transitology, would alter the character and mission of the US public high school. Historically the high school has been envisaged and constructed as a quintessentially public institution, with a civic mission, providing a free and common public education for all, and performing multiple, albeit sometimes contradictory functions. Amongst these, as laid out in several texts beginning with the famous and influential 1918 Report of the NEA Commission on the Reorganization of Secondary Education titled *Cardinal Principles of Secondary Education*, have been such goals as:

1.   social, civic and cultural goals;
2.   moral and ethical character;
3.   citizenship; and
4.   'emotional and physical well-being, creativity and aesthetic expression, and self-realization' (NEA, 1918; 1938; Goodlad, 1983).

Clearly, the trajectory charted in the epoch under study would lead to a reconstructed school whose paramount role would be to cater to the needs more of a free and rather elitist 'enterprise culture' rather than a liberal social democratic 'civic culture'.

The modernist discourse adumbrated in '*A Nation at Risk*, 1983 and all that' had a considerable impact, as noted above, on the reform movement that accelerated afterwards. In subsequent 'policy talk' and 'policy action' in the 1980s and the 1990s, surrounding public education, one can easily detect similar or kindred 'crisis and reform' sagas and policy directions as those of the transitology of concern here. Among these one would include the following:

1.   the emphasis on excellence, higher national and world-class standards;
2.   the continued obsession with accountability, testing and measuring of student progress;
3.   the overemphasis on the economic purposes of public education;
4.   the involvement of corporate America in the business of schooling; and
5.   the trend towards devolution, deregulation and choice in education (Whitty *et al*, 1998).

In conclusion, it should be noted that since the 1980s other dramatic scenarios are being enacted on the 'crisis and reform' stage of US public education. Prominent amongst them are the so-called culture wars, multiculturalism, the critique of Eurocentric education and culture, feminist epistemology, and critical pedagogy. At this historical juncture, these discourses are running parallel to the one we attended to here. Whether the reform pendulum will swing in a postmodernist direction towards the constellation of values that this entails remains to be seen.

References

Apple, M W (1990) What reform talk does: creating new inequalities in education, in *Education Reform: Making sense of it all*, ed S B Bacharach, Allyn and Bacon, Boston

Armstrong, P, Glyn, A and Harrison, J (1984) *Capitalism Since World War II*, Collins, London

Berliner, D C and Biddle, B J (1997) *The Manufactured Crisis: Myths, fraud and the attack on America's public schools*, Longman, New York

Bowles, S and Gintis, H (1976) *Schooling in Capitalist America: Educational Reform and the Contradictions of Economic Life*, Basic Books, New York

Callahan, R E (1962) *Education and the Cult of Efficiency*, The University of Chicago Press, Chicago

Carnegie Forum on Education and the Economy (1986) *A Nation Prepared: Teachers for the 21st century*, Carnegie Foundation, Hyattsville, Maryland

Cohen, D K and Lazerson, M (1977) Education and the corporate order, in *Power, Ideology and Education*, ed J Karabel and A H Halsey, Oxford University Press, New York

Cohen, J and Rogers, J (1983) *On Democracy*, Harmondsworth, Penguin

Cremin, L A (1988) *American Education: The metropolitan experience 1876–1980*, Harper and Row, New York

Finn, C E (1989) 'A nation still at risk', *Commentary*, 2

Goodlad, J (1983) *A Place Called School: Prospects for the future*, McGraw-Hill, Hightown, NJ

Hobsbawm, E (1994) *Age of Extremes: The short twentieth century, 1914–1991*, Michael Joseph, London, translated into Greek by Vasilis Kapetanyiannis (1995), Themelio, Athens

Jennings, J F (1987) The Sputnik of the eighties, *Phi Delta Kappan*

Kaestle, C (1985) Education reform and the swinging pendulum, *Phi Delta Kappan*

Karabel, J and Halsey, A H (eds) (1977) *Power, Ideology and Education*, Oxford University Press, New York

Kliebard, H M (1986) *The Struggle for the American Curriculum, 1893–1958*, Routledge, London and New York

Kliebard, H M (1990) Vocational education as symbolic action: connecting schooling with the workplace, *American Educational Research Journal*, 1

Konstantellou, E (1992) Beyond the limits of humanistic and technocratic ideologies in education: a critique of the Greek and American models, PhD dissertation, Columbus, Ohio

Mishra, R (1984) *The Welfare State in Crisis: Social thought and social change*, Wheatsheaf Books, Brighton

National Commission on Excellence in Education (1983) *A Nation at Risk: The imperative for educational reform*, US Government Printing Office, Washington, DC

National Commission on the Reform of Secondary Education (1973) *The Reform of Secondary Education: A report to the public and the profession*, US Government Printing Office, Washington, DC

National Science Board Commission on Precollege Education in Mathematics, Science and Technology (1993) *Educating Americans for the 21st Century: A plan of action for improving mathematics, science and technology education for all American elementary and secondary students so that their achievement is the best in the world by 1995*, A Report to the American People and the National Science Board, National Science Board, Washington, DC

NEA, Commission on the Reorganization of Secondary Education (1918) *Cardinal Principles of Secondary Education*, Washington, DC

Peterson, P E (1985) Why commissions say what they do, in *The Great School Debate: Which way for American education?*, ed B Gross, Simon & Schuster, New York

Ravitch, D (1983) The educational pendulum, in *Education 85/86*, ed F Schultz, Dushkin Publishing, New York

Spring, J (1982) *American Education: An introduction to social and political aspects*, Longman, New York & London

Task Force on Education for Economic Growth (1983) *Action for Excellence: A comprehensive plan to improve our nation's schools*, The Education Commission of the States, Washington, DC

Timpane, M (1984) Business has rediscovered public schools, *Phi Delta Kappan*

Tyack, D B and Cuban, L (1995) *Tinkering Toward Utopia: A century of public school reform*, Harvard University Press, Cambridge, MA

Tyack, D B, Kirst, M W and Hansot, E (1980) Educational reform: retrospect and prospect, *Teachers College Record*, **81** (3)

Whitty, G, Power, S and Halpin, D (1988) *Devolution and Choice in Education: The school, the state and the market*, Open University Press, Buckingham and Philadelphia

Wirth, A J (1983) *Productive Work in Industry and Schools: Becoming persons again*, University Press of America, Lanham, MD

Index